W9-BWJ-844

CLASSIC CAR RESTORER'S
HANDBOOK

RESTORATION TIPS AND TECHNIQUES FOR OWNERS AND RESTORERS OF CLASSIC AND COLLECTIBLE AUTOMOBILES

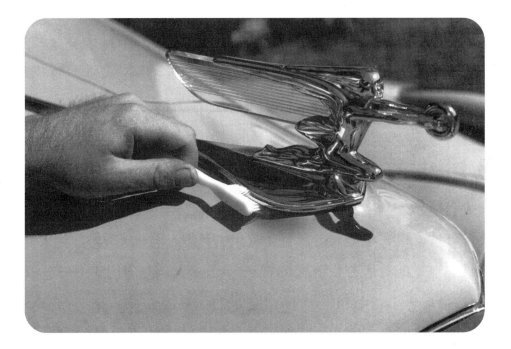

Jim Richardson

HPBooks

HPBooks
are published by
The Berkley Publishing Group
200 Madison Avenue
New York, New York 10016
First Edition: November 1994
© 1994 Jim Richardson
10 9 8 7 6 5 4 3 2 1

Library of Congress Cataloging-in-Publication Data

Richardson, Jim.
    Classic car restorer's handbook : restoration tips and
techniques for owners and restorers of classic and collectible automobiles/Jim
Richardson.
       p. cm.
    Includes index.
    ISBN 1-55788-194-4
    1. Antique and classic cars–Conservation and restoration.
  2. Automobiles–Maintenance and repair.   I. Title.
TL152.2.R53   1994
629.28' 72–dc20   94-19094
                                                                  CIP

Book Design & Production by Bird Studios
Cover photo by Michael Lutfy
Back cover photos by Leslie Bird and Jim Richardson
Interior photos by Jim Richardson unless otherwise noted

ACKNOWLEDGMENTS

I wish to thank my good friend Steve Kimball for giving me my first opportunity to write, and for his patience and tutelage over the years. I also want to thank Michael Lutfy, HPBooks' Automotive Editorial Director, for giving me the chance to write this book, and for his careful editing, good advice and help. I am deeply grateful to restoration pros Paul Schinnerer, Cal Soest, Al Escalante, Jack Cooley and Charles Whiteley for their wise counsel, helpful suggestions and willingness to share their vast knowledge of classic cars. Finally, I owe a great debt of gratitude to my sons Scott and Steve for helping with the wrenching and photography, and my wife Bette for putting up with all the mess and the solitary evenings while I worked.

CONTENTS

INTRODUCTION

Would you like to own and drive a piece of automotive history, such as a Packard or Cadillac? Well . . . you can have one; or you can have a showroom perfect '47 Lincoln Continental, or a pristine '37 Packard. There's just one catch. They don't make them anymore, and the ones that do exist are either old and tired, or restored and expensive. So unless you are very fortunate financially, you'll need to do a bit of work to get such a car. But it's exciting work; you'll be learning new things all the time, and you'll be meeting interesting people in the process. And the best part is, when you're finished, you will have the classic or collectable car of your dreams. Brand new.

And I don't mean just new appearing. There are plenty of gorgeous looking older cars that have had expensive paint jobs and some chrome work done, but under the hood, they are still 20, 30 or 50 years old. They are not pleasant to drive, they are not dependable, and they are not restored. Their wiring is a fire hazard, they are prone to overheating, their shock absorbers have long since failed, and their brakes are marginal.

It's a pity, because for less than the price of a new Nissan Maxima—plus some hard, but enjoyable work—you can make any one of the above collector cars new.

And, when you're finished, you'll have a vehicle that will be distinctive and unique. And it will probably go up in value instead of down like a modern car. You don't have to be a pro to do the work, and you usually don't need a lot of experience either.

Lesson number one is to buy the right car. Make sure it is the model you want, and that it is complete without extensive rust. Photo by Michael Lutfy.

If you've always wanted to restore and drive an old car, but weren't sure how to go about it, this book is for you. It is intended for the new kid on the block, the hobbyist restorer, doing a car for the first time—and on a limited budget. It is also intended for those who love the process, the adventure, and the challenge of working on collector cars. Each chapter is written in an easy to follow, step-by-step format, so you can prop the book open on a fender, or your workbench, and do the job without having to wade through a lot of extraneous information, and possibly lose track and make an error as a result. There are no long, tedious history lessons either.

Shop manuals will tell you how to fix all of the mechanical parts of your car, and the directions on automotive paint cans will tell you how to do a paint job. Restorers should read these items carefully, as well as purchase specific skill-building books, e.g. a book on paint and body or welding, to become familiar with the techniques necessary to perform these tasks. But these sources of information don't tell you how to do things without the use of a lot of expensive equipment, and they don't always steer you away from possible mistakes. That's the reason for this book. Having been a hobbyist restorer for a number of years, and having made most of the mistakes it is possible to make, I can now offer you the benefits of my costly education at a fraction of the price I paid. The following are some of the lessons I've learned.

BUY THE RIGHT CAR

I don't mean that Fords are better than Chevrolets or Chryslers are better than Pontiacs. Any make or year of car is worth restoring if you love it. You must be happy and satisfied with the make and model car you want. This is a personal choice I can't help you with. However, what I really mean by buying the right car is start with a complete car that isn't badly rusted—especially if this is your first restoration. Extensive rust means expensive panel replacement, or at least a lot of careful cutting and welding. If a car is incomplete, especially if it is missing trim items, you will have to spend a lot of time and a lot of money to obtain the lost parts. How much depends on the rarity and age of your car.

Four-door sedans can be more expensive to restore, not only because of the extra sheet metal and upholstery, but also they offer the least return for the money because most people prefer more glamorous models. Coupes are probably the least expensive to redo, and offer a pretty good return, depending on the desirability of the make and year of the car. Convertibles of any kind are excellent investments, but hard to find and expensive to buy. Woodies are next in desirability, but offer their own unique restoration problems. However, rules were meant to be broken. Money isn't everything. I restored a 1936 Packard four-door sedan that I absolutely love and wouldn't sell for twice what it is worth.

Whichever year, make and model you restore, do it because you like the activity and you will enjoy owning and driving the car. Don't do it for money. Mutual funds are much better investments. However, old cars have their compensations too. You can't take friends out for breakfast on a sunny Sunday morning in a mutual fund.

SET UP A SHOP

Don't try to restore your car in your driveway or your back yard. You need at least a two-car garage, and you need plenty of light and good ventilation. You also need shelves. The average vintage car has more than 5000 parts. When you take yours apart, you will need a place to store these parts in an organized fashion. A big workbench is a must. So is a complete set of automotive hand tools. Virtual necessities are: an engine hoist, an engine stand, a two-horsepower compressor and an oxyacetylene torch. The reason I say virtual necessities, is because these items can be rented.

Of course, how much equipment you need depends on whether you just want to make your car look and run as it should or plan a bumper-to-bumper, ground-up, show-quality restoration. A good, original, low-mileage car should be left that way. No car is as correct as an original. And if your car is a common make and model, and it only needs a little work to make it right, it would be a waste of money and time to tear it all to pieces

10 rules to follow when BUYING A CLASSIC

1) Take a friend

Before you start looking for the vehicle of your dreams, read up on its specifications, color combinations and engine and transmission options so you can make sure you are getting what you are paying for. Bel Airs get turned into Impalas all the time merely by adding a little cosmetic trim, and any Fairlane can become a 427 by adding the little emblems on the fenders. Recently, a 1941 Packard 120 convertible was doctored up and sold in the Los Angeles area as a Super Eight. A Super Eight is a rare and valuable classic, whereas a 120 is not. The purchaser of the car was duped into paying 20 thousand dollars more than his purchase was worth. So be careful.

The best way to avoid an expensive mistake is to join the club for your marque and get to know the cars and the experts on them. Then take a knowledgeable friend or colleague with you when you are ready to consider a purchase, even if you have to pay him for the advice. It's less expensive to learn from the mistakes of others than from your own.

2) Check the body

Most novice restorers don't realize that collector car mechanical items are and restore it. But if your car is 25 to 60 years old, and has had a long service life, chances are it needs everything restored.

DO A LITTLE AT A TIME

Any old car buff that has been in the hobby for a few years has had opportunities to buy basketcases. They usually pass them up because they don't know which parts are missing, and they can't tell how things go back together, unless they are an expert on the car. Trouble is, neither can the owner. Basketcases usually aren't bargains, even if they are free, except as sources of parts for someone else's restoration. Don't make your car into one.

It's easy to do. If you tear into it without taking pictures, making notes, and storing things in an organized, logical way, you'll soon get lost and disheartened. And your car won't be a car anymore. It'll just be parts. A basketcase. Professional restoration shops often tear cars all to pieces when they restore them, but even they take pictures, make notes, and store things carefully. And they have a small army of trained, experienced, professionals who each know their area of the job as well as you know your living room.

So make your car into a series of little victories instead of one big defeat. Get your feet wet on one small task, such as doing the brakes. When you have that done, do another area. It may take a little longer to do a restoration that way, but your chances of success are much greater. Also, it is easier on your wallet.

DO THE MECHANICAL FIRST

At a recent, rather prestigious concours, a car won first place in its class, even though it barely ran. I know, because a few months later it was in a local repair shop having its engine overhauled and its steering and front suspension rebuilt. The owner made a sad mistake. Because in order to get the engine out, the front end had to be taken off of the car. And there was no way to do that without chipping the car's hand-rubbed lacquer paintwork, no matter how careful the mechanic was. Of course, the mechanic was careful—because he was paid to be—at the rate of $49 an hour! That adds up fast.

So go through your car's engine, driveline, brakes and other systems before doing the paint, chrome and upholstery. You don't want rusty water blowing all over your pretty paint job because you neglected the cooling system. And you don't want to slam into the back end of an ill-tempered attorney's BMW because you didn't do the brakes. Nor do you want your dreams to go up in smoke because you never got around to replacing that old, faulty wiring.

That's about all of the general advice I have to offer, so let's get specific. The sooner we start, the sooner we'll be on the road, turning heads, in that new '56 Eldorado, '40 Ford, or '65 GTO.

—*Jim Richardson*

---

generally less expensive, and easier to repair, than major body panel problems. Before you seriously consider any car as a prospective project, pull it out into the sun, or better yet, under some bright fluorescent lights, then squat down and sight along the length of each side of the body. Is it wavy or rumpled? Are there funny lumps and bulges? These are indications of collision damage. If so, the panels will need to be fixed. Depending on the extent of the problem, a good body and fender repair person may be able to fix it, but it is quite possible that the only way to make the car look right will be to unbolt, or cut off the bad panels and replace them. Such work can get very expensive.

Next, check to make sure the doors, hood and trunk lid fit squarely and align properly with surrounding panels. Also check to make sure the bumpers aren't slanted, sagging or deformed. These items could be indicative of extensive damage and a bent frame.

Make sure all the trim pieces are there and in good shape. These are some of the hardest items to find for any classic. If pieces are missing, you may want to assure yourself that you can get replacements and find out how much they would cost before you make an offer on the car.

3) Look for rust & filler

Take along a magnet or the Spot Rot gauge by Pro Motorcar Products (813-726-6587) when you go out to inspect a prospective purchase. Assuming the car has a steel body (a few sports cars are made of aluminum or fiberglass) a magnet should stick to it. Run your magnet over areas that are likely to have suffered an impact or to have rusted out. Fenders and doors get hit a lot, and kick panels, door sills and aprons under trunk lids are especially vulnerable to rust. If your magnet doesn't stick to a spot, you may have discovered a thick patch of body filler. If you do find such a spot, try to look at the back side of the panel. You may be able to see what the problem is.

Poorly repaired dents or rusted areas in themselves may not preclude the purchase of a car, providing it is what you want, you can get it for the right price, and you are prepared to make the necessary repairs. But you need to know about these problems before negotiating a deal. If you don't, you lose, and sometimes you lose big. I once was shown what looked like a nicely restored '40 Chevrolet coupe that a fellow had purchased for a healthy price, on which the trunk apron had rusted away completely. The previous owner had reconstructed the apron with wire mesh and Bondo. It looked perfect for a while, but not for long.

4) Try the electrics

Inspect the wire harness under the hood, in the trunk, and under the dash. Are wires frayed, cracked, or disconnected? If so, you will need to install a new harness in order to make the car safe and dependable to operate. Try each electrical accessory to make sure it works properly. Don't forget electric windows, dimmer switches, horns and door locks.

5) Inspect the engine

Read the diagnostic section in Chapter 1 for engines. There are some tips in it that can help you determine any engine's condition. Check the oil. It is okay if it is black because most detergent oil is if it has been in the engine any length of time. But if it is gray and muddy, it may be full of sludge due to a cracked block or blown head gasket. Start the engine up and check for smoke or steam. Black smoke may just be an over-rich carburetor, but bluish smoke means crankcase blowby due to worn piston rings or valve guides.

A great deal of steam, on the other hand, could mean that water is getting into the combustion chambers due to a cracked head or block, or possibly a blown head gasket. If the car has been operated this way for long the engine

Another tip: Make sure you do the mechanical end of the restoration first. You'll be more than a bit disappointed if your expensive, show-winning bodywork and paint is chipped, dented and scratched while rebuilding the engine. Do the engine, chassis and drivetrain first, then turn your attention to sheet metal, trim and upholstery. Photo by Michael Lutfy.

may have been badly damaged.

Do a compression check. Cars are costly. It is well worth the little time and trouble that is involved to check the compression on any car you are seriously considering buying. Many classic car engines, especially inline 6s and 8s, will sound very smooth even when they are worn out. A compression check is the best way to be sure of their condition. Anyone who is serious about selling his car should be willing to allow a compression check in his presence, provided the individual doing the checking is careful with the car.

Also, you will want to read up on how your favorite car's engine, transmission and differential were numbered so you can verify whether the car has its original equipment or not. Cars with matching numbers are worth more than those whose numbers don't match, but if the price is right, and the engine is correct for that year of car, you may want to buy it anyway. If you are just looking for a nice driver, numbers aren't so important.

6) Check the cooling system

Read the troubleshooting section of the cooling system chapter of this book for tips in this area. Remove the radiator cap and look for rust. Ideally the water should be clear or the color of coolant. Older cars that were made to run with only water in them may show a little rusty discoloration, but the rust should not be thick. Warm the car up for about 20 minutes to see if it overheats. Remove the radiator cap and see if the coolant is flowing freely in the upper reservoir of the radiator. Check the freeze plugs for leaks. Also check the coolant for traces of oil. If the engine has a cracked block or blown head gasket, oil will sometimes get into the cooling system.

7) Check the shocks

Give the car the bounce test. Press on the front fender or bumper to get the car oscillating up and down. When you quit bouncing it, the car should come back up, then settle slightly and stop. If it keeps on bouncing, the shock absorbers need rebuilding or replacing. Do the same test at the back of the car.

8) Test the brakes

Take the car for a test drive and try the brakes. The car should stop smoothly with no fading (diminishing of stopping power) and it should track in a straight line. If you hear a grinding or scraping noise, the brakes may be worn down past the linings. If that is the case, you may have to replace a drum. Brake drums for heavier, older American cars aren't easy to find.

If the car pulls to one side, or the pedal goes down slowly, the hydraulic system may have a leak. With a flashlight, check the back of each wheel for signs of leaking brake fluid. Also inspect the master cylinder. A complete brake job on a vintage car could cost as much as $400 to $600 so you need to know what you are getting into. If the brakes fade when you step on them, the drums may have been turned too many times, or there may be condensation in the brake lines.

9) Try the steering

Take any prospective purchase for a good long drive of half an hour or more, and try it out under different conditions. Does the steering wheel shimmy at certain speeds? If so, the front end may need rebuilding. Does the car wander? The verdict is the same for this problem. Is there a lot of play, or slop, in the steering wheel before the car starts to turn? If so, the steering linkage may be worn, or the steering box may need an overhaul. Parts are generally available for most classic car front ends, but a rebuild can cost $500 on some cars.

10) Know your market

Before you buy, check classic car price guides to see what the car of your dreams is going for. Classic car price guides usually only tell you what such a car sold for at auction last time around, so they can't be relied upon completely. Watch such publications as *Hemmings Motor News* and *Classic Auto Restorer* to establish price benchmarks. Club publications are helpful too.

Old pros in the restoration business will tell you that any collector car is only worth what someone will pay for it, not what an appraiser says it's worth, or what a price guide decrees. Condition is the most important single factor. A perfectly restored or exceptional original car is worth much more than one that needs a lot of work. Year, make and model are very important to a car's worth too. A '57 Thunderbird is worth much more than a '58. A show-quality '57 goes for around $46,000 at this writing, but a '58 convertible in the same shape is only worth around $28,000. Prices can vary considerably even from one year to the next, so do your homework before you start writing checks.

Rarity doesn't necessarily make a car valuable. A '57 Studebaker Scotsman is much rarer than a '57 Chevrolet, but Chevys are worth more because they are as popular today as they were when they were made, whereas the Scotsman wasn't popular when it was made, and is all but forgotten today. Generally, cars that were held in high esteem in their own time are still popular, whether they were rare and costly or quite common. The Model A Ford is an example of a car that has never been rare, but is still extremely popular and can command a good price. ■

ENGINE OVERHAULING

Although no part of your classic's driveline is more important to the car's operation than any other, the engine ends up getting the most attention. This is probably because it is the one assembly in the running gear that keeps your classic from being an expensive paperweight. Nothing can happen without it, so we tend to look after it. But the main reason the engine requires so much care is because it is the most dynamic mechanism in your car. While most of the parts in your car's driveline just spin, the parts in your engine move in strange ways. Pistons get slammed down and shoved up; pushrods, rocker arms and valves jump around at a furious rate; and connecting rods get pivoted from side to side. All of this takes place thousands of times per minute in a very hot environment.

Hundreds, and usually thousands, of small explosions occur within a gasoline or diesel engine every minute it is running. The heat in the combustion chambers is intense, and can be especially hard on valves, heads, and the tops of pistons. Your car's cooling system is able to control this heat adequately, provided it is in good working order, and provided that the fuel-to-air mixture and the ignition timing are correct.

But even under ideal operating conditions, the top end of every piston engine eventually succumbs to heat and wear. The valves burn, their guides wear out, the heads warp, and the pistons collapse and become loose. The piston rings and cylinder bores in the block wear out too because of the up-and-down friction of the rings, and the slight wobbling back and forth of the pistons on their wrist pins.

The bottom end (crankshaft and connecting rods) gets pushed around as

With careful planning, the right parts and proper tools, it is possible to rebuild your own engine. In addition to the tips that follow, locate a shop manual for your car. Don't compromise here: without a properly running, reliable engine, your classic becomes an expensive piece of furniture. Photo by Michael Lutfy.

well. Fast-moving parts are supported by bearings that take a pounding from the reciprocating action of the engine. Over time, these bearings wear out of round, so their clearances become too wide in places. Oil pressure drops as a result. At this point, the engine will require attention or it will expire.

But how do you determine if your engine has reached this point? Actually, it's not that difficult. A little detective work will tell you a great deal, and there are tests you can run at home with inexpensive equipment that will give you a pretty accurate picture of the situation. To begin with, let's give your engine a complete physical examination and a compression check.

INSPECTION

You can tell a lot about an engine's condition just by examining it carefully. Start by inspecting where the heads mate to the block. Do you see any wet or rusty streaks running down the block? If you do, you may have a blown head gasket. In that case, the head will have to be removed, the gasket replaced, and the head re-torqued into place. Check around the soft plugs (freeze plugs) to see if any of them are weeping. If so, the offender

will need to be removed and a new one installed.

Next, check for oil leaks at all of the mating surfaces between the heads, block, valve covers, pan and timing gear cover. Crawl under your classic and look for leaks around the front, and especially the rear main bearings at each end of the oil pan. Most oil leaks can be fixed simply by replacing a defective seal, but main bearing leaks are a much bigger problem. On many engines, you will have to pull the crankshaft out in order to get at them.

Remove the radiator cap and inspect the coolant. Is it full of rust and reddish muck? Flushing the system may be all that is necessary to get rid of it, but it is quite possible that rust has accumulated in the waterjackets of the engine, especially in the areas furthest from the water pump. If that is the case, you will have to pull the engine from the car, clean out the rust, and have the block hot-tanked at a machine shop.

If you find that your coolant looks a lot like chocolate pudding—dark, thick and gooey—you may have a blown head gasket or cracked block. The goo is likely a result of oil mixing with coolant in your engine due to these problems. These two

fluids are supposed to remain separate at all times. Check your oil. If it has a similar look, it probably has coolant in it as well. In either case, the verdict is the same. You will need to replace the blown head gasket, or replace or repair the cracked block.

Checking Spark Plugs

Remove the spark plugs and look them over. If any are wet or rusty, again, a leaking head gasket or cracked block may be the cause. On the other hand, if the plugs are black and exceptionally sooty or coated with oil, you probably have worn piston rings, or worn valve guides in the case of an overhead valve engine. However, if the plugs are dry, but black and caked with carbon, it may be that the air/fuel mixture from your carburetor is too rich. See the chapter on carburetors for help with this problem.

Healthy plugs usually mean a healthy engine. Bottom end bearings could still be worn or damaged, but the valves, pistons and rings are probably okay if the plugs show a little discoloration at the base of their porcelain insulators and their electrodes and metal bases have a slightly sooty deposit on them. But if the plugs

Spark plugs can tell you a lot about your engine's condition. The one on the left is ash gray, indicating too lean a fuel mixture. Its electrode will soon burn. The plug in the center is wet with oil indicating worn rings or valve guides. The plug on the right is healthy because it has a light coating of soot and a slightly discolored porcelain insulator around its electrode.

White aluminum oxide on this piston indicates moisture getting into combustion chambers. It is usually the result of a leaking head gasket or a cracked block or head.

are ash gray or the electrodes burned, your engine is running too lean.

Inspecting the Oil

Start your engine and run it until it is thoroughly warm. Now drain the oil. If it has been in the engine for awhile, it should be black, but it should not contain water or fine metal particles. Either of these unwanted ingredients spell trouble. Water indicates a leaking head gasket or cracked block. Metal particles mean bearings may be self-destructing. But a fine gray streak in your oil as it runs out of the pan is nothing to worry about. It is a byproduct of combustion and it only means your oil needs changing. But if you can feel particles in the oil when you rub it between your fingers, it means trouble. An overhaul is probably in order. The following are definitions of symptoms that can be diagnosed by oil inspection.

Oil Smoke—Black or dark gray smoke is usually the result of an overly rich fuel mixture resulting in too much fuel getting into the combustion chambers. This problem can be caused by a carburetor with a sticking choke or one that is out of adjustment. Also, in the case of cars equipped with a compound mechanical fuel pump, oil may be leaking into the fuel system through a torn diaphragm in the pump chamber. Such problems are easily remedied. Chokes and carburetors can be cleaned and adjusted, and fuel pumps overhauled. But blue and bluish white smoke tells another story.

It generally indicates that the oil and compression rings on your pistons are worn and, as a result, oil is seeping up past them. This condition is known as *blowby*. Advertising claims to the contrary, nothing sold in a can will fix, or even help, this condition. The engine needs rebuilding. But blue smoke can, in the case of an overhead valve engine, also mean that your valve guides are worn, allowing oil to run down into the combustion chambers from the valvetrain above.

Oil Consumption—If you've owned and driven such a car for awhile, you will have probably noticed that in addition to blue smoke you have experienced unacceptable oil consumption. How much is unacceptable? If your car uses a quart or more every thousand miles, you have cause to worry. If the engine isn't leaking it, it must be burning it. Repairs are in order.

Broken pistons and rings will allow oil to seep into the combustion chamber. Blue smoke is a sign of such trouble. It can also mean that rings are badly worn and need to be replaced, or that the valve guides in an overhead valve engine are worn, allowing oil to seep past them.

Steam—Steam emanating from the tailpipe of a fully warmed engine is another ominous sign. Water, and water vapor, commonly comes out the tailpipe of a car just after it is started, but if steam issues from an engine that is up to full operating temperature, it often means a leaking head gasket or a cracked block. Of course, on a cold day, a certain amount of steamy condensation can be expected. It is only when you see a great deal of it that you have to worry.

Low Oil Pressure—Other sure signs of serious problems are: low oil pressure, especially at idle; lack of power, and hard starting. (Assuming the engine is in proper tune.) Such symptoms usually mean that the rod and crankshaft bearings are worn, so their clearances are loose, and that the valves are no longer sealing properly, meaning that the engine is generally tired. In addition to these signs of problems, if you know what to listen for, funny noises can tip you off to problems as well.

Noises—A low clunking or rumbling sound under load usually means worn main bearings, and a clacking or clanging sound on acceleration indicates *piston slap*. A compound rattle, especially at certain engine speeds, means worn rod bearings, and a sudden clatter when backing off the throttle is likely to be worn wrist pins. Sometimes the location of such problems can be pinpointed using a special engine stethoscope or by simply pressing a long screwdriver or length of hose against the block in different areas and listening carefully at the other end of it.

A commonly heard symptom of trouble is a rhythmic "chuffing" sound when the engine is idling. It usually means a burned exhaust valve. Of course, it could also mean that the valves are only badly out of adjustment, or that there is a broken valve spring or a bent pushrod. If your engine has mechanical lifters, do a valve adjustment as outlined in Chapter 21. Doing a valve adjustment is a good idea anyway, because any diagnostic tests you run will only be accurate if the valves are set properly. If an adjustment doesn't

smooth and quiet your engine, pop off the valve covers and side plates and look things over carefully. With the engine running, slip a slot-head screwdriver in between the coils of each valve spring and twist slightly. If the noise goes away, or diminishes, you have weak valve springs.

Piston slap is a dull or hollow sound. The piston is actually wobbling around inside the bore. A collapsed piston skirt causes a similar but much louder noise. This can best be heard when the engine is cold. It decreases as the engine warms up and the piston expands to reduce piston-to-bore clearance. To check for piston slap, retard the spark. Loosen the distributor lock-down bolt and rotate the distributor a few degrees counter clockwise. If you're suffering piston slap, this should reduce the noise. Don't forget to reset the distributor after this test.

A light knocking or pounding noise that's not related to detonation or preignition is probably due to excess connecting rod bearing-to-journal clearance. This means the bearing is worn out. Finally, a light tapping or clicking noise may indicate excess pin-bore clearance in a piston.

To confirm and pinpoint a particular bottom-end noise, disconnect and reconnect the spark plugs one at a time. When you disconnect the wire from the bad cylinder, that cylinder is unloaded. Power is eliminated with the cylinder and the piston-and-rod assembly "relaxes," eliminating or reducing the noise it was making. The noise should disappear or be greatly reduced. If this test is being performed on a car with a solid-state (electronic) ignition, be sure the plug wire is grounded. If not, you run the risk of damaging the electronic control module.

Kits are available that make this a simple task. They consist of jumpers, or short wire springs, that snap over the plug end and into the plug wires. The cylinder can then be disabled by touching the spring with an insulated wire grounded to the engine.

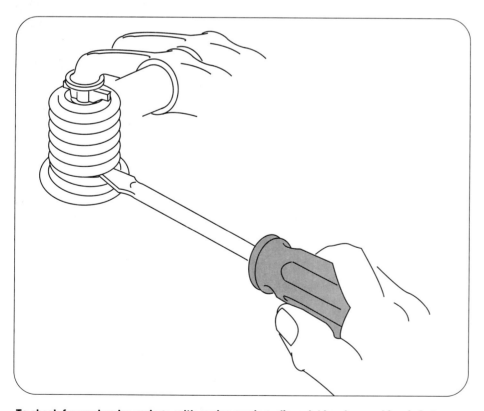

To check for weak valve springs, with engine running, slip a slot-head screwdriver in between the coils of each valve spring and twist. If the clicking goes away, the valve spring is weak.

Noises at Half-Engine Speed—If you're hearing a sharp clacking or rapping noise at half-engine speed, this indicates your engine probably has a collapsed hydraulic lifter. If the noise is a light clicking, it's probably excess clearance in one of the valve mechanisms. If this clicking gradually diminishes or disappears after the engine is started in the morning, for example, the problem is a lifter with excessive *leakdown*. Due to wear, oil leaks out of the lifter and it collapses under the load of the valve spring. When the lifter is pumped up—pressurized with oil—the noise goes away, but a completely failed lifter will not pump up.

To double-check a noisy valve lifter, remove the valve cover on the noisy side. With the engine idling, insert a feeler gauge between each rocker arm and its valve stem one at a time. When you get to the offending valve, the noise will stop or change pitch considerably because the feeler gauge has taken up the clearance. Suspect a malfunctioning lifter or bent pushrod, particularly if the engine has been over-revved.

Obviously, any engine that has done a lot of miles without an overhaul should probably be refurbished. How many miles are a lot? That depends. Cars made before the 1950's rarely went much beyond 100,000 without major work. Cars from the Brass Era and early twenties needed overhauls every year. But, thanks to better lubricants and better alloys, cars made in the last 20 years can sometimes go in excess of 200,000 miles without a complete overhaul. The best way to judge how many miles is a lot for your car is to get to know people who own the same brand and year and work on the car themselves. They will be able to tell you what to expect.

TESTING

The detective work outlined above can give you a general idea of your engine's

A compression test will tell you a great deal about your engine and is easy to perform. Follow the steps outlined in this section and note each cylinder's compression. Don't forget to set the gauge back to zero between cylinders. Compression should be consistent, and should be within specifications established by the manufacturer.

condition, but there are some simple tests that can really get to the heart of the matter. All you need in order to perform them are a couple of inexpensive gauges available at most auto supply stores. We'll also tell you about a more esoteric test, called a *leakdown test,* that is commonly used on reciprocating aircraft engines. It has found favor with street rodders because of its accuracy. You may want to try it yourself.

Compression Testing

The most commonly used test to determine an automotive engine's condition is the *compression test,* an indicator of a cylinder's sealing capability. It has been around since the horseless carriage days, it is simple to perform, and it is accurate enough to tell you almost everything you need to know. But before attempting it, make sure your engine is in proper tune, its valves correctly adjusted, and its battery fully charged. Otherwise, your readings could be faulty.

Warm It Up—Compression should always be checked with the engine at full operating temperature. Take your car out for at least a 20 minute drive so all of its metal parts can warm up and expand to their correct clearances. Check a shop manual to see what the compression should be for your engine.

Test the Cylinders—Shut the engine off, block the choke and throttle wide open, then remove the spark plugs. Now have a friend crank the engine while you check the compression. Push the nipple of the gauge into a spark plug hole while the engine turns over several times. Note each cylinder's reading, then return the gauge to zero.

A difference of up to 6 psi is acceptable from one cylinder to another; and if your engine is consistently a few pounds lower than the specified compression in your shop manual it just means it has aged due to use. But if any of the cylinders are more than 10 pounds low, your engine needs work. And if they are all 10 pounds low or lower, you're probably in for an overhaul.

Is It Piston Rings?—If your compression checked out low on any cylinder, the problem could be in the rings, or valves, or a combination of the two. To determine if you have worn rings, squirt a little oil in the spark plug hole for that cylinder, then test it again. If the compression test reads normal, worn piston rings are the problem.

Is It Valves?—If the compression does not come up on re-testing, burned valves or a blown head gasket are the likely problem. However, if you didn't adjust your valves before performing the test, they may only need to have their clearances set. Before tearing your engine apart, adjust your valves properly and do another compression test.

Is It Rings & Valves?—If the compression comes up a little upon oiling and re-testing, but not enough, the problem may be rings and valves.

Is It a Blown Head Gasket?—If the compression is down in two adjacent cylinders, the problem is likely to be a blown head gasket. Sometimes, re-torquing the head will solve the problem, but most likely you will need to remove the head and replace the gasket.

Is It a Stuck Lifter or Broken Valve Spring?—Hydraulic valve lifters will sometimes get dirt in them and collapse or stick. There are products available that can be poured into the crankcase oil that will sometimes free stuck lifters; but usually, bad lifters must be removed and cleaned or rebuilt. Broken valve springs are another possible source of problems. Remove the valve covers on your engine and check the springs by prying them with a screwdriver. They should be tightly held in the valve actuating mechanisms.

Are the Rings Stuck in Their Grooves?—Sometimes piston rings will stick in their grooves due to carbon buildup. Shoot a little solvent or kerosene into the cylinder and see if it loosens them up. If not, a ring job is probably in order.

Vacuum Gauge

Because an internal combustion engine is essentially a big air pump, much can be learned about its condition by monitoring the flow of air being sucked into it during operation. For that you need a vacuum gauge. A vacuum gauge indicates the difference between the air pressure inside the intake manifold and the atmospheric pressure outside the manifold. If you know how to use one, a vacuum gauge can tell you a number of things about your engine. It can provide information about leaks and burned valves, late ignition timing, poor carburetor adjustment and exhaust backpressure problems. For our purposes in this chapter, we'll be using it to determine your engine's overall

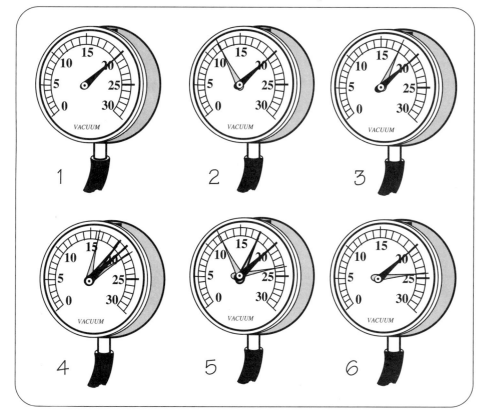

These are some of the readings you should get when you run a compression test. (1) An engine that is in good condition should indicate a steady 18-22 inches of vacuum pressure at sea level with the engine idling. (2) If needle fluctuates below normal with engine idling it could indicate an air leak at the intake manifold gasket, or at the carburetor gasket. It could also indicate a leaking head gasket. (3) A regular, intermittent drop below normal indicates valve leakage. (4) Rapid intermittent dropping from normal indicates sticking valves. Try vacuum readings with open and closed throttle. (5) Fluctuations increasing with engine speed indicate weak valve springs. (6) If, with engine idling, fast vibrations, but normal vacuum are evident, it is an indication of ignition trouble. Slow movement at normal vacuum indicates incorrect carburetor adjustment.

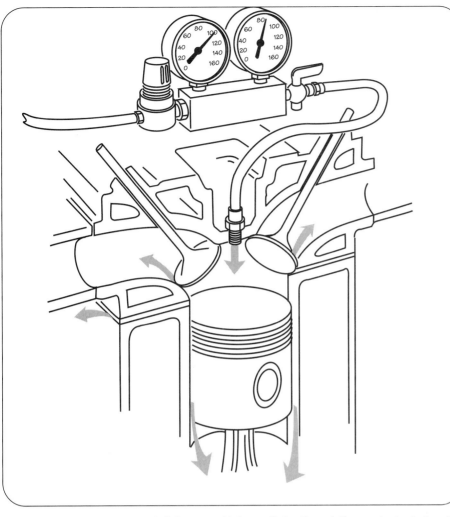

In a leakdown test, compressed air is pumped into a cylinder through the spark plug hole until 100 psi is reached on a gauge, then a second gauge attached to the testing device measures how long it takes for compressed air to leak out around valves and piston rings.

cars with vacuum-operated windshield wipers, you can simply disconnect the wiper motor and tie into its tubing. On cars equipped with a vacuum booster pump on the top of the fuel pump, you will need to disconnect the booster pump. Make sure you have a good seal at the gauge tubing connections before beginning your test.

Set the Idle—Warm the engine thoroughly before beginning the test. The best way to warm the car up is to drive it for 20 minutes or so. Don't just go by your temperature gauge, because it can't tell you enough. A tachometer can be handy to make sure your engine is idling at the correct speed while testing (a shop manual can give you the exact figure to expect). Or, on most older cars, you can simply adjust the throttle so the car will roll along at about 7 to 10 miles an hour in low gear with your foot off of the gas. Assuming the test is being done at sea level, the vacuum gauge should show a steady reading of from 18 to 22 inches if your engine is in good condition.

To isolate problems, consult the illustration on page 6. The black needle indicates a steady reading, and the white needles indicate fluctuations. If you have never used a vacuum gauge before, find someone who has, and ask them to give you a second opinion as to your findings. Another way to get a feel for the use of a

condition, but it would pay any novice mechanic to learn how to use one for the other things too.

Due to the fact that a vacuum gauge measures the difference between atmospheric pressure and the pressure in your intake manifold rather than measuring from some fixed benchmark, if you live above sea level you need to take into account the lower atmospheric pressure when you use your gauge. See the chart nearby to adjust for the readings at different altitudes. The readings are measured in inches, which refers to the number of inches the pressure would cause mercury to move up a glass tube in an old-fashioned barometric gauge.

Hook It Up—To use a vacuum gauge, you will need to remove a plug on the intake manifold and install a fitting that will let you hook up the rubber tubing from your vacuum gauge. On some earlier

VACUUM GAUGE READINGS AT DIFFERENT ALTITUDES

The following figures are for a well-tuned engine at idle.

Sea level to 1,000 feet	18 to 22 inches
1,000 to 2,000	17 to 21
2,000 to 3,000	16 to 20
3,000 to 4,000	15 to 19
4,000 to 5,000	14 to 18
5,000 to 6,000	13 to 17

On many cars of the '20s, '30s and '40s the front clip, consisting of the front fenders, grille, radiator and cowl, can be removed as a unit, making engine work easy. On later model cars, you will need to leave the front sheetmetal in place, remove the hood, and lift the engine up and out carefully with a cherry picker.

the sealing qualities of the cylinder by filling it with compressed air. The advantage is that outside air pressure and variable internal engine specifications don't affect the readings, therefore it is more accurate. It actually measures how much air is leaking past the rings, valves, etc. Although each manufacturer has different scales of readings, generally, a good cylinder will have between 5 and 10% leakage of the recommended test pressure.

Literature accompanying the device will tell you how to use the tester, and what the result of your test means. Leakdown testers can be ordered from larger auto supply stores or performance and speed shops.

vacuum gauge is to set up your engine to exhibit certain symptoms, such as ignition trouble or manifold leaks, then observe the consequences on your gauge.

Leakdown Testing

A test that is not as commonly used to determine engine condition as the compression test, but is much more accurate, is a leakdown test. Mechanics who work on reciprocating aircraft engines have used this test for years to determine the condition of an engine's top end, and racers and street rodders looking for that winner's edge have adopted it too. Manley and Moroso offer these gauges. If you do decide to purchase one, you'll need a compressed air supply of 80 psi minimum to perform the test.

Essentially, a leakdown test determines

DISASSEMBLY

There's only one way to disassemble an engine—carefully. If you get hurried and disorganized, you'll turn a fun project into a big problem. Basic rules are: Don't bang on things, keep parts organized and clean, and take photos, make sketches or take notes of parts and systems as they come off. These are general, basic rules. Specific procedures for step-by-step removal are beyond the scope of this book, which focuses on general tips. For specific procedures, you'll have to locate an engine manual for

THINGS YOU'LL NEED:

- Cherry picker engine hoist
- Wrenches (open, boxed, combination, socket) from 3/8" to 7/8" for American made cars)
- Assorted screwdrivers

- Flare-nut (tubing wrenches)
- Pieces of cardboard or carpet (to protect radiator and fenders during removal)
- Channel-lock pliers
- Shallow drain pan

- Engine stand
- Sharp putty knife
- Gasket remover
- Propane or acetylene torch
- Small ballpeen hammer

your car. However, there really isn't any mystery involved in yanking an engine from a car. The following tips should get you there if you use some mechanical common sense.

But before we don our grubbies and whip out the socket set and start wrenching, let's get things ready. First, if you don't have a good engine hoist, borrow or rent one. The easiest to use are the "cherry picker" types which cantilever an arm over the car and will roll on wheels. Don't be tempted to suspend a chainfall from your garage rafters to remove your engine. Old-car cast-iron engines can weigh as much as 1000 lbs. Even a little Chevy 6 weighs 500 lbs. fully assembled, so you'll be flirting with a disaster if you attempt to lift out your motor using this method.

While you're at it, obtain an engine stand too. You want one that will let you rotate the engine on its crankshaft axis so you can work on the bottom end as well as the top. It should roll on wheels or casters so you can move it around. Pickup some containers to hold the old motor oil and coolant as well. Environmental regulations stipulate that you must dispose of these fluids at an approved facility. Furthermore, they must be kept separate. Failure to do this can result in a very hefty fine. Finally, round up a healthy assistant who isn't afraid to get his hands dirty to help you with the task.

Removal

Engines can sometimes be overhauled without removing them from the chassis on cars made before World War II. Motors from the era of Model A Fords can easily be overhauled in the chassis provided they don't need new bearings poured or their cylinders rebored. But usually, in order to make an engine better than new after it has been in service for years, you will need to take it out of the car and rebuild it from the block up.

Before you start wrenching, as we said

in the beginning of this chapter, get a shop guide or an old *MoTors* manual, and read up on how your car was designed. You need answers to such questions as: Do you pull the engine and transmission together? And do they come out the top, or do you lower them out the bottom? Late thirties cars with inline engines, such as some Oldsmobiles and small series Packards, were designed to have their engines lowered into pits. Back then, garages usually had pits rather than hydraulic lifts for working under cars. It was easier to lower the engine and transmission out the bottom as a unit into the pit and thus avoid damaging the front end and radiator. But there are a couple of things you need to do before you begin.

Take a few Polaroids to show how things are arranged under the hood before removing your engine's accessories. Disconnect and remove the battery from your car. Be careful not to break the poles loose in the battery. Use two wrenches working against each other so as not to put any torque on them. Now wash your engine down with a commercial degreaser such as tri-sodium phosphate (T.S.P.), or just use a strong mixture of laundry detergent and water.

Drain Fluids—Drain the coolant and oil and dispose of them according to local laws. (Chances are, a nearby gas station or oil and lube center will take them for a small fee). Radiators usually have a petcock on their bottom tanks. If the petcock is stuck, shoot on a little WD-40 on it, tap on it very gently and try again. Don't apply muscle—you'll probably break it off if you do because chances are it is made of brass, and brass is soft. If the petcock still won't budge, pull the lower

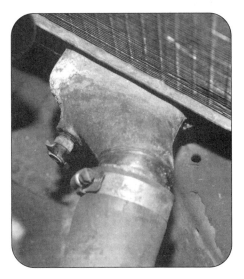

Drain the radiator coolant from the petcock if one is installed. Chances are, it is also stuck. If it is, spray some WD-40 on it and tap it very gently. Have your drain pan ready!

Many old cars have the rear motor mounts on the transmission. If your car is made this way, you will need to support the engine before making them loose. Support it at the mounting flanges, not at the oil pan, because the pan will not support its weight.

radiator hose loose, but be prepared for a flood. If the hose has bonded itself to the radiator flange, cut the hose, rather than poking around where it attaches to the radiator with a screwdriver. You don't want to damage the flange.

Radiator & Water Pump Removal— Remove the fan-shroud bolts, then lay the shroud back over the fan. If the car has an automatic transmission and a transmission cooler, disconnect the transmission cooler lines from the bottom of the radiator tank. A flare-nut or line wrench will help prevent rounding the corners of the nut. When the lines are disconnected they'll leak automatic transmission fluid (ATF) so have your drain pan under them. ATF may siphon from the transmission through these lines. To prevent this, push a short piece of fuel line over the end of each tube, fold the hose back on itself and wire it in place. This will ensure the 13 quarts of ATF stay in the tranny.

To protect the fins, tape a piece of cardboard to the back of the radiator. Remove the radiator mounting bolts, then lift the radiator straight up and out. Be careful as the cooling fins are very delicate and easily bent if dragged across anything. While you have the radiator in your hands, check for signs of leaks— noted by rust stains—a bent or poorly repaired core, loose fins or any other signs of potential problems. Unless the radiator is in top condition, I suggest you have it reconditioned. It would be terrible to fry a brand-new engine because of a leaking radiator. With the radiator out, remove the thermostat housing and top radiator hose as a unit.

Remove Accessories— Remove such items as the generator, starter, distributor, carburetor and fuel pump and store them carefully with the respective fasteners labeled and attached. Store these items in plastic bags for overhauling later. Remove these items before taking the engine loose from its mounts. (Sometimes the easiest thing to do after you remove a part is to put fasteners back

in place so you won't mix them up.) These accessories can easily get bumped and ruined if left in place when you lift the engine out. Before you remove the distributor, mark it with a china marker as to which nipple on the distributor cap is the number one cylinder. Don't use a pencil because graphite conducts electricity, so it may cause a short later. If possible, remove the cap with the wires still intact.

Hood— Draw around where the hood attaches to its hinges before attempting to remove it. If you forget to do this, lining your hood up when you reinstall it can be a major undertaking. Also, wire any shims you find between the hood and hinge to the hinge so you won't lose them or mix them up.

Lift Out Engine— The following operations must be strictly adhered to for safe and easy engine removal. If you're using a chain, it should be at least three-feet long. The chain should have at least 3/16-in. diameter welded links.

A chain that's too long can always be hooked up shorter—adjusted so the engine will clear the car before the cherry picker reaches its maximum height. The excess chain can be piled on the engine.

There is a good reason for the minimum-length chain. If the chain is too short, or hooked up too short, the engine could slide forward or backward through the hook due to the small angle of the chain. More important, the shallow angle places excessive loads on the chain, bolts and engine-attaching points. This greatly increases the danger of chain breakage and injury.

To avoid this problem, don't hook the chain up any shorter than necessary, certainly no shorter than three feet and use a fender washer between each bolt head and the chain. A fender washer is a large-diameter washer with a small hole.

Fasten the chain to the left front and right rear of the engine. Make a final check for any wires, lines, hoses, bolts or other items you may have forgotten or

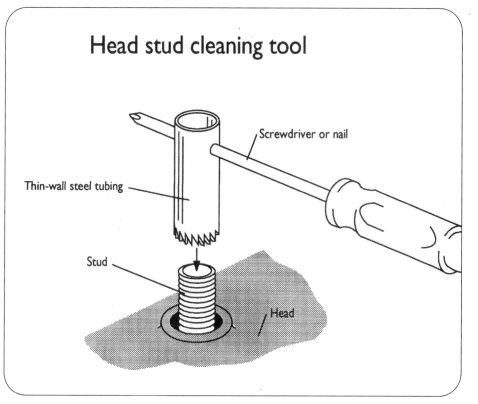

Head stud cleaning tool

Screwdriver or nail

Thin-wall steel tubing

Stud

Head

A tool can easily be made to clean corrosion from around studs on cylinder heads by filing notches into one end of a piece of thin-wall steel tubing, then drilling a hole and putting a nail or Phillips screwdriver in the other end so you can turn the tool. Slip the tool down over the stud and turn it to remove rust. Head will usually come off easily after use of this tool.

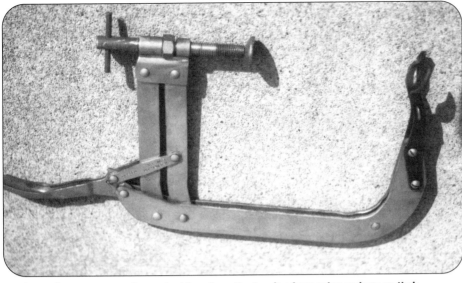

A valve spring compressor is required to relieve the tension from valve springs on their keepers. Use the tool to compress each valve spring, then pull its keeper out of the slot in the end of the valve. The valve and spring can now be lifted out easily.

overlooked. When you're sure everything is ready, position the cherry picker or hoist over the engine. Place the hook under the chain or through the lifting-plate loop and slowly start lifting the engine.

As the engine lifts, the front end of the car will rise with it. This is normal, because the front suspension is being unloaded. At this point, place the jack under the transmission. Keep the jack under the transmission until the engine is out. This keeps the front end of the transmission from dropping and damaging the transmission mount, U-joints or shift linkage.

Raise the engine until the engine mounts clear the frame. Rock the engine from side-to-side to separate it from the bellhousing. If it won't separate, coax the engine and bellhousing apart with a large screwdriver or small prybar. Double check to make sure all the bolts are out first. When they separate, continue to raise the engine and pull forward. If the car is equipped with a manual transmission, the engine will have to come forward enough for the input shaft to clear the clutch.

Raise the engine high enough to clear the front of the car and wheel it out, or roll the car from under the engine. But before you move the car, tie the transmission up

to the firewall. Old coat hangers are great for this. Now you can lower the car and remove the jack.

While the engine is suspended from the hoist or cherry picker, bolt the engine-stand plate to the rear of the block using the bellhousing bolt holes. Place the engine stand onto the engine-stand plate

To make your life easier, pick up a can of gasket remover, such as this brand from Permatex. It will help you scrape off the old gasket residue on the block and heads, as well as on other mating surfaces. Photo by Don Taylor.

and lower it and the engine as one assembly.

Remove the Head(s)—Heads can be difficult to get off, but not because—as some believe—they are stuck to the block. Usually the problem is due to corrosion between the heads and the mounting studs. Remove the head nuts, then use a putty knife to pop the heads off. If they don't want to budge, shoot a little penetrating oil between the studs and the head, let it soak in, then gently tap the studs with a ballpeen hammer. The object isn't to bash things loose, but to set up a vibration that will crack the corrosion between the head and the studs.

If the above method doesn't help, find a short piece of thinwall steel tubing that just fits over the head studs. File saw teeth in one end of the tubing. Now drill a hole in the other end and insert a nail or screwdriver, cross-ways, to use as a handle (see illustration on p. 10). Hold your new tool up next to the edge of a head and mark how deep you want it to cut. Avoid cutting so deeply that you damage the block when you twist the tube down over each stud to remove the corrosion. If the head still doesn't come off, shoot some more penetrating oil down the studs and try again. Be patient, and don't bang or pry too aggressively. Replacement heads for most classics, if they are even available, can be expensive. If your engine has overhead valves, remove the pushrods at this point and put them aside.

Remove the Valves—On overhead valve engines, the valve mechanisms come off with the head and can be disassembled now or later. But if your engine is a flathead, you will want to remove the valves at this point. Before you start disassembly, find a thin plank of wood about 3 feet long and 6-in. wide and drill holes in it in two parallel lines, one row for intake and one for exhaust valves. Number each pair of holes according to cylinders, so you won't get anything mixed up.

Main caps should be numbered before you remove them (if they are not already numbered), with a hammer and punch. It is imperative they go back in their original journals facing the right direction. Photo by Don Taylor.

Use a valve compressor to take the load off of the valve keepers on the ends of the valves. Slip the keepers out of their slots and store them in a container so they won't get misplaced. Release the valve compressor tool, then slip the spring off. Keep all of the intake valve springs together and keep the exhaust valve springs in a separate container unless you know they are all the same type and tension of spring.

On overhead valve engines, before you take the rocker arm assemblies apart, label each rocker arm with a string tag as to where it goes in the line up. On many engines, there are right and left rocker arms as well as intakes and exhausts.

Remove Oil Pan & Pump—It is best to remove the oil pan with the engine right-side-up. Chances are, it still contains a residue of oil and sludge that you will not want all over your garage floor. Loosen its bolts evenly, then pop off the pan with a putty knife. Clean it out thoroughly with solvent, then put it in a plastic trash bag to keep it clean. Remove the basket and scavenge line from the oil pump and clean them. Remove the oil pump and inspect it for wear, then clean it too. Store these items in the bag with the pan.

Label Main Caps—If the rod and main bearing caps aren't numbered, you will have to mark them before removing them. It is absolutely crucial that they go back on their original journals and that they face the right direction. Get a punch and a ballpeen hammer and number each main, working from front to back. Use one nick for the front main, two nicks for the second and so on. Mark each cap on the right (or left) of the cap so you will know which way it should face when it's time to reinstall it. Now do the rod caps the same way.

Remove Bore Ridges—Is there a ridge at the top of the cylinder bores, above where the piston rings slide up and down? If so, you will need to remove it with a ridge reamer so you can get the pistons out. Because cylinders only wear in the areas where they contact the piston rings, the top 1/4" to 1/2" of the cylinder does not wear at all, creating a ridge. The rings press out against the cylinder walls, so the rings hang up against the ridge when you try to push them out from underneath. If you are experiencing this problem, purchase or rent a ridge reamer at a large auto supply or hardware store. Shoot a little light oil on the cylinder wall at the ridge. Insert the ridge cutter, adjust it to remove just a little metal at a time, then turn it in each cylinder using a wrench. Keep working and adjusting the cutter until the ridges are removed.

Remove the Pistons—Mark the pistons the same way you did the bearings, unless you know you will not be using them again. If the cylinders don't need to be rebored, and the pistons are in good condition, you may only need to

When we got the head off of this old Packard 8 we noticed the heavy ridges at the tops of the cylinders, which told us this engine has been in service a long time without an overhaul. A ridge reamer was required to remove the pistons.

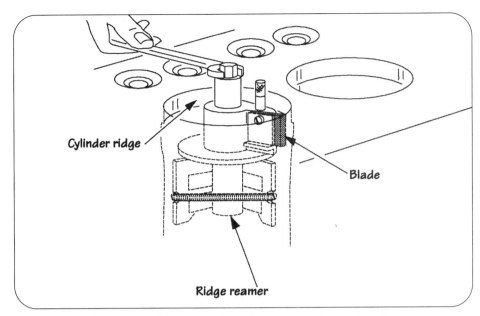

In order to get pistons out, a ridge reamer is needed to remove the ridge at the tops of cylinders on engines that have seen long service. Insert the tool and adjust its blade to cut a little at a time. Shoot a little oil on the cutter and the cylinder wall, then turn the cutter in the cylinder to remove the ridge.

Like the main caps, mark the rod caps in sequence before removing them. Use a hammer and punch. Also, make sure you mark them in such a way as to indicate which way the cap should face when reinstalled.

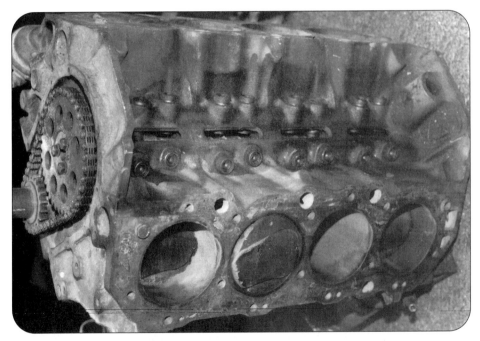

Mark pistons as to which cylinder they go to before removing them. Use a hammer and punch, but be gentle. Most pistons are made of aluminum which is softer than cast-iron parts.

belong, and don't mix them up.

Early Fords, Hudsons, Buicks and Chevrolets, as late as 1952, did not have oil pumped to their connecting rod bearings. Instead, a scoop was installed on each connecting rod, and oil was dipped from the pan as the engine spun. This was known as the *splash system*. If your car's engine uses splash lubrication, note which way the scoops face on the ends of the connecting rods. If your rods have poured babbitt bearings in them, carefully save any shims you find between the bearing caps and rods, and don't mix them up. They will be vital to establishing the correct bearing clearance

Use a hammer and punch to mark the timing gears in relation to one another before removing them. Some timing gear assemblies can be slipped off of their shafts easily. Others require a special puller.

knock the glaze off of the bores with a hone and re-ring and reinstall the pistons. Remove rings with a pair of ring pliers.

Rod caps and rods will also need to be marked with respect to location and direction. With the respective rod at bottom dead center, unbolt each rod bearing cap, slip the piston out the top of the engine, then reinstall the cap on its

connecting rod. Save any locking devices used on the nuts for the cap bolts. Some engines on early cars have rod bearing journals that will not fit through the cylinder bores. If your engine is made this way, you will need to pull the pistons out the bottom after the crankshaft is removed. If your engine has insert rod bearings, identify them as to where they

Crankshafts on old inline sixes and eights can be quite heavy. Even those on modern V8s aren't light. Get a friend to help lift it out so you won't bump or nick anything or injure yourself in the process of removing it.

RECONDITIONING

Now that we have the engine apart, let's determine what it needs to make it new again. Chances are, unless your classic's engine has been abused, it can be rebuilt. Most vintage car engines can be rebored and remachined without too much trouble. The key is to select a good machine shop. You'll need to find one who will take the time to do your job carefully.

Check with other classic car enthusiasts about local machine shops. You can also ask professional mechanics for a recommendation. Don't overlook speed shops. Many have excellent machining facilities. But wherever you go, before you place your precious parts on the pile, take a look around their facility. Is it clean and orderly? Does the machinery appear to be fairly new and in good

when you reassemble your engine.

Remove Timing Gears—Remove the vibration damper, then the timing gear cover. Determine if the timing gears are marked as to their relationship to one another. If they are not, nick them with a punch, or mark them in some way so you can get them back on correctly. In many cases, you will need to rent or buy a gear puller to remove the timing gears.

Remove the Crank—Loosen the main bearing caps, then, unless you are a very big guy working on a very small engine, get a friend to help lift the crankshaft out of its journals. Leave the flywheel attached and store your crankshaft vertically by attaching it with wire to a post or side wall in your garage. Do not lay it on its side, because there is the possibility it will warp and sag under its own weight. When you do have to remove the flywheel to have it resurfaced, if it is an early flathead Ford V8, mark it so you can put it back on the same way it came off. Most engines are made so the flywheel can only go on one way, but check yours to make sure.

Remove the Cam—A good tip for removing the cam is to screw a 4-in. bolt into the nose of the cam to serve as a handle. Hold the lifters up out of the way

with clothespins, then slide the cam out slowly, taking care not to bump any journals, lobes or bearings. Wipe it clean, and store it upright like the crankshaft.

A crankshaft you can lift out easily by yourself is the one in a Model A Ford. It has no counterweights, so it is quite light. Cars made in later years all have counterweighted crankshafts that make them run more smoothly, but later crankshafts are also much heavier and harder to handle.

The block is the most important part of your car's engine. Look it over carefully. If you find cracks, a replacement is your best bet. A rebuildable block was not hard to find for this Model A Ford. If you need one for your car, check the classifieds in hobby publications such as *Hemmings* or *Classic Auto Restorer* magazine.

14

Your block (as well as the heads) should be Magnaflux-inspected to check for cracks. A large magnet is placed on the block, and magnetic powder is sprinkled on the surface. The powder forms a line along any cracks. Photo by Don Taylor.

repair? (Very old and tired machinery may not stay within tolerances.) Can they do all of the work at their shop, or will they be sending some of it out? If so, where? And finally, does anyone there remember Hudsons, Studebakers or whatever it is you are restoring? Old car engines often have requirements that are unique to them so it could pay to find out. But before you take your engine to the shop, let's determine what it will need.

Cylinder Block

The block is arguably the most important part of your engine. If it is corroded, cracked, warped or worn out, it will need to be repaired or replaced before an overhaul can be performed.

Check for Cracks—They can happen almost anywhere in an engine, but appear most commonly between cylinders, around valve seats, and in bearing saddles. You can often spot them with the naked eye, but not always. To be safe, have a good machine shop Magnaflux inspect your block, connecting rods and crankshaft to make sure they are fracture free. Magnaflux creates a magnetic field in the piece being checked.

Iron powder is then sprinkled over the surface. The particles group around any cracks and show up as a fine, white line.

This process will reveal even the smallest hairline crack which, if left unattended, could result in engine failure after the rebuild. A good machine shop will do this automatically when reconditioning a block.

Another method you can perform at home is *Spotcheck*. Spotcheck seeks the same end as Magnaflux but uses a dye to indicate cracks. Spotcheck consists of a penetrant—a liquid red dye—and a developer—a white powder. Cleaner is

also included to clean the surface prior to and after the test. Spotcheck can also be used to check rods, heads, pistons and crank. The major advantages of Spotcheck are its ability to check non-magnetic parts such as pistons, and its convenience. Spotcheck is available from Magnaflux Corporation, 7301 West Ainslie, Harwood Heights, IL 60656. (708) 867-8000.

If you or the machine shop find any cracks, the best way to handle the problem is to find another block. This may sound like extreme advice, but good blocks are not usually that hard to find for most cars produced in quantity in the last fifty years, and they are by far the most reliable fix for cracked blocks. Most old car engines are made of cast iron, which is difficult to weld. There are services that specialize in their repair, but it is an expensive process. To weld a cast-iron block, it must first be brought up to very high temperatures in a kiln. Doing so can cause it to warp out of alignment.

Sometimes, blocks can be *pinned* if the crack is between cylinders, but pinning seldom works between valve seats. Pinning is done by drilling a hole at the

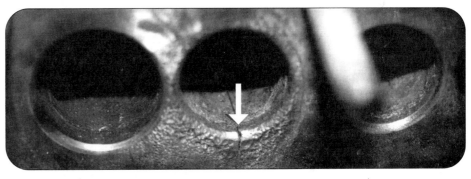

A wide crack at the valve seat in this old flathead block means a replacement will have to be found. Fixing such cracks is very difficult to do, and the repairs don't usually hold in this critical area. Note extensive corrosion as a result of coolant leaking from the waterjacket.

end of the crack to contain its progress, tapping it, then tightening a threaded, tapered plug into the hole. A second hole is then drilled, overlapping the first, and plugged. This process is continued until the crack is filled. The pins are then cut off and machined level with the block.

If the deck of the block is warped in any spot more than .0007-in., it must be milled. Photo by Don Taylor.

your problem.

Check for Warp—To check for deck warp, select a machined straight-edge as long as the block deck. Set this on the deck and use a feeler gauge to check for gaps between the straight-edge and the deck.

Measure several different places along the straight-edge, locating it at various angles across the deck. If any gap exceeds 0.007-in. the block will have to be *decked* or, using the more popular term, *milled*.

Although the most accurate measurements will be made with a long straight-edge, a 12-in. one will suffice. Instead of the 0.007-in. maximum, use 0.003-in. If warp or notching exceeds 0.015-in., the block should be discarded. Removing more than 0.015-in. could result in insufficient deck clearance—distance between the top of the piston and the block's deck surface.

Ask your machine shop to see that your block's main bearing journals are in alignment, and to align-bore them if they aren't. Also have them mill the mating surfaces for the heads and manifolds if they need it.

Measuring Bore Wear—Engine blocks are seldom worn out. They often

Clean Out Corrosion—To check for rust, pop out the soft (freeze) plugs. Dig all of the loose rust out of the waterjackets with a screwdriver. If there is a metal stripping service near you, have them dunk your block and heads. The alkaline bath most such services employ will remove every bit of rust and filth. Your parts will come out clean and rust-free. The next best answer to rust in the waterjacket is to have your engine hot-tanked at the machine shop. If your block or heads are badly corroded around water passages or around the soft plug openings, new metal can be welded into place, but again, finding a good rebuildable block (or good heads) to substitute for your rusty one is probably the best solution to

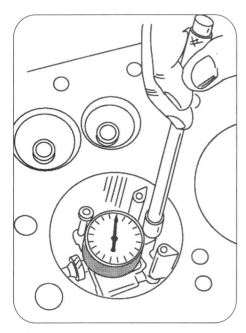

Cylinder bore taper can be checked using a special tool with a dial indicator such as this, or with an inside micrometer. If your cylinders are out of round more than .005 inch, your block will need to be re-bored and new pistons fitted. If the taper is over .015 inch the verdict is the same.

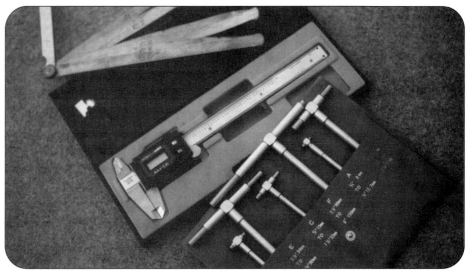

Long feeler gauges at top are used to measure piston fit in cylinders. Vernier caliper in center is used to measure crankshaft journals. This one has a handy digital read-out. Measure journals from top-to-bottom and from right-to-left to see if they are out of round. Inside micrometers can be used to measure cylinder bores in order to check for taper. A dial indicator will do this job too.

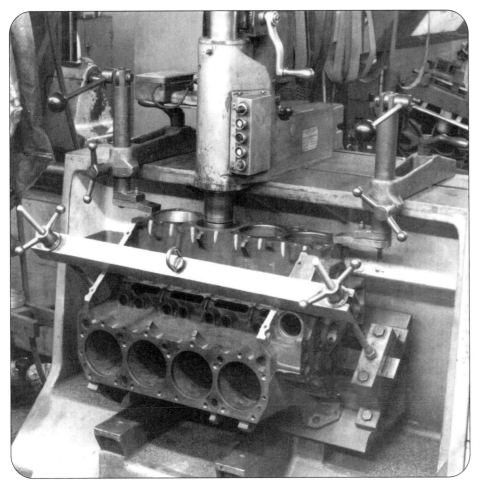

If cylinder bores are out of round by more than .005-inch, the block needs to be re-bored and fitted with the proper oversize pistons. Get the pistons first, then take the block to the shop and have them machine each bore to match each piston. Photo by Don Taylor.

If taper is within specs, you can clean up cylinder bores with a hone. Use a variable-speed electric drill and apply a little oil on the cylinder walls and the cutting stones. Be careful not to go so far down in the bores that the stones slip out the bottom. Even if cylinders are within tolerances, you will still need to rough them up slightly so new rings will seat.

have to be bored to make the cylinders straight and round again, but such work is routine at any good machine shop. Healthy cylinder bores will have an almost mirror-like shine after having been in service for any length of time. Signs of trouble are scoring, discoloration, grooves and roughness.

As an engine runs, its pistons pivot on their wrist pins. Over time, the cylinder bores wear at the tops more than at the bottoms (taper) and at right angles to the wrist pins due to friction, heat and compression (roundness). There are a couple of ways to tell if your block needs to be bored. If you had to remove a heavy ridge in order to get the pistons out, your block will probably need boring, and you will need to replace your pistons with larger ones. More sophisticated checks for roundness and taper require a dial indicator or an inside micrometer. To check for roundness, take readings at right angles to each other near the tops of the cylinders. To check for taper, measure near the tops and bottoms of the cylinders. If you are using a dial indicator, place it at a slight angle in the bore, then tip it slowly up and down while noting the measurement. The lowest reading is the one to note.

If your cylinders are out of round more than .005-inch, the block needs to be re-bored and fitted with new pistons. If the taper is over .015-inch, the verdict is the same. If your engine does need to be re-bored, take it to the machine shop and have them double check it and tell you which size pistons to order. But don't have them do the machine work until you are able to furnish them with the new pistons, then have them bore each cylinder to a particular piston's diameter. This is a more accurate method then boring the block to a nominal dimension.

Scuff the Bores—If your cylinders are within tolerances on bore and taper, they will still need to be *honed* to knock the glaze off of their walls so new rings will seat properly. A machine shop can do this for you, or you can do it yourself. Pick up a cylinder hone that will fit an electric hand drill at your local auto supply. If your journals and rod and main bearing surfaces are in good condition there is no need to remove your crankshaft. But be sure to cover the lower end of your engine with rags to keep grit out. Coat the stones and pads of the hone as well as the cylinder walls with light machine oil, then slip the hone into a bore. Start the drill and move the hone slowly up and down in the cylinder, but be careful not to let it slip out the bottom. If you do, its stones will shatter, and your crankshaft could be damaged.

Valve stems sometimes stick in their guides and get bent. Engine abuse can cause this problem too. Also, if edges of valve are knife-edged or notched, replace them. If they aren't bent, remove all carbon buildup.

Valvetrain

Valves—Scrape away carbon from the head, pistons and valves. Often you can spot burned or warped valves by the soot pattern around them on their seats. Also check to see if the valve seats are deeply recessed. If so, you may want to have them machined out and install modern, hardened insert seats as a defense against unleaded fuel. Roll the valve stems on a flat table. If any of them wobble, it's because their stems are bent. They will have to be replaced. Notice the edges of the valves. If they are thin and knife-edged or notched and burned, purchase

Many cars from the '30s and '40s used mushroom tappets that rotated as the cam lobe actuated them. They must be ground so they are slightly rounded in order for them to work. These were ground on a special machine that your machine shop may not have. If it doesn't, you can grind them yourself.

new ones. Get modern stainless steel replacements that will hold up on a diet of today's no-lead fuel.

Valve Springs—Valve springs take a lot of punishment. If your engine has been in service for many years, replace them. Otherwise, check them with a metal ruler to make sure they still extend to the correct height and that they are square. Also, have the machine shop check them for resilience when compressed. Weak or broken valve springs will be noisy and will cause an engine to be down on power.

Lifters—If your engine has hydraulic lifters, replace or rebuild them if they have a lot of miles on them. It is very

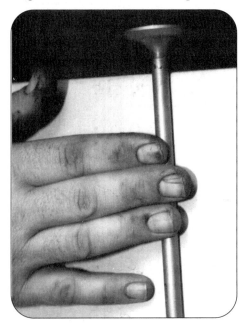

Roll valves on a flat table or bench to check for straightness. Replace any bent ones.

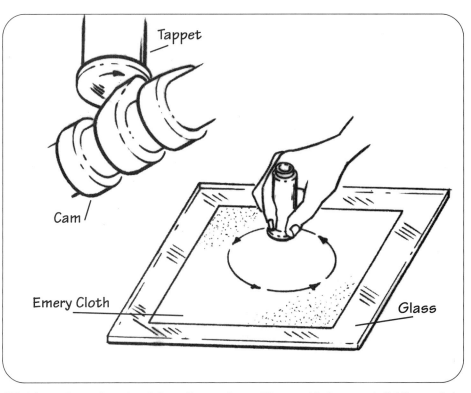

Old-style mushroom tappets rotate as the cam turns. They need to be ground slightly rounded to operate properly. Grind mushroom tappets using fine (#360) emery cloth on a piece of glass for flatness. Use a little oil to help the cloth cut. Work in a circular motion and rotate the tappet regularly.

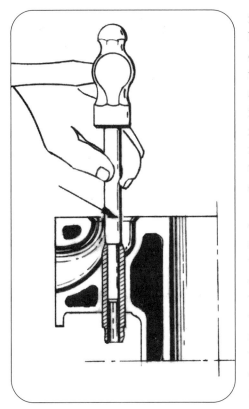

Worn out valve guides will need to be driven out using a hammer and pilot drift. Your machine shop can install new ones or you can do it, but be careful not to damage your guides or cause a burr to form in the process.

On later overhead engines only, after a new guide is inserted it must be cut flush with a cutting tool such as this one. Then the inside diameter must be reamed to the correct size. Photo by Don Taylor.

important that rebuilt hydraulic lifters go back in the same lifter bores they came out of. Don't mix them up. If you decide to rebuild them at home, keep your work area absolutely clean, and seal each lifter in a plastic bag until you are ready to install it, so it will not get any dirt or grit in it. Problems with hydraulic lifters are usually a result of scoring or wear due to dirty engine oil.

Mushroom Tappets—Many classic car engines use mushroom tappets to actuate their valves. The ends of the tappets that ride on the cam are slightly dome shaped and must be smooth and unpitted if they are to rotate properly on the cam. There aren't many machine shops that can regrind these old-style tappets to their correct profile, but you can do it at home with a piece of glass and some fine emery cloth. Place the emery cloth on the glass to insure absolute flatness (a pane of glass is about as flat a surface as you'll find this side of a precision machine shop), shoot a little oil on it, then grind the tappet around in circles on the emery cloth. Rotate the tappet in your hand after every five circles. Never grind mushroom tappets flat; if you do, they will not rotate properly and will wear rapidly.

Valve Guides—Bad valve guides can result in high oil consumption, especially on overhead valve engines. Look for signs of oil leakage and wear. Move valves from side-to-side in their guides and measure the movement with a dial indicator. Verify whether they are within tolerance according to the specifications in your shop manual. Often, if they are not badly worn, guides can be knurled at the machine shop to bring them back to specs. An added plus is that the grid pattern left by the knurling process will help hold oil and increase lubrication.

If your valve guides are badly worn, replace them. Consider using bronze guides. They are more expensive, but generally last much longer than the original cast iron. Guides can be driven

out with a hammer and a drift of the correct diameter. Drive in new guides with the same tools, or have the machine shop do the job. Either way, make sure that the upper shoulders of new guides are the correct height from the inner surface of the valve chamber.

Rocker Arms—Check the rocker arms and shafts for wear and galling. If they are badly worn, replace them, or have them sleeved with bronze if replacements aren't available. Use emery cloth to polish any pitting from the ends of rocker arms. Roll pushrods on a flat table. If there is any wobble, it means they are bent. Replace them if possible.

Pistons

Pistons are constantly pounded and suffer considerable abuse. Modern engines use aluminum pistons, but many classics used cast iron. Iron pistons are more stable at high temperatures and they last longer than aluminum, but they are much heavier. Consequently, engines equipped with them cannot handle high revs, and when cast-iron jugs are worn, they usually can't be re-ringed. Also, piston slap is a major problem with old cast-iron pistons.

Groove in piston skirt is to allow for expansion. Most aluminum pistons are cam ground, so they are not round when they are cold. Measure them for wear at right angles to their wrist pins near the top and bottom.

Aluminum pistons are usually *cam ground*, which means they aren't round when they are cold. As they expand during engine warm up, they become round in the bore. Such pistons must be measured differently than round ones. Some aluminum pistons have steel reinforcing struts, so they expand at a different rate than pistons not equipped with them.

Measure for Wear—Check your shop manual to determine the best way to measure your engine's pistons. Pistons are easily measured using outside micrometers. Measure cam-ground pistons at right angles to the wrist pins and near their tops and bottoms. The lower parts of pistons are called *skirts*. Piston skirts can shrink or collapse if your engine overheats.

Check Clearances—Piston fit varies from one engine to another, and aluminum pistons require more clearance than cast-iron. Consult a shop manual for your engine to determine the optimum tolerance. Check piston-to-cylinder clearance by placing the piston (without

rings installed) in the bore along with an extra long feeler gauge of the correct dimension. The thickest gauge that will allow the piston to slip in and out is the clearance.

If you discover that your engine needs new pistons, replace them with N.O.S. (new old stock) originals if you can. Otherwise, try to obtain forged replacement pistons. In many cases, cast-iron pistons can be successfully replaced with aluminum—and it is usually advantageous to do so—but your crankshaft will have to be balanced to accept them.

Fit Wrist Pins—If your wrist pins and rod bushings are worn, have them replaced at the machine shop. Specialized tools are often required to do the job, so it is seldom done at home by the hobbyist restorer.

Rings

Piston rings maintain compression and prevent crankcase oil from seeping into the combustion chambers. Piston rings should always be replaced when

overhauling an engine, even if you use the original pistons. The clearances between the rings and their piston grooves are critical, as are the gaps at the ends of the rings. On older engines use the three-piece oil rings especially designed to prevent high oil consumption.

Clean the Grooves—If you are using your original pistons, clean all of the carbon out of their ring grooves using a special tool for the purpose (available at auto parts stores). Or you can break off a piece of an old ring and grind the end of it to a sharp edge and use it to scrape out the deposits.

Check End Gaps—If the end gaps in the piston rings are too small, or the rings are too tight in their grooves, when the engine heats up during operation the pistons will expand and the rings will have no place to go. The result will be a seized engine. To check a ring's end gap, slip it into a cylinder bore, square it up with a piston so it is perpendicular to the bore, then measure the gap with a feeler gauge. If it is too tight, place the ring in a smooth-jawed vise and dress the ends with a fine file until the correct clearance is obtained.

Check Ring Groove Clearance—Slip the side of a ring, along with a feeler

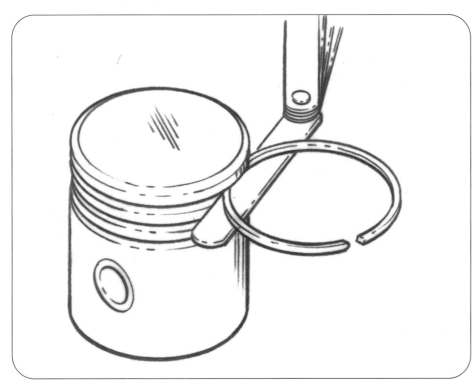

When fitting new rings to old pistons, ring clearance must be checked to make sure rings have enough room to expand during operation. Use a feeler gauge of the correct thickness as specified in your shop manual and slip it and the ring into its groove to check clearance.

Most wrist pins need to be pressed out (or installed) with a hydraulic press. Never hammer pins out! Photo by Don Taylor.

gauge of the correct thickness according to your shop manual, into its groove on the piston. If the rings prove too thick, carefully grind them thinner on a piece of fine emery cloth placed on a piece of glass for flatness. Rotate the rings under your fingers every few strokes so material will be removed uniformly. Check your work frequently so you don't remove too much metal.

Connecting Rods

When you take your piston and rod assemblies to the machine shop to have the wrist pins fitted, tell them to check your connecting rods and to straighten them if they are misaligned or bent. If you are restoring a sports or muscle car with an engine that may have been run at high revs, have your rods Magnaflux inspected to check for hairline cracks. Rod bores should be sized and honed on engines with insert bearings. Also, rods should be balanced with the crank and pistons, at the machine shop.

Camshafts

The lobes and bearing journals on your

This is a severely worn rod bearing. Pits, grooves and signs of the bronze backing mean this bearing took a pounding, which indicates the crank journal probably is worn.

engine's cam should be smooth and shiny with no sign of grooving, pits or wear. A machine shop can verify that your cam is within specs. If you are doing a complete overhaul, have new cam bearings installed in the block, and have your cam ground and Parkerized to harden it and help lubricate it for the break-in process.

Crankshaft

Long crankshafts used in inline-six and

straight-eight engines are especially prone to warping. To check them, put the end main insert bearings back in place, set the crankshaft into them and tighten the caps to the correct torque specification. Set up a dial indicator and magnetic stand at one of the center main bearing journals to measure wobble, then turn the crankshaft. If there is any deviation, have your crankshaft straightened at the machine shop. If you do not have a dial indicator, the machinist can check your crankshaft to see if it is straight.

Inspect the Bearings—If they are healthy, they will appear polished to a satin sheen. If they are discolored, pitted, or have metal particles embedded in them, they will need to be replaced. Worn insert bearings often have a very shallow oil groove down the center, and occasionally, in extreme cases, the backing shell will actually show through the lining.

Check Journals Wear—As reciprocating engines run, their bearings take a heavy pounding as a result of the up-and-down motion of the pistons. Crankshafts in engines that are run at high rpm will wear differently than engines operated at low rpm under heavy loads.

Using an outside micrometer, check each bearing journal on your crankshaft for out of round. If the difference is more

If crankshaft is ground, new undersized bearings must be installed. Be sure to check if the proper undersize bearings are available before you have the crank machined. Photo by Don Taylor.

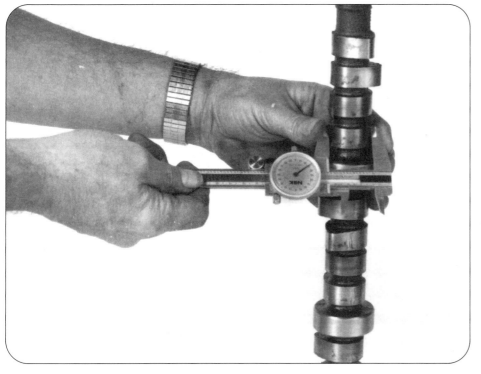

Camshaft journals and lobes must be checked to make sure they are within specifications. If they are, the cam should be ground and Parkerized. Photo by Don Taylor.

than .0015-inch on journals up to 1.75-inch in diameter, or more than .002-inch on journals two inches in diameter and larger, the crankshaft will have to be machined and new, undersized bearings obtained to fit it. But before you have your crankshaft ground, determine which sizes of bearings are still available for it. Rod and main bearings with sloppy tolerances will not hold oil pressure and will soon fail.

ASSEMBLY

The biggest challenge of an engine overhaul is to put it back together right, and the greatest joy is to fire it up for the first time. These processes involve patience and precision, but the rewards are great.

If you've followed the instructions in the previous sections on engine inspection, removal, disassembly and machining, you already know how to measure tolerances, and you've familiarized yourself with your engine's design. But just to be on the safe side, read through your shop manual again and note any special instructions. (No general book such as this can cover all the things you need to know for each engine.) Then follow these steps as a guide.

Check Clearances

Before beginning assembly, use a long feeler gauge or inside and outside micrometers to verify piston-to-bore clearance. Make sure they are within the tolerances specified by the piston manufacturer. If pistons are too tight, the engine will be hard to start, and may overheat and seize. If they are too loose, your engine will develop noisy piston slap and consume oil. If you find problems with piston clearances, take everything back to the machine shop and have them remedy the problem. If pistons are only slightly too loose, they can be knurled, or super-sized at the machine shop to bring them out to the correct diameter. If pistons are too tight in their bores, cylinders can be honed to the correct size.

Next, check the ring gap clearances as described on page 20. Slip each piston ring into a cylinder bore, make sure it is perfectly perpendicular to the bore, then measure the gap to make sure it meets the specification set by the ring's manufacturer. If it is too small, clamp the ring in a vise between pieces of soft wood, then use a fine file to open the gap to the correct dimension. Rings have gaps to allow for heat expansion as the engine warms up. If the gap is too small, the ring will have no place to go; the engine will overheat and seize.

Finally, check to see that the space between the rings and their grooves on the pistons are adequate. Do this by placing the edge of the ring in the groove accompanied by a feeler gauge of the correct thickness (see illustration on p. 20). The two should just slide in without force, but should not be at all sloppy.

Clean it Up

Before you begin assembling your engine, make sure everything is clean, and when I say clean, I mean clean. That includes your work area and all of your engine's parts. Otherwise, even a few particles of grit will make short work of your efforts. Put new carpet pieces or clean cardboard down on your workbench so you won't dent or nick soft metal parts such as aluminum pistons or soft bearing surfaces.

Use a rifle cleaning kit to cleanse all of the little oil galleries in your block, connecting rods and crankshaft. Wet the bore brush with oil and scrub each passage until you can insert a cotton swab and pull it out clean. When machine work is done on your engine it leaves sharp metal particles in these small passages. If they are not removed, they will be washed into your rod and main bearings during operation where they will embed themselves in the soft babbitt metal and score your crankshaft. Don't use compressed air to blow out the galleries; it will not do a thorough enough job. Also, you run the risk of eye injury from flying metal flakes.

Paint Your Parts—After all parts are sterile, wipe down the block, heads, oil

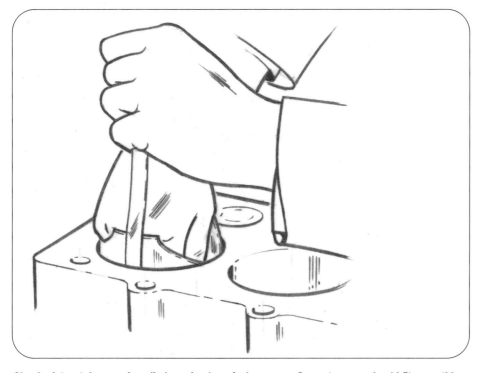

Check piston tolerance in cylinder using long feeler gauge. Correct gauge should fit smoothly, but next size up shouldn't clear. If it does, pistons will need to be knurled or super-sized at machine shop to expand them.

Paint your engine parts before assembly. That way you won't paint over gasket edges or parts that are not supposed to be painted. Wash your parts down with lacquer thinner to get any oil or grease off of them, then spray them using engine enamel in the correct color for your year and make. Give them a day or two to dry before you begin assembly.

With a small file, chamfer the edges of oil holes in your crank journals to prevent scoring bearings. Wash journals down with lacquer thinner to remove any grit. Coat them with Maltby's assembly lube before setting crank in place.

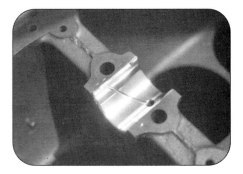

New bearings were poured in this Model A Ford block. Buicks and Chevrolets of the '30s and '40s as well as early Fords all had poured babbitt bearings. If your engine needs new poured bearings you'll have to get expert help; check hobby publications such as *Hemmings Motor News* for people who can perform this service.

When crankshaft is torqued in place in main bearings, it should turn with just a little effort applied to it. If it spins effortlessly or is hard to turn, it is because bearing clearances are not correct.

pan, intake manifold and side plates with lacquer thinner, then spray them with engine enamel of the correct color for your make of car. Use pieces of cardboard to mask mating surfaces and areas you don't want painted. Engine enamel is available in aerosol cans and doesn't usually require primer. A good source is The Eastwood Company. Eastwood also sells high temperature exhaust manifold paint, as well as special accessory enamels in the correct colors and proper matte finish.

Crankshaft

Mount the block in the engine stand, then wipe each of the main bearing saddles clean with lacquer thinner. Also, clean the backs of the bearing shells just as carefully. This is a very important step, because one little particle of grit can distort the clearance between the bearing and the crank. The result will be that the bearing will not get enough oil due to the decreased tolerance and will overheat and burn.

Soak front and rear main bearing seals in oil overnight. To install them, follow a shop manual for your engine. Now slip the main bearing shells into their saddles. The ends of the shells will stick up very slightly in order to insure a crush fit when the caps are tightened into place. A crush fit insures that the bearing shells will fit tightly against their saddles so they can conduct heat away from the bearing surfaces.

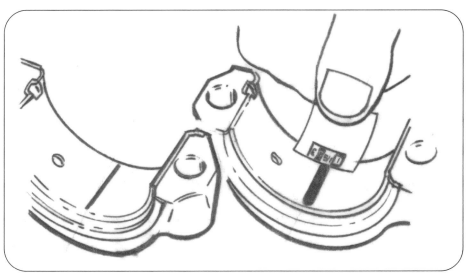

Use Plastigage to check bearing clearances. Tighten bearing with thin strip of plastic into place to the correct specs, then remove the bearing cap and measure the width of the plastic strip with the paper gauge provided. If bearings are too tight they won't get enough oil and will heat up and burn. If they are too loose, they won't hold correct oil pressure.

Rod bearing caps must go back on same rod they came from and must face the right direction. Also, any shims required between rod and cap must be put back in place. If your connecting rod bolts have castellated nuts on them as shown here, you may have to file the bottoms of them to get them to torque to the right specifications and still line up with the holes in the rod bolts. Be sure to install new cotter keys of the correct size after they are torqued in place.

If your engine is an oldie that requires the pistons to be installed from the bottom, put them in now. On some makes, you can knock out the wrist pins, push the rods up from the bottom, then re-attach the pistons to them and slide them into the bores from the top using a ring compressor.

Next, wipe the crankshaft bearing journals clean with lacquer thinner and smear a little Maltby Assembly Lube or similar product on them. Now get a friend to help you set the crankshaft carefully in place. Loosely install the bearing caps, making sure they are on the right bearing, and facing the right direction. Be sure to place new locking devices under the cap bolts, then tighten them down finger-tight. With a good torque wrench, tighten all of the bearing

caps down evenly in at least three stages, working from the center of the engine out. On the final go-around, tighten them to the specifications stated in your shop manual. (As an example, small-block Chevy V8s with four-bolt mains should be torqued to 65 ft-lbs.)

If your main bearing caps are held in place by castellated nuts, you may have to file the bottoms of the nuts enough to allow you to torque them to the correct specification and still allow the insertion of a cotter key.

As a final check, turn the crankshaft using only your hands. It should turn easily. If it doesn't, remove the bearing caps, clean off the assembly lube with lacquer thinner, then check the clearances with *Plastigage*. Put a small piece of the material in the bearing you wish to check, then reinstall the bearing cap and torque it to specs. Remove the bearing cap, then determine the tolerance by checking how much the plastic was flattened. The paper wrapper in which the Plastigage was wrapped has a gauge printed on it that will tell you what you need to know. Your parts supplier may have given you the wrong size bearings.

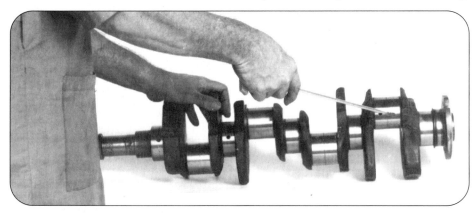

Clean all oil passages in the crank with a rifle bore cleaning kit. Keep working until you can insert a cotton wad and bring it out clean. You should do the same with all passages in the block and rods, too. Photo by Don Taylor.

Camshaft

Coat the lifters with engine oil, smear the ends with assembly lube, then put them in place. Use clothespins to keep them up, out of the way of the cam.

Put a coat of camshaft moly assembly lube on the cam bushings and lobes too. Gently guide the cam in place, being extra careful not to ding the lobes against the cam bearings.

Soak a new timing chain in oil. (Timing chains should be replaced when doing an overhaul if possible.) Install the timing gears and chain, making sure the gears are oriented correctly according to their location marks. On engines that use meshed timing gears, check their alignment, and check the lash with a feeler gauge.

Cam is installed. Note dull gray Parkerizing coating. It protects the cam's lobes during the break-in process. This mechanic is using a special homemade tool to check lifter clearance.

Make sure you cover the rod bolts with fuel line or sleeves to protect the bore and crank journal. Photo by Don Taylor.

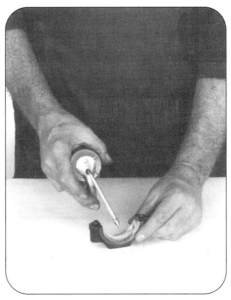

Clean the saddles of the rod caps, then insert the bearing shells and coat with oil or assembly lube. Photo by Don Taylor.

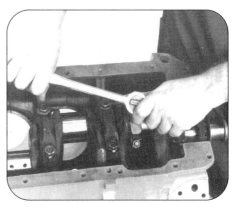

Install new locking devices on rod and main bearing bolts. Torque bolts in place using a good torque wrench. Tighten them evenly in three stages. Photo by Don Taylor.

Dip the piston in oil, then gently guide it down the bore. Use a ring compressor, and once the rings clear, you can use the butt of a hammer to push it down through. Photo by Don Taylor.

Some pistons come marked with arrows to tell you which way they should face. Other numbers shown tell how much these new replacement pistons are oversize. Note that bores have been scuffed to help rings seat properly.

Pistons

Mount the rings in their respective grooves using a ring expander. On all but very early engines, pistons can be installed down from the top of the engine. But before installing your pistons, make sure the ring gaps are staggered at 10:00, 2:00 and 6:00 on the piston to prevent a blowby situation. Coat the bores, pistons, rings and wrist pins with oil. (You can just dunk the whole piston assembly into a can of oil, then drain off the excess). Wrap the bottom ends of your connecting rods with a rag and make sure you cover the rod bolts with plastic sleeves or an old piece of fuel hose. This will prevent scraping the bores or the crankshaft journals.

Use a well-oiled ring compressor to hold the rings while you tap the pistons into their cylinders using a wooden hammer handle. Make sure you put the right rods in the right holes, and make sure the pistons are facing the right direction. On many engines, the expansion slot in the piston skirt faces the cam, but yours may differ.

Install Rod Caps—Clean the saddles and the backs of the bearings with lacquer thinner, then put the bearing shells in place. Coat each one with assembly lube. Normally, as with main bearings, they will protrude a little above the bearing saddles. This is to insure a crush fit, so heat will be conducted away from the bearing surfaces. Now install the bearing caps, making sure they are on the correct rods facing the right way per your punch marks. Use new locking devices on the rod bolts and nuts, and torque your connecting rod bearings in place in three stages according to the specifications in your shop manual. Install the oil pump if it is internal on your engine, and make sure its drive rod is aligned properly. Then install the scavenge line and strainer basket.

Flywheel

On most cars it can only go on one way, but on some Ford products it is possible to put it on wrong. Use the proper heat-treated bolts and new locking devices or lock washers. Don't be tempted to substitute ordinary hardware store bolts, as they could create a potentially deadly situation if they fail.

This Cadillac flathead V8 is almost finished. Note builder's marks to tell him which way pistons should face. Deck on which head attaches has been machined flat for a good fit.

Timing Gear Cover & Oil Pan

Now install the timing gear cover. Use a little *Gaskacinch* on the seal and tighten the cover evenly in place. Don't over-tighten the bolts, because you could deform the cover and cause oil leaks. Now install the vibration damper using new locking devices on the bolts. You can use a length of 2 x 4 to hold the crankshaft still while you are torquing the bolts.

Coat the oil pan and its gasket with Gaskacinch on the pan side only, then press the gasket onto the pan, making sure the holes line up correctly. Carefully place the pan on the block, then install three of its bolts finger-tight. Space them evenly around the pan. Now install the rest of the pan bolts and tighten them finger-tight. Next, working from the center of the pan out to the corners,

When you install timing gear, pan, or valve covers, only snug up bolts or screws. If you over-tighten them you will warp such parts and cause leaks.

26

Be sure you put rocker arms back on shafts in their proper order. On many cars there are rights and lefts as well as intakes and exhausts. Oil everything as you work, or coat bearing surfaces with assembly lube.

tighten the bolts evenly. If your pan gasket is made of cork, be especially careful not to over-tighten the bolts, because the gasket will just squeeze out the sides and be ruined.

Valves

If your engine is a later model, overhead valve type, the machine shop will probably have already installed the valves, springs and keepers. But on flatheads and earlier overhead valve engines, you will have to do it. Before you put the valves back in, check the valve guide shoulder height, especially if

you had the machine shop install your valve guides. The machine shop probably installed new guides, but they may not have lined them up properly. How far the guide shoulder should protrude into the valve chamber varies from engine to engine, so check a shop manual for the right spec. Use a hammer and drift to adjust the dimension.

Now oil the stems and drop the valves into their guides. Slip a washer and valve spring on each valve, then compress the spring with a valve spring compressor. Slip the keeper in place, then release the tension.

If your engine has solid lifters, you will need to adjust the valves. Check your shop manual for the tolerance, then bring each piston up to top dead center on its compression stroke, and make the adjustment. Both valves will be closed at this point. As soon as you have the engine back in the car and running, you will need to readjust them. See Chapter 21 for how to do it.

If your car is an older overhead valve engine, be careful not to mix up the rocker arms when reassembling the valvetrain. They come in rights and lefts as well as intakes and exhausts.

This Chevy head came back from the machine shop all built up. Unless you are familiar with checking installed height, shimming, coil bind, etc., you probably should have the shop assemble your heads.

Cylinder Heads

If you need to replace the head-to-block studs, make sure you get the correct type for your car. Often, the threaded part that goes into the block is supposed to be tapered. Coat the threads of the studs with a little Permatex before tightening them into place. Two nuts can be tightened against one another on a stud, then the upper one is used to tighten the stud into place.

Check your new head gasket(s) against the old one to make sure they have all of the necessary holes. If they don't, return them and get the proper ones. Coat the head gasket with Gaskacinch on both sides and set it into place. Make sure you have it oriented the right way, then set the head gently in place.

Torque the head nuts in three stages to the specification in your shop manual. If there is a sequence diagram in your manual, follow it. If there is no diagram, tighten the head nut in the center on the head, then the two on either side of it, then alternate front and back down the center of the head until you reach each end. Then do the ones on either side of those,

alternating left to right, then front to back, until you reach the ends of the head. Install some old spark plugs loosely into the head to keep debris out.

Manifolds

If you choose to use your old manifold studs, chase their threads with a die. Put the gaskets in place, then slide the manifolds onto the studs. No liquid sealer is required. If your engine is inline, with the manifolds attached to one another, bolt them together loosely, then slide them into place and tighten everything evenly. Work from the center out to the ends of the manifolds.

Pumps

If there is a water distribution tube in your engine, install a new one now. If you cannot locate a new one, make sure yours is clean and rust-free. Now install the water pump. Make sure you put the bolts in the right holes. On many water pumps they are of different lengths; if you try to tighten a long bolt into a short hole, you may punch through into the waterjacket.

Coat the oil pump gasket with Gaskacinch on both sides and slip it into place. Fill the oil pump with oil, then attach it to the engine. Do not turn your engine upside down after this, because the oil will run out of the pump. Without oil in it to prime it, it may not pick any up from the pan when you start the engine.

Put sealer on the fuel pump gasket (assuming your car is equipped with a cam-driven mechanical fuel pump) then put it in place. Install the pump, making sure its lever is riding properly on the cam.

INSTALLING THE ENGINE

Whether you install the engine, clutch and transmission as a unit, or set the engine in place and then install the transmission, depends on the design of your car. The following assumes that you install them together.

Bellhousing & Clutch

Grease or replace the pilot bearing in the flywheel. Do the same with the clutch release bearing. Most mechanics replace or rebuild the clutch when they have the driveline apart, because it is so hard to get to it once the car is back together. Make sure the disk assembly is facing the correct direction, and that you use the proper heat-treated bolts to attach the clutch mechanism when you install it. Tighten the bolts down evenly in a crisscross pattern to the correct specification using a torque wrench. When you install the bellhousing, make sure you put any shims that were under the mounting bolts back in the same place so you won't have alignment problems when you install the transmission.

Transmission

Find a couple of long bolts that will screw into the transmission mounting holes on your bellhousing, and cut off their heads. Cut slots in the tops for a screwdriver with a hacksaw. Now screw

Cast-iron manifolds should be sand blasted and painted with high temperature coating while they are off the engine. Make sure the heat-riser flap moves freely and be sure to install a new spring before installing manifold. Tighten manifold nuts evenly working from center out to ends.

them into the upper mounting holes on the bellhousing so they can act as guides when you slide the transmission into place. Make sure the clutch is properly aligned, then push the transmission in. You may have to do a bit of fiddling to get the pilot shaft of the transmission to line up. Install the lower transmission bolts, then remove the guides and install the upper ones.

Up & In

Now set the engine back in the car and attach the motor mounts. Attach the temperature gauge sending unit and the oil gauge sending unit after coating their threads with oil. Reinstall the carburetor, then hook up its linkage. Attach the pulleys and fan at the front of the engine, then attach the starter and generator. Bring the number one piston up to top dead center, then insert the distributor so the rotor is pointing to the nipple for the number one spark plug wire.

FINAL PREPARATION

Add fresh oil to your new engine. In most cases, 10w30 is just fine, but check with people who are familiar with your engine as to which oil is best. Add coolant to the system. Do not hook up the fuel line from the tank to the fuel pump just yet. Now look everything over carefully to make sure you haven't missed anything.

Initial Start-Up

Remove the spark plugs and crank the engine until a little oil pressure shows at the gauge. Now reinstall the plugs and hook up the fuel line from the tank to the pump. Have a friend watch the engine for leaks or problems when you start it. After it starts, let it warm up, then adjust the idle speed at the carburetor, then set the ignition timing. Also adjust the valves if necessary. Keep an eye on the temperature gauge while you are working, as fresh

engines sometimes overheat. After the engine comes up to temperature, shut it down and check all lines, fluid levels, and look for leaks under the hood. If all checks out, you can take the car for a test drive.

When you begin driving the car again, keep the revs down and vary your speed. Do not accelerate hard. Cruise around and listen for any bumps, grinds, whistles or groans. As soon as the engine is up to normal operating temperature, scoot back home to check things under the hood. Look again for leaks, check all fluid levels and give it a thorough inspection. Then re-torque the cylinder heads, intake and exhaust manifolds. Don't forget to change the oil after the first five hundred miles.

Unless your engine has adjustable rocker arms and you wish to perform a hot lash adjustment, you can now congratulate yourself for a job well done! ■

CARBURETORS

2

The first internal combustion engines were developed in the middle of the 19th century, and their technology advanced on a parallel track with steam engines. These gasoline, kerosene, and alcohol-burning engines were actually used before the automobile was invented by farmers as stationary power sources. They were primitive devices that operated at a low, constant rpm, so fuel metering wasn't terribly difficult to deal with.

But when people like the Duryea brothers in the United States, and Daimler and Benz in Europe, tried to adapt these powerplants to carriages, they soon learned that they needed a better way to control the air/fuel mixture entering the combustion chambers at various engine speeds. On the stationary farm engines, gas was dripped into the chambers, much like with a giant eye-dropper. A refinement of that approach was to drip the fuel onto a heated metal plate to vaporize it before it entered the combustion chamber. This allowed for more even and thorough burning of the fuel.

However, neither of these methods offered any throttle control. Eventually, a clever, early automotive engineer (no one knows for sure who) figured out how to use the engine's vacuum and a venturi to atomize the fuel. He may have been goofing around with his wife's perfume sprayers at the time and gotten his idea from them, because they operate on the same principle, which is: Air rushing past a vertical tube filled nearly full of

fluid will create a vacuum at the mouth of that tube and suck the fluid out into the air current, vaporizing it as it does so. A further refinement (the venturi) consisted of decreasing the diameter of the throat of the air horn just below the jet so as to constrict the air slightly in order to create a greater vacuum below where it rushes past the fuel tube.

Although this design produced a consistent air/fuel mixture, it still didn't provide throttle control. For that, a flap-

This is what a typical Stromberg two-barrel carburetor looks like. They were used on everything from Fords to Cadillacs for over 40 years. The general procedures are the same for any carburetor, but yours may differ considerably in detail, so read a shop manual on it and check the availability of rebuild kits before tearing it down.

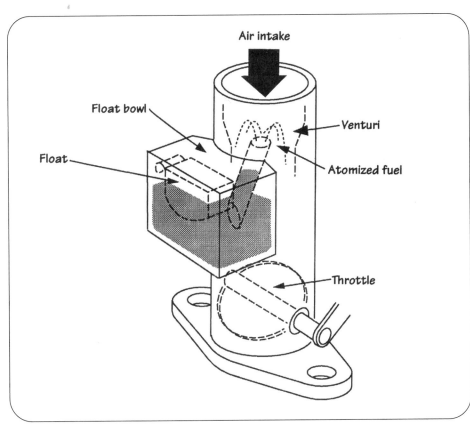

Air intake

Float bowl

Venturi

Float

Atomized fuel

Throttle

Fuel is pulled into air stream by vacuum from engine. Slight decrease in diameter of carburetor's throat causes venturi effect which pulls fuel out of the jet and atomizes it. A chamber with a float in it insures a constant supply of gas. Float shuts off fuel when reservoir is full. Throttle plate regulates vacuum to control engine speed.

THINGS YOU'LL NEED:

- Carburetor overhaul kit (Make sure you get the overhaul kit, not the tune-up kit)
- Carburetor cleaner (McKay Parts Dip is a good one)
- Neoprene gloves and protective goggles
- Fine brass wire and bristle brushes
- Cookie baking pan, small trays or flat dishes
- Needle-nose pliers
- Screwdrivers (Small, narrow slot-head, and wide slot-head with notch filed in its center)
- Flashlight
- Masking tape

like plate, often referred to as a *butterfly valve*, was needed beyond the venturi to control the flow of the air/fuel mixture, and thus the speed of the engine. With this addition to the basic venturi, a device was created that vaporizes gasoline effectively and allows an increase or decrease in rpm as needed, provided the engine is thoroughly warmed up, and the person doing the driving doesn't require rapid acceleration.

One problem with a venturi carburetor is that the loss of pressure created by the venturi causes a sudden lowering of the temperature of the air/fuel mixture due to the lack of pressure. It is much like when you spray paint using an aerosol can. As the contents of the can shoot out, there is a loss of pressure in the can, so it gets cold. The problem becomes serious with carburetors because they can actually ice up. To prevent this, early manufacturers often put the intake manifold on top of the exhaust manifold, and use a flap in the exhaust manifold called a *heat riser* to regulate the temperature of the carburetor. There are some other methods used to keep the carb warm, and they vary with engine design, but they all have the same purpose.

Another problem with a simple carburetor is that it cannot cope with a sudden tromp on the gas pedal. For an internal combustion engine to speed up suddenly, it needs a big blast of fuel; hence the *accelerator pump*, which consists of a fuel-filled cylindrical chamber with a piston at the top that can be plunged down to force fuel into the engine when needed. The accelerator pump is also the reason that pumping the gas pedal a couple of times helps start your car when it is cold. Doing so primes the combustion chambers. Just don't overdo it. Pumping the accelerator more than a couple of times will flood the engine, making ignition impossible, and will send raw gasoline sloshing down the cylinder walls, which will wash off vital lubricants.

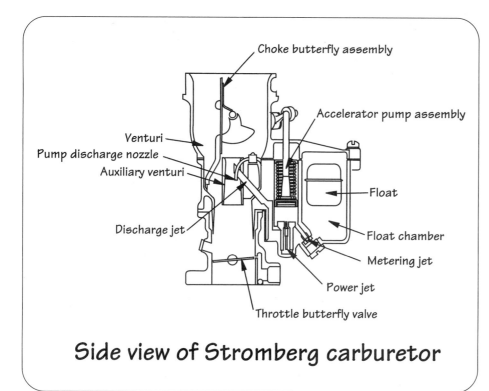

Side view of Stromberg carburetor

Choke butterfly assembly
Accelerator pump assembly
Venturi
Pump discharge nozzle
Auxiliary venturi
Float
Discharge jet
Float chamber
Metering jet
Power jet
Throttle butterfly valve

Side view of Stromberg carburetor showing its various parts. Use this as a guide for rebuilding yours.

There were a couple of other problems that needed to be solved before the basic carburetor could function efficiently. First, there was the fact that a cold engine needs a much richer mixture (more fuel, less air) in order to run properly. This problem was solved by putting another butterfly valve, commonly referred to as a *choke*, ahead of the venturi to constrict the flow of air. By doing so, a greater vacuum could be created at the jet, so more gas could be sucked into the engine.

The last big problem was the fact that an idling engine doesn't produce enough vacuum to draw a rich enough fuel mixture into it to keep it healthy. (An engine that runs too lean will overheat and burn valves and pistons.) To solve this problem, an idling or low speed jet needed to be added below the main jet to introduce more fuel at low rpm. If you look up your carburetor from underneath, you'll see a little hole in each throat, situated just above the throttle plate. That is the port for the idling jet.

What I have just described is the basic design of the earliest carburetors. Many

innovations have been added over the years to make the device work better for various applications. Some of the big four-barrel models of the late '50s and '60s are quite complex, perhaps even to the point of being a bit more of a challenge to rebuild than most of us would want to undertake. But the majority of carburetors made in the last 60 years are fairly simple and can be overhauled by the hobbyist restorer. However, before you attempt to overhaul your carburetor, read up on how it is designed, what procedures need to be followed, and whether it requires special tools in order to work on it.

TROUBLESHOOTING

For some reason, novice mechanics blame a car's carburetor as the cause of just about every engine problem. And worse than that, they usually twiddle with the idle jet settings and the idle speed adjuster screw to try and correct the problem. Ironically, the carb is almost never at fault. Carburetors usually give

long, trouble-free service, provided they are kept clean. But because carburetors are relatively accessible, beginners usually mess with them first and often create more problems for themselves. Actually, many engine malfunctions can be traced to the ignition system, especially if the car is equipped with a breaker-point distributor. So before you aim an accusing finger at your car's carburetor, check its ignition system thoroughly. Also, do a valve adjustment and check your engine's compression, as outlined in other chapters of this book. Chances are, your problem will turn up in one of these areas.

Even if you have a strong suspicion that your car's fuel system is at fault, check the fuel filter, fuel pump and fuel lines before tearing into the carburetor. Only after eliminating all of these other factors should you consider a carburetor overhaul. And an overhaul is almost always the next step, because there isn't much you can do to a carb on the average older American collector car while it is mounted on the engine. (Don't bother with those magic potions they sell at the supermarket that you are supposed to pour down your carb's throat to clean it. They are totally ineffective and can actually make problems worse.)

What to Look For

If your car runs rough and produces an unhealthy looking black smoke, your carburetor may be providing a mixture that is too rich in fuel. Another indication of a mixture that is too rich is sooty spark plugs. Check to make sure your choke is in proper adjustment and is operating freely.

If your choke is operating properly, the float may be stuck, or it may have developed a pin hole and lost buoyancy. Also, the needle valve that it opens and closes may be dirty or worn, in which case the mechanism will have to be replaced. A stuck float can sometimes be fixed by removing the top of the carburetor and cleaning the needle valve mechanism, but chances are you will want to disassemble, clean and rebuild the entire carburetor.

If the float in your carb has developed a leak, it will have to be replaced. The following admonition is stated in the overhaul section, but I will repeat it here—never try to solder a carburetor float. You risk an explosion if you do, because the metal is permeated with gasoline.

If your engine produces a popping sound in the throat of the carburetor and you are plagued with overheating and poor acceleration, the carburetor is providing an air-to-fuel mixture that is too lean. The problem may be dirt in the jets or a float that is adjusted so it is too low in the fuel reservoir. The problem could also be air leaks due to bad gaskets in the carburetor, or between the carburetor and the intake manifold, or even between the intake manifold and the engine. It could also be an air leak around the throttle shaft due to wear. Use a vacuum gauge to test for air leaks.

Dirt, rust, or condensation in the float chamber or jets will cause an engine to sputter, run rough, and even stall. A complete disassembly and cleaning is the remedy. And since you are going to that much trouble, you might as well overhaul it completely.

REBUILDING

Chances are, if your vintage vehicle has been in service for awhile, its carburetor is probably worn, dirty and working less efficiently than it should. Rebuilding it can make a big difference to your classic's smoothness, dependability and fuel economy. And if you are doing a complete restoration, you will want to renew the carburetor in any case. Many carburetors can be rebuilt in a matter of hours using basic tools. As an example, I'll demonstrate a rebuild of the Stromberg two-barrel. These carbs

appeared on just about every brand of American automobile from Buick to Studebaker, with Dodge, Ford and Cadillac in between. They were used extensively in the industry from the mid '30s into the late '60s. Your car's carburetor may differ considerably in detail from our example, but the basic overhaul procedure is the same. To begin, you'll need the materials listed in the sidebar on page 31.

Disassembly

Set the cookie pan out on your workbench and place the carburetor in the middle of it. Have a flashlight handy. The cookie pan is to minimize the loss of tiny springs, clips, needle valves and other small items. The flashlight is to help you find them if you do. If you need to look for a lost part on the floor, hold the light down at a low level so the item will cast a shadow. Flashlights are also good for peering into the small orifices of a carb. Stick small items to strips of masking tape in the order they come apart, as you remove them. That way you won't lose them or get them mixed up. If your carburetor is extremely dirty and corroded, soak it overnight in a solution of

Mark which way is up before removing choke butterfly assembly. It is possible to install it upside down and backwards if you don't know how it goes. Tap gently on stubborn screws to loosen them.

2 parts WD-40 to 1 part brake cleaning alcohol before trying to take it apart.

Remove Air Horn—On the outside of the carburetor, disconnect the choke linkage, then unscrew the rocker arm that actuates the accelerator pump. *Note:* On the Stromberg, it unscrews clockwise, unlike

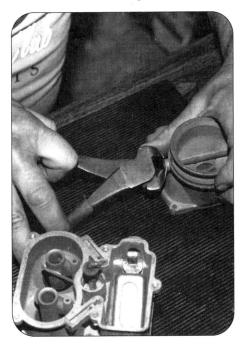

After you get the choke assembly off, remove the choke butterfly shaft with a pair of pliers.

To remove the float assembly, unscrew the hinge pin.

Be careful not to lose these tiny parts.

most screws. Remove the cotter pin that connects the rocker arm to the accelerator pump plunger. Unscrew the air horn and choke butterfly assembly from the top of the carburetor. Lift it off carefully. The accelerator pump plunger comes out with it.

Disassemble Choke Butterfly— Make a small sketch or take a Polaroid of how the butterfly is oriented in the air horn. That's so you can get it back in right. It is possible to install it upside down and backwards on some Strombergs.

Disassemble the accelerator pump and stick the small items to a strip of masking tape in the order they came off.

Remove the Float Assembly— With a small screwdriver, unscrew the hinge pin for the float. The float will come out along with the needle valve. Also remove the needle valve seat.

Unscrew Idle Jets— They are in the two small holes on either side of the accelerator pump. You'll need a very narrow screwdriver to get at them. Work as carefully as possible so you don't

damage them. If the tiny orifices at the bottoms of the tubes are clogged, clean them with toothpicks rather than wire. Wire might enlarge the diameter of the orifice.

Remove Power Jet— The power jet is down at the bottom of the large center tube that the accelerator pump was in. A wide screwdriver with a notch filed in the center of the blade is needed to remove and install it without damaging it. Don't be tempted to use a normal screwdriver for this operation, because if you force the little raised tip in the center of the power jet down too far you will ruin its mechanism. This is important, because unless you were able to find a N.O.S. (new old stock) overhaul kit, the one you have may not contain a power valve and idle jets, in which case you will need to clean and reuse your old ones.

Remove Drain Plugs— Turn the carb over and remove the three brass drain plugs jutting diagonally out of the float bowl. Under the center plug will be the accelerator check valve. Unscrew it carefully with a narrow screwdriver. Below the drain plugs are the idle mixture adjustment screws. Unscrew them, then clean the tiny orifices in the throttle body with toothpicks.

Remove power jet using a large slot-head screwdriver with a notch filed into its center so as not to damage the jet.

Remove metering jet plugs.

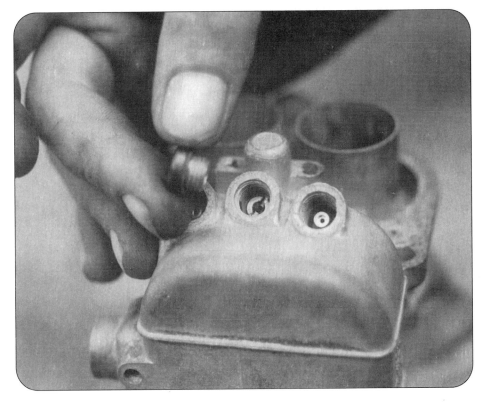

Accelerator pump check valve is under center plug. Remove it using a screwdriver.

Remove Throttle Body—Remove the screws that hold the throttle body to the float chamber casting.

Cleaning & Inspection

Get everything clean first by soaking it in a metal basket placed in a big can filled with parts cleaner. McKay is my favorite brand. You won't want to be fishing in this nasty, toxic stuff with your fingers even if you have gloves on. If, after letting things soak, they still aren't completely clean of varnish, put on some rubber gloves and eye protection, then get out your soft wire brush and scrub them. Rinse all of your parts in water, then dry them with compressed air, if you have it. Be careful not to accidentally blow small items into oblivion.

Check for Flatness—Place the air horn in position on the float chamber casting and make sure the mating surface of the air horn isn't warped from over-tightening. If it is, heat it to 350 degrees in an oven, then gently press it flat in a vice between two blocks of soft wood, or take it to a machine shop and have them

dress it on a surface grinder.

Check for Wear—Work the throttle back and forth and note whether the throttle body casting is worn out-of-round,

and whether the shaft is worn. If the throttle body casting is worn out-of-round, it will have to be reamed and bushed at a machine shop. If the shaft is worn, a new or good used one will have to be found.

Check the Float—Look it over to make sure it doesn't have any pinholes. If it does, you will need to replace it. Never try to solder a hole in a float. The metal is permeated with gasoline, so an explosion is a good possibility if you try to heat it up.

Inspect Accelerator Pump Bore—If it is rough or pitted, ream it with a dowel of the right diameter wrapped in fine emery cloth. Chase all of the threads in the float chamber and throttle body castings with a tap too.

Reassembly & Adjustment

Put the carburetor back together reversing the order of the disassembly steps noted above. Leave the air horn off and the accelerator pump out until you adjust the float level. Soak fiber gaskets in gasoline before installing them but don't use any liquid sealant. Don't

Gently clean orifices using an old dull drill bit.

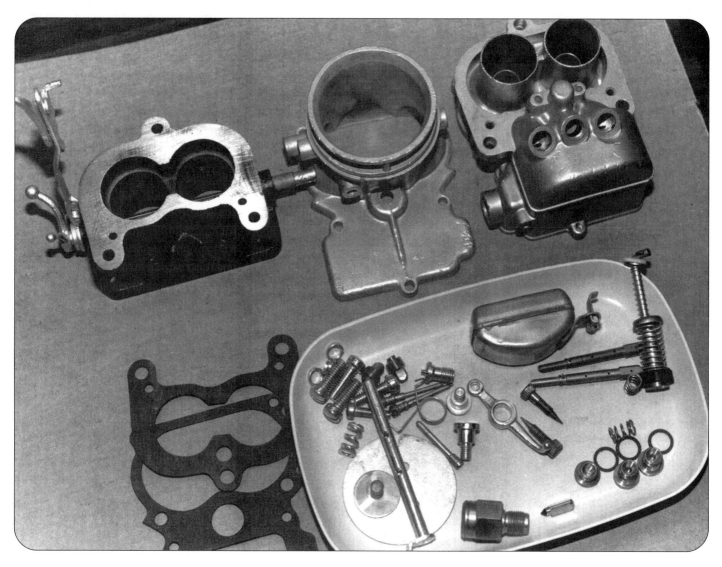

It pays to be organized—carburetors are complex devices. Here is the Stromberg ready for assembly.

lubricate the choke mechanism, because the oil will just turn to carbon from the engine heat and restrict the movement of the mechanism. Make sure the choke assembly operates freely. Be careful not to over-tighten screws, because you risk warping your carburetor's castings if you do. Set the idle screws 1-1/2 turns out, as a preliminary adjustment.

Set Float Level—Most carbs allow adjustment of the float level before installing the carb. You merely set the level of the float by bending its tine at the pivot, and you measure from the top of the float bowl to the top of the float. Stromberg didn't make it that easy. However, they used to sell a special tool for setting float levels, but good luck finding one today. Stromberg carburetors

Partially reassembled carb showing metering jet plugs and idle adjustment screws. Set idle adjustment screws at 1-1/2 turns from closed until you can adjust them on the car.

Check gaskets to make sure they have all of the proper holes. Parts in kits are usually intended to fit several carburetors. Hole had to be cut in gasket for choke in this application.

After carb is installed, make sure the choke mechanism doesn't bind.

require that you measure the *fuel level* in the float bowl. To do that, you need to install the carburetor on the car. If you have a back-up electric fuel pump mounted somewhere on your car's frame, as recommended in Chapter 3, you only need to flip on its switch and pump the fuel into the carb. The float and needle valve will shut it off at the right moment. Otherwise, you will have to start the car (it can be done without the air horn and accelerator pump installed on the carb) and measure the fuel level with the engine running, which is a very dangerous procedure.

You will need to check a shop manual for the float setting on your particular carb. Measure from the top mating surface of the float bowl down to the level of the gasoline when the float is up and the needle valve closed. Don't measure right next to the side of the float bowl, because capillary action makes the fuel creep up the side a little. Instead, make yourself a cardboard template in the shape of a T with the vertical leg of the T cut to the right length. Bend the limiter tine on the float so it stops the gas from entering the float bowl at the right point.

Final Adjustments—Install the accelerator pump, the float bowl cover and the accelerator pump rocker arm. Hook up the choke mechanism and make sure it doesn't bind. Now start the car and warm it up until the choke is fully open. Adjust the idle mixture screws together, in or out, a half-turn at a time until the engine idles smoothly. Finally, set the idle speed by turning the adjustment screw on the linkage. Many older cars can be adjusted down to a very low idle speed and still run smoothly. Setting your idle this low is a bad idea. The cylinder walls of your engine will be starved for oil if you do. ■

Accelerator pump and float assembly in place. Note felt washer at top of accelerator pump to prevent leaks.

FUEL SYSTEMS

3

We went through the carburetor in the previous chapter, but now we need to make sure the rest of the system is in proper working order. Problems with any component of the fuel system amount to the same thing; being stuck beside the road. Classics and collectibles usually do a lot of sitting around waiting for good weather or the next club tour or show. During that idle time the gasoline in the tank deteriorates, condensation forms, and rust develops. But even when old cars are driven regularly, problems can develop due to dirty fuel, diaphragm failure in the fuel pump and occasionally, vapor lock on hot days. To prevent these misfortunes from befalling you, let's work our way back through the system and make sure everything is as it needs to be before hitting the highway.

Does your old car behave like it's running out of gas, even though the gauge says the tank is half full? The problem may be a dirty fuel filter, a clogged fuel line, or even vapor lock—or it might be a bad fuel pump. Before you start replacing things, run some simple tests. If it turns out to be your pump, it's no big deal. You can rebuild it in an hour or two. Of course, if you are doing a full restoration, you'll want to overhaul the fuel pump along with everything else as a matter of course.

DIAGNOSIS

Make sure you have gas. Sometimes the float on the gas gauge sending unit in

This Model A Ford gas tank presents its own unique problems because it is also the car's dashboard.

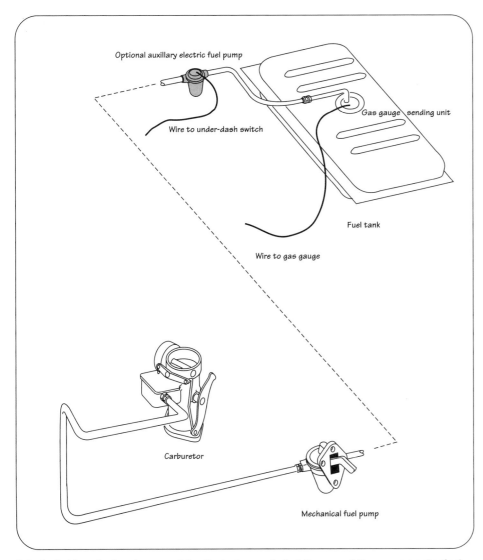

A typical old car fuel system consists of a tank mounted at the rear of the car, a mechanical, cam actuated fuel pump mounted on the engine block, and a carburetor. An optional electric pump can be added at the rear of the car near the gas tank and actuated by a switch under the dashboard. Such pumps are useful if your mechanical one fails and can be used to prime the carburetor when the car has been idle for a long period.

the gas tank hangs up and doesn't drop as fuel is pulled from the tank. Even though the gauge says you have plenty of fuel, you may be out of gas. Remove the gas cap and rock the car from side to side. You should hear a faint sloshing sound. If you don't hear anything, add some gas to the tank and try again to start the car.

Vapor Lock—If stalling occurs only when you've been running the car at speed and the engine is hot, you may have a vapor lock problem. Vapor lock is when the fuel in the carburetor, fuel lines or fuel pump gets so hot it vaporizes. If you think this might be your problem, try

installing a thicker gasket between the carb and the intake manifold. If fuel lines run near manifolding or heat-producing parts of the engine, move them away. A thicker gasket where the fuel pump mounts to the engine may help too.

Check the Choke—If your choke hangs up in the closed position after the engine is warmed up, the engine will get plenty of fuel, but no air. Either way you're stuck. Make sure the choke moves freely, is in proper adjustment, and that its spring is healthy.

Inspect the Fuel Filter—Can you see sediment in it? If so, clean it—in the

case of the old fashioned type—or replace it if it is the disposable kind. Even if you can't see any debris in the filter, clean it anyway. And if your car has a disposable filter, unless it is fairly new, replace it. Fuel filters are very effective at doing their job, but they eventually clog.

Clean the Air Filter—If it is exceptionally dirty, it could be causing your problem. Clean it, or replace it in the case of a paper disposable one. Air filters need regular attention if they are to perform properly and not compromise performance.

Check Fuel Lines—Hoses on gas station pumps sometimes disintegrate from the inside. Chunks of neoprene are washed into the fuel. The scavenge line in the tank picks them up and sucks them into the system. There are other substances that can cause the same problem, such as deteriorating gas tank anti-corrosion liners, or dirt from a defective underground storage tank. If you suspect fuel line blockage, disconnect each line at both ends and blow it out with compressed air. Inspect the full length of the fuel lines for leaks or rust spots. Even if a fuel line isn't apparently leaking gas, a tiny pinhole or crack in a flex-hose could allow air into the system and cause the fuel pump to cavitate. The result: You go nowhere fast. Replace any questionable tubing. Fuel lines sometimes get pinched or dented by flying stones. A constriction is likely to cause a build up of sediment and blockage. Replace dented lines.

Flush Fuel Tank—If there was dirt in the fuel filter, or a blockage in the fuel lines, drain and flush the tank. I'll tell you how later in this chapter.

Test the Pump—Take the rotor out of the distributor so a stray spark from your ignition system won't cause an explosion, then disconnect the fuel line at the carburetor. Find a metal container the size of a 1-lb. coffee can and hold it in front of the line. Have a friend crank the engine. The fuel should shoot out in a steady stream at the rate of about one pint in 20

To rebuild your fuel pump you only need a few hand tools, some sealer, parts dip and an overhaul kit. Pans or dishes to help keep parts organized are a good idea too. Just make sure you get the correct kit for your pump.

car won't warm up properly and will get poor gas mileage.

REBUILDING YOUR PUMP

If your fuel pump won't pump fuel, don't despair. Mechanical fuel pumps are usually easy to rebuild. Just pick up a kit at an auto supply store, or order one from an old car parts house and go to it. You'll be on the road in no time. The example used for our photographs is an AC single diaphragm type used on many different makes of car from the '30s into the '70s.

Disassembly

Remove the Pump—Disconnect the fuel lines, then unbolt the pump. Be careful not to drop it, because it may have a glass sediment bowl on the bottom that will shatter on impact. If the bolts holding the pump in place are of differing lengths, note on pieces of tape where they go, or attach string tags with the same information. If there are any ceramic or fiber insulators between the bolts and the pump, save them and reinstall them. They help prevent vapor lock.

Order a Kit—Scrub your pump with lacquer thinner to get the grime off of it,

to 30 seconds. Hold your thumb over the end of the line and have your friend crank again. You should feel pressure. A pressure gauge, as well as some types of vacuum gauges, can be used to do a more precise test. You will need to tie the gauge into your system with a T fitting, and you will need to make sure its connections are tight. Some of the problems common to mechanical fuel pumps are: A torn or de-laminated diaphragm, worn rocker arm or pivot pin, and dirt in the valves. You can bench check a fuel pump after you've removed it from the car by attaching lengths of clear neoprene fuel line to the outlet and inlet then immersing the ends in a can of gasoline. Work the pump arm up and down several times. The pump should pick up fuel and pump it back into the can.

Check Jets—Take the top off of the carburetor and inspect the float chamber for rust and sediment. Also check the jets. A little dirt clogs a carb in a hurry.

Check for Manifold Leaks—Air leaking into an intake manifold can disturb the fuel mixture and cause the engine to run badly or not at all. A

leaking windshield wiper vacuum line on a compound fuel/vacuum pump will also cause problems. Finally, check the exhaust manifold heat riser to make sure it moves freely. If the heat riser is stuck in the wrong position, the car won't warm up properly. If it is stuck closed, there will be unnecessary backpressure and excessive heat. If it is stuck open, your

When you order your overhaul kit, you will want to tell the supplier the manufacturer of your pump, the make and year of your car and which engine it has, and the serial number of the fuel pump, which is usually cast in the side or stamped on the pump body.

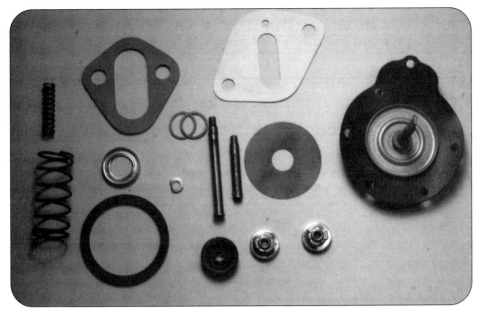

A typical fuel pump kit consists of a new diaphragm and actuating spring, filter screen, valves and assorted hardware and gaskets.

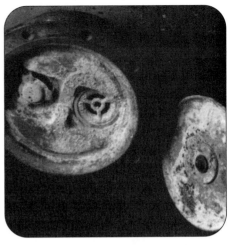

Moisture buildup in this pump created oxides and corrosion that wreaked havoc with the carburetor. If you find this in your pump, absolutely every bit of it must be removed during the overhaul process to prevent further problems.

then make a note of the part number. It's usually stamped along the top of the pump body, or on the mounting flange. The parts house will need to know the year and make of your car, the part number of your pump and who manufactured it. It was not unusual, years ago, for an auto maker to use two or three different brands of fuel pumps in a single year's production, so be specific when you request your kit. A good source of old car parts is: Egge Machine, 8403 Allport Ave. #C, Santa Fe Springs, CA 90670. (800) 866-EGGE.

Mark It—Scratch a line across the flanges of the diaphragm chamber so you will be able to get the two pieces back together in proper relationship to one another when you reassemble the pump.

Remove the Rocker Arm—Drill away the peened-over end of the pin that holds the cam rocker arm in place. Tap out the pin using a punch or drift.

Remove Diaphragm—Evenly unscrew the pump body halves in a cross pattern. The pump body should come apart easily, but if it doesn't, use a putty

Mark the two halves of the diaphragm chamber before disassembling them so you can line them up correctly during reassembly. You can file a small notch in them with a fine file.

Cam-driven rocker arm is removed by drilling away peened end of pivot pin then driving it out with a hammer and punch.

knife to gently pry it apart. Don't mar or nick the mating surfaces. Gently push up on the diaphragm with the palm of your hand and turn a quarter turn to unhook it from its linkage. Slip it down out of its oil seal.

Disconnect Linkage—Remove the rocker arm, link, tension spring, spacer washers and bushings (if any) from the upper pump body casting. If the pump body is badly worn where the rocker arm pivots, you will need to have the opening drilled out and bushings pressed in. A good engine machine shop can usually do this for you.

Undo Sediment Bowl—Unscrew the sediment bowl on the bottom of the pump. Your fingers may be slippery with gasoline, so be careful not to drop the glass bowl. You may be surprised at how much filth and water is in it.

Remove Valves—Make a small drawing showing how the valves are arranged in the lower half of your pump. You will need to know which one is the intake and which is the outlet when you install new ones. Loosen the screw, then remove the valve retainer and valves. Loosely put the retainer back in place.

Pull Out Seal—Gently pull out its retainer, then remove the oil seal in the

41

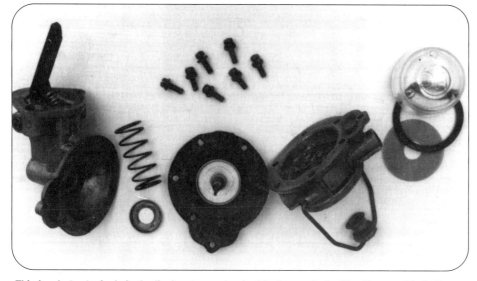

This is what a typical single diaphragm mechanical fuel pump looks like disassembled. Be especially careful handling the glass sediment bowl. A little gasoline can make it slippery and easy to drop—and there are no replacements.

Put the spring retainer in place at the base of the diaphragm, actuating rod dished side up, then add spring.

upper pump body. Make a note of which way the seal faces.

Scrub Clean—Throw all of the castings in your can of parts dip and let them soak. If they are really filthy, clean them with a stiff bristle brush. Rinse them thoroughly with water, then blow dry with compressed air.

Reface Valve Seats—If the seats that the valves ride in are pitted or corroded, glue a disk of fine emery cloth on the end of a dowel of the correct size and gently rotate it in the seat to smooth it.

Reassembly

The first step is to install the rocker arm. Slide the rocker arm, linkage, spring and retainers in place, then insert a drift into the hole. Now drive the drift out using the new pivot pin. Drive the pin through until it projects out the other side. Place the head of the pin on a hard surface, such as the end of a vise, and place a washer on the end of the pin. Make sure the spring is seated properly, then peen over the end of the pin with a hammer and small punch.

Insert Oil Seal—Push the oil seal up into the pump body casting. Make sure its lip is facing the right way according to the diagram with the overhaul kit or shop manual. Now gently tap in its retaining ring. A socket of the correct diameter can be used as a drift to make the retainer seat squarely.

Attach the Diaphragm—First, place the metal spring retainer in place at the base of the diaphragm pull rod, dished side up. Next, install the spring in the dished seat of the retainer. Now slip the diaphragm pull rod up through the oil seal in the pump body. Make sure the tension spring is seated properly, then press the diaphragm assembly up with the palm of your hand and turn it a quarter turn to hook it on to the linkage. This procedure requires a little patience. Be careful not to deform or dislocate the oil seal.

Put neoprene diaphragm actuating rod oil seal in facing the correct way, then tap in its retaining ring. A socket the diameter of the outside edge of the retaining ring is handy for this purpose. Shoot a drop of oil on the seal.

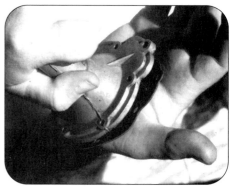

Install the diaphragm by pressing it gently into the seal and turning it a quarter turn using the palm of your hand.

Before installing pump valves, use your finger to check to see if their disks open and close crisply. If they don't, you will want to obtain valves that do.

Install valves making sure you have them facing the right way per your diagram. Install their keeper dished side up.

and down three or four times through its full range of operation. On the final stroke, hold the rocker arm down so the diaphragm is pulled up fully against its spring. Tighten four of the screws at even points around the circumference of the flanges. Now tighten the others evenly in a cross pattern. This procedure insures that the diaphragm will be able to operate to its fullest capacity without fatiguing and tearing.

Installation

Smear a little silicone sealer on the pump gasket, the pump mounting flange, and the engine block. Let it skin over. Now install the pump, making sure that any insulators are put back in place. And don't be tempted to leave off that heat shield that made the pump so difficult to remove. It protects the pump from vapor lock. Connect the fuel line then start the

Check the Valves—Before installing the new valves, check to see that they open and close properly by pressing in on the little disks in their centers. They should open freely and close securely. If they check out okay, install the outlet valve with its three-legged cage down, and the inlet valve with its cage up. Now install the valve retainer clip in so its hump is up. Tighten it into place.

Assemble the Sediment Bowl—Slip in a new screen at the top of the bowl, install a new gasket, then put the bowl in place and tighten the retainer into place. Do not use any sealing compound on the bowl gasket.

Put It Together—Carefully turn the diaphragm so its holes line up with those in the pump body. Now place the lower half of the pump on the upper part so your marks line up. Put the screws back in, then tighten them in a cross pattern until their heads almost contact the lock washers. Now work the rocker arm up

Install a new screen and neoprene gasket before adding sediment bowl. A little bearing grease on the gasket will help it seal.

An auxiliary electric fuel pump mounted on the frame near the gas tank is handy for filling the carburetor float chamber after car has been idle for a long time. It can also help overcome vapor lock on hot days. Make sure you get one that is designed for the correct voltage for your car. Install a disposable fuel filter with it for extra protection. An added benefit of an electric pump is that it can be used to empty the gas tank if necessary.

Installing an Auxiliary Electric Pump

Most older American cars use mechanical fuel pumps that are driven by the camshaft. Such pumps are reliable, but have some disadvantages. For instance, when a car is stored for any length of time, fuel evaporates out of the carburetor float bowl. When you return the car to service, the fuel pump must fill it again before the engine will start. A mechanical fuel pump takes a long time to do this. That's why it takes so much cranking to get old cars going. An electric fuel pump will get you started in a hurry because it will fill the float bowl quickly without having to turn the engine over. Also, electric fuel pumps will overcome vapor lock on hot days.

An electric fuel pump can be used to prime the carburetor, then be shut off with a switch under the dash of your car so you can operate normally using the factory correct one. Both the pump and the switch can be installed in places where they won't spoil the original appearance of the vehicle.

Purchase an electric fuel pump at your local auto parts store, or by mail-order through hobby publications such as *Hemmings Motor News* or *Classic Auto Restorer*. Get a pump that operates on the same voltage as your car's electrical system (6 or 12 volts), and make sure it is set up to be positive or negative ground as required for your vehicle. Also, while you're at the auto supply, pick up about 3 feet of neoprene fuel line and an inline fuel filter.

Mount the pump on a crossmember or inside the frame at the back of the car near the fuel tank. Electric fuel pumps work best when placed near the tank, and even the fussiest car show judge won't look for them back there. Make sure the pump is properly grounded to the frame. (I like to install an auxiliary ground strap.) Then run a wire along the existing harness to the dash. Wrap the wire with several layers of electrical tape, or run it through a grommet in places where it is likely to chafe against any surrounding metal surfaces.

Install a toggle switch under the dash and attach the wire from your pump. Now run a wire from the switch to a hot terminal on your ignition switch, in such a way that the pump will only operate with the ignition on.

Next, cut the fuel line with a tubing cutter where it comes out above your gas tank. Don't cut it below the tank level because fuel will siphon out and cause a very dangerous situation. Now flare the tubing slightly, then push the neoprene fuel line onto it and clamp it in position with a hose clamp. Put the inline filter in the line ahead of the electric pump. Attach the other end of the line to the nipple of the pump marked "in." Finally, flare the end of the fuel line going to the front of the car and install a length of neoprene tubing between it and the nipple marked "out" on the pump.

Flip the switch and let your fuel pump run until it fills the carburetor, then check for leaks. If you don't find any, you're all set. (If you do, check for burrs at metal unions, then make sure all connections are tight before trying the system again.) Now you can prime your carb easily, get home if your mechanical pump fails, and more to the point of this chapter, pump the fuel out of your gas tank so you can remove it and make repairs. All you have to do is disconnect the fuel line from the pump to the engine, stick it into a gas can, and flip the switch under the dash.

engine and check for leaks. It may take a bit of cranking to get your pump to fill the carburetor float bowl.

FUEL TANKS

If your vintage vehicle's gas tank is rusted and leaking, you have a potentially explosive situation on your hands. And if you are restoring your car, why not head fuel tank problems off before they ruin your day?

Most old cars need to have their gas tanks cleaned and repaired sooner or later. As a car's engine runs, it pulls fuel from the tank at a steady rate. Air is sucked in to replace it due to the vacuum created. Moisture in the air, upon contact with the cool gasoline and the metal sides of the tank, condenses and settles to the bottom where it does its insidious work. Also, water splashes up and runs down onto the fuel tank during normal driving and causes the tank to rust on the outside. As a result, sooner or later, most vintage vehicle owners are faced with removing their car's gas tank and repairing it,

resealing it or replacing it. The task isn't usually difficult or expensive, but you must proceed cautiously. Don't forget for a minute that gasoline is more dangerous than dynamite. Don't smoke, do all work outdoors, and be careful not to cause a spark while handling your tank. If you must work inside, make sure all pilot lights from items such as water heaters or laundry dryers are off.

Many old cars have drain plugs at the bottoms of their gas tanks that makes emptying them easy. All you have to do is drain the fuel into gas cans and pour it into another car. Remove the gas cap from the filler neck so the fuel will drain faster. Use two cans for the job, but be careful not to drop the drain plug into the can as you remove it. Have a friend close by to help shuttle fuel, and be sure to keep a fire extinguisher at hand.

More modern cars don't usually have drain plugs on their gas tanks. To empty them, you will need to pump, or siphon the fuel. You can pick up a plastic, accordion-pleated, siphon and hose at an auto supply store that will do the trick, or

you can install an auxiliary electric fuel pump on your car and use it to pump your tank dry (see sidebar on page 44). But don't try the old trick of siphoning by sucking on a hose to get the fuel started. Gasoline is toxic—and you might accidentally get a mouthful.

Reconditioning the Fuel Tank

Once you have all the gas out of the tank, either by siphoning or hopefully by pumping it out with your newly installed electric pump, you're ready to pull it out of the car. Disconnect the fuel line and the wire from the gas gauge sending unit. Open the trunk and detach any flexible hose between the tank and the filler neck. Finally, loosen the bolts on the straps holding the tank in place, then lower the tank out of the car.

Inspect the exterior, top and bottom of the tank for problem areas. Look for wet spots and rusty circular patches. Also check around the filler neck weld for holes. Tip the tank so the sun shines in the hole for the sending unit. A healthy tank will have bright, clean metal inside.

Most classic car fuel tanks have a drain plug for emptying fuel. Get a friend to help, use two gas cans, work outdoors, don't smoke, and make sure you have a fire extinguisher at hand. Always keep in mind that gasoline is more dangerous than dynamite.

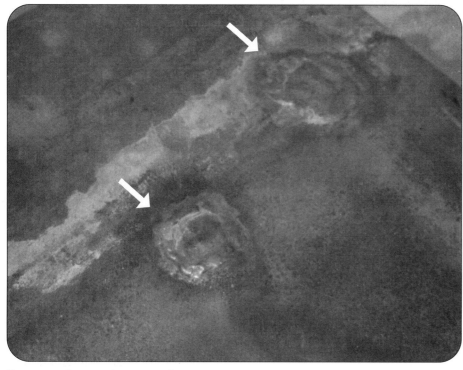

Put your tank on saw horses and fill it up to the filler neck with water. Look for slow dripping and widening circles of moisture. Don't forget to check the top of the tank for leaks too. Circle any leaks with a marker pen, then take your tank to a radiator shop to be fixed. Never try to solder or braze your tank at home. You risk an explosion if you do. Shown here are two patches that were brazed in.

When you get your tank back from the radiator shop you are ready to clean, seal and paint it. Bill Hirsch's Gas Tank Sealer and Miracle Paint are an ideal combination for rehabilitating your rusty, leaky tank. Follow the instructions on the sealer and make sure you give your tank enough curing time before reinstalling it.

If yours doesn't look so good, don't despair. Many old gas tanks aren't healthy, but most of them can be saved. Don't use a trouble light or flashlight for your inspection, because they might make a spark that could cause the fumes in your tank to ignite.

Clean Out Tank—Carefully washed pea gravel or a can of mixed bolts, nuts and washers will do a good job of de-rusting a dirty tank. Put a little water in the tank, then pour in the gravel, or fasteners, and slosh them around vigorously to break the corrosion loose. Rinse out the tank and repeat the process until the wash water comes out clear. Another way to sanitize the tank is to have it hot tanked at a radiator shop or metal stripping facility. A metal stripper will return your tank cleaned to bright metal and ready for sealing.

Check for Leaks—Place your tank on a couple of sawhorses, then duct tape over the sending unit hole. Now fill the tank with water up into the filler neck. Small leaks will show up in the form of fine spray or widening wet spots. Circle each hole with a grease pencil, then take your tank to a radiator shop and have them solder up the holes. Never try to solder them yourself, because the metal of any used gasoline tank will be permeated with potentially explosive material.

Sealing—Another very good way to seal and fix a tank with a couple of minor pinholes is to coat it with Bill Hirsch's gas tank sealer. You can order it by mail from: Bill Hirsch, 396 Littleton Ave., Newark, NJ 07103. (800) 828-2061 or (201) 642-2404. Even if your tank doesn't leak, if it is at all rusty inside it is a good idea to coat it with sealer anyway. Get the alcohol-resistant kind. The non-resistant sealer can come loose and get into your fuel system if it is attacked by alcohol, and spiked fuel is becoming more common.

To seal your tank, just follow the directions on the can. Bill says to be sure the sealer is sloshed onto every interior

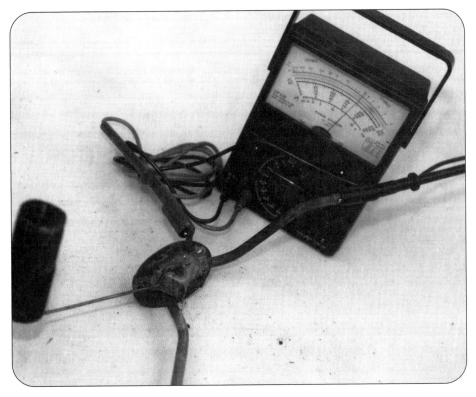

Test your fuel tank sending unit with a multimeter set on ohms. As you move the float on the unit up or down the meter should fluctuate accordingly. If it doesn't, you may need a new unit.

Clean pickup tubes on your sending unit, then soak its cork float in shellac to preserve it before reinstalling the unit. Make sure you let the shellac dry first.

surface of the tank. A thin coat is best. Pour the surplus back into its container and put a lid on it. Let the sealer dry for a day, then apply another coat. Give your tank a few days to cure before returning it to service.

Painting—If your tank was painted black originally, a couple of coats of black Rustoleum will restore it to its former look. Rustoleum has the correct semi-gloss finish used on most older cars, and is rust resistant. Bill Hirsch's Miracle Paint works well too. If your tank was galvanized originally, paint it light gray, then pat on silver paint with an artificial sponge. You'll be surprised at how authentic tanks painted with this process can look.

Restore the Sending Unit—Most gas gauge sending units are just a rheostat switch actuated by a float. It is a good idea to check such units and clean them before reinstalling them. First, clean the electrical connections so they will make good contact; then check the rheostat with a multimeter. It should read zero at empty, and the needle should rise smoothly as you move the float upwards. If the float is made of cork, let it dry out thoroughly, then dip it in shellac to seal it. Finally, make a new gasket and reinstall the unit.

Reinstall the Tank—Get a friend to help; gas tanks are big and unwieldy, and it can be tricky to snake the filler neck back into place. It may be necessary to attach the electrical lead to the sending unit before raising the tank into place. Tighten the strap bolts evenly, then hook up the fuel line. Replace the filler neck flex-hose and insert the filler neck into the tank to the correct height. Now start the car and run it for a while to check for leaks.

That's all there is to it. But, just to be safe, always carry a fire extinguisher in your old car anyway. Fires are not uncommon with vintage vehicles. Besides, many clubs now require extinguishers onboard when participating in their tours. ∎

COOLING SYSTEMS

4

It's important that your car's cooling system be overhauled at the same time as its engine. After that, regular maintenance will help keep your classic cool.

HOW IT WORKS

Your car's radiator, water pump, thermostat, and waterjacket are more of a temperature regulating apparatus than a cooling system. Actually, the hotter an engine runs, the better, short of any engine damage of course. Many race cars, like Indy cars, are on the verge of overheating all the time. That's because they produce the maximum possible power that way. Energy is produced each time a spark plug fires, igniting the gas/air charge. Even in the most sophisticated engines, some of that energy is lost due to heat dissipation through the block, heads and waterjackets. So engines that run too cold will not operate to maximum potential because the energy they produce is siphoned off. That's why your old car is designed to quickly heat up to a temperature in the neighborhood of 190 degrees Fahrenheit and stay there during normal operation.

All but the early cars, such as those from the teens and early twenties, have thermostats in the upper water outlets of their engines that stop the flow of coolant until it has warmed to optimum operating

White or green powdery corrosion is a sure sign of radiator leaks. A radiator shop can solder them up and rod out the tubes while they are at it. Don't have the shop paint your radiator. You can do a better job yourself, but don't shoot more than a fine mist on the cooling fins because paint will hold the heat in the radiator.

temperature. Some classics from the thirties had a thermostat that operated a set of shutters in front of the radiator that stopped the flow of air over its cooling fins. Air is what ultimately cools any engine, so it was an effective setup, though more expensive to manufacture.

As soon as the thermostat opens, coolant is pushed out of the top of the engine and fed into the upper tank of the radiator. From there it trickles down through numerous small tubes that are covered with thin metal cooling fins. Air passes over the tubes and fins as a result of the fan's action and the forward motion of the vehicle. It carries excess heat back and down under the car. When the coolant reaches the bottom reservoir of the radiator, it is pulled back into the engine by the water pump to begin its task again.

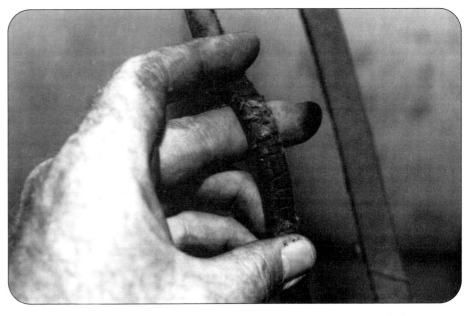

Rotten hoses and belts are often overlooked cooling system problems that can leak or snap and cause serious problems. Replace them with the correct length and type for your car.

SOLVING OVERHEATING PROBLEMS

Before you tear apart your cooling system, especially if it is in good shape,

Some older cars have a petcock mounted on the block that allows you to drain the waterjacket. Be careful trying to open it. Don't apply too much pressure because chances are it is made of brass and will break off if you do.

you might want to perform a series of tests and maintenance procedures to see if any of them cure your overheating problems.

Check Belts & Hoses—Replace any belts that are frayed, cracked or slipping. A loose fan belt can slip on the water pump pulley; and even if an old belt isn't

slipping, it is likely to break at the worst possible time.

Look over hoses for cracks, swelling, checking and signs of leakage. Hoses should be supple, but firm enough not to collapse in use. If belts or hoses are more than five years old, replace them. They are the weakest link in a cooling system.

Inspect the Core Plugs—They're usually on the side of the block opposite the manifolds on inline engines, and on both sides below the heads on V8s. Don't forget to check for one at the back of the block too. Weeping core plugs (sometimes known incorrectly as freeze plugs) may well be the cause of your overheating blues.

If you find a bad one, puncture it with a screwdriver, then pop it out. Put a little silicone sealer or Permatex around the lip on the block, then gently tap in a new plug using a short piece of pipe or socket as a drift. When the plug is seated properly, give it a sharp rap at its center with a small ballpeen hammer to expand it into place.

Check the Radiator—Is it full of bugs and dirt at the front? If so, blow them out with a garden hose from the back. Do you see signs of leaks? Look

for white or green deposits at the corners of the tanks. Is the radiator cap sealing properly? Make sure its washer is in good shape and that it will hold the correct pressure. If it is old, replace it. Cars with pressurized cooling systems will boil over if the pressure drops.

Start the engine and let it warm up. Carefully place your hand in various places on the front of the radiator and feel for cold spots. A healthy radiator should be warm at the top and cooler at the bottom. Cool spots on the core indicate blockages in the cooling tubes. As a further check, disconnect the lower hose on your radiator, then run water in at the top. It should run out the bottom at the same rate. If it doesn't, the radiator will have to be backflushed or removed and taken to a specialist who can unsolder the tanks and rod out the core. Never try to rod out a radiator at home; your chances of ruining it are very high.

Radiators generally have drains on their bottom tanks. Be careful not to overstress them because they can break off easily. If yours won't open, pull the bottom radiator hose instead. But be prepared for the flood.

Thermostat is usually situated directly under hose outlet to upper radiator tank. If it sticks open, your car won't warm up properly on cold days. If it sticks closed your engine will overheat in short order. It should be replaced every couple of years. Be sure to put the thermostat back in facing the right way.

Often, backflushing a radiator is all that is necessary to return it to good operating condition. Disconnect the lower radiator hose, remove the radiator cap, then wrap a garden hose with rags and stuff it in the lower radiator opening. Have a friend turn on the water full blast. Backflushing is a messy operation, but it is far more effective than merely opening the petcock on your radiator and running water through it. You should also backflush your engine block while you are at it. Disconnect the upper radiator hose, remove the thermostat and force water into the engine from the top. There are kits complete with chemicals and pressurizing fittings if you want to do a professional-quality job. If you don't even want to mess with it, most repair shops have a pressurized backflushing system.

Test the Thermostat—If your thermostat is stuck open, your engine will not warm up properly on cold mornings and will run rich. If your thermostat is stuck closed, the situation is much worse. Your engine will overheat in a hurry, because coolant will not be able to circulate through the cooling system. The only way to tell if your thermostat is defective is to take it out and test it. On most modern cars, the thermostat is located in the hose outlet casting on top of the engine. Some of the classics of the '20s and '30s had thermostats mounted in the upper tanks of their radiators. These were called *sylphon thermostats* and they actuated a rod that opened and closed a set of shutters in front of the radiator.

To test an in-block thermostat, take it out and suspend it with wire in a saucepan of water. Heat the water on the stove. The thermostat should start opening at about 150 degrees Fahrenheit and open completely at about 190-195 degrees Fahrenheit. A kitchen thermometer can tell you exactly at what temperature it opens, but usually you can assume the thermostat is good if it pops open before the water boils.

A sylphon thermostat can be tested the same way, but you will have to limit its expansion using a U-shaped bracket and a C-clamp. Otherwise, the little gas-filled chamber that actuates it will stretch to the point of no return. If your thermostat fails, you'll have to replace it. For some tips on selection, see the thermostat section under the overhauling part of this chapter.

Check Head Gasket—If there is coolant in your engine's oil, or oil in its coolant, you have a blown head gasket. If coolant is leaking out from between the block and the head, the verdict is the same. But sometimes, head gasket problems aren't so obvious. If you suspect a bad head gasket, run a compression test (see Chapter 1). If the compression is down in two adjacent cylinders, replace the gasket. If a

Rust and crust builds up in any old car's engine. When you have yours apart, be sure to dig out as much of it as you can before sending the engine to be hot tanked and machined. A large screwdriver is handy for this purpose.

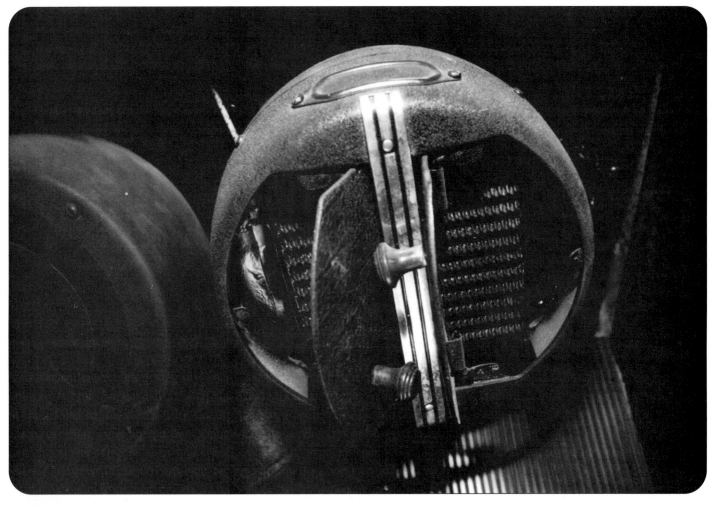

When refurbishing your old car's cooling system, don't forget to check for leaks and clean the small radiator core inside the heater before reinstalling it. You won't want your new custom carpets ruined by rusty water.

compression test tells you what you want to know, there is one sure way to tell if a head gasket is leaking.

Remove the top hose, outlet neck and thermostat. Now reinstall the outlet neck and fill the engine until water is showing at the neck opening just above the level of the head. Disconnect the fan belt. Now start the engine and have a friend rev it quickly while you watch the water level in the outlet neck. If the water rises, or you see bubbles, replace the head gasket.

Check Timing & Adjust Carburetor—Sometimes overheating isn't caused by cooling system problems at all. If an engine's ignition timing is too advanced, it will ping and knock under load and will sizzle. An engine will also get hot if the ignition is retarded too far. Use a timing light and set your engine to the manufacturer's specifications. If your carburetor is running too lean, your engine will stumble and cough on acceleration and will overheat. Adjust the mixture accordingly.

COOLING SYSTEM OVERHAUL

If any of the above tests still don't solve your overheating problems, then a complete overhaul is the only answer. If any part of the cooling system is malfunctioning, your car will not run its best, and most likely you'll eventually be stuck, steaming and stinking, beside the road. If you have the engine apart, overhaul the cooling system as well.

Hot Tank Block

Chances are your engine's block and heads are full of rust if they are made of cast iron and have been running for a long time without a rebuild. If you have the engine disassembled, remove the core plugs and, using a big screwdriver, dig out as much of the crusty corrosion as possible. Then have the block and heads hot tanked, or better yet, take them to a paint stripping service such as Redi-Strip and have them dipped before you begin the machine work. They'll come back clean as new.

Before you reassemble the engine, check the block and heads for cracks from previous overheating mishaps. Blue aniline dye, available at auto stores, is fairly effective for this purpose, but the best way to find them is to have everything Magnaflux inspected at a machine shop. If you discover cracks in your block or a head, try to find a

Water pumps can't easily be rebuilt at home. New bushings and packing are usually needed.

Foam will form as a result, and foam doesn't cool well. Also, bearings on your pump shaft should be tight, with no play in them. If you're doing a frame-up restoration, it makes sense to have your water pump rebuilt. Who wants a cracked block as a result of overheating, or, for that matter, rusty water blowing all over a new hand-rubbed lacquer paint job? Unless you have an arbor press and are experienced with such things, you should have your pump rebuilt professionally.

Replace Belts & Hoses—Such items have a relatively short service life, are inexpensive to replace, and can force you to walk if they fail while you're out on the road. Use only hoses of the proper length, and correctly formed for the application. On many older cars, two short hoses and a metal tube are used to go from the bottom tank of the radiator to the water pump. Never use a single, long hose for this connection. Suction from the water pump will cause a long hose to collapse and cause the water supply to your engine to be cut off.

If you are going to be competing in shows, use only the types of hose clamps, hoses and belts that were used by the manufacturer when the car was built, if possible. Smear a little hose shellac on the mating surfaces when you install your new hoses to insure against leaks. Adjust fan and accessory belts according to the specifications for your car. If belts are too tight they will put unnecessary stress on bearings and they will break from stress. If they are too loose, they will slip and cause the accessories they drive to perform inadequately.

Recondition the Heater—Automotive hot water heaters are nothing but miniature radiators with fans in front of them. If you are doing a complete restoration, you'll want to restore the heater too. Take the core in and have a radiator shop boil it out and check it for leaks. You won't want rusty water all over your new wool carpets. ■

replacement or have them properly repaired by someone who knows how to do it correctly.

Recondition Radiator

Old radiators generally have restricted passages due to rust and scale buildup. Take your radiator to a repair shop and have them boil it out and pressure-test it. Have them solder any leaks too, and repair or reweld any fittings or hose necks. However you can probably do a better, less expensive job of painting it yourself, so tell them not to do it.

Brighten the upper and lower radiator tanks with #360-grit sandpaper then spray them with a coat of primer. Top coat them with black Rustoleum, or use Eastwood Products' semi-gloss engine enamel for an authentic look. Only lightly mist your radiator's cooling fins with paint. Too much of it will act as an insulating blanket and interfere with cooling.

Replace the Thermostat—Thermo-stats can wreak such havoc with an engine if they stick in the closed position that it is wise to replace them every two years in normal use, and most certainly when the engine is down for overhaul. Replace a bad thermostat with one of the same temperature range. On some makes, such as early Chrysler products, in-block thermostats must face a certain direction, so be careful how you install them. Don't be tempted to leave the thermostat out completely. If your thermostat sticks in the closed position when you are in the middle of nowhere, it is okay to run without it until you can get a replacement. But don't operate your engine without one for an extended time, because the coolant won't stay in the radiator long enough to cool properly. Also, your engine won't warm up properly on a cool day, and your fuel economy will suffer as a result.

Rebuild the Water Pump—Leaking water pumps can allow coolant to leak out and air to leak into the system.

CLUTCHES

5

On front-engine, rear-drive cars with a manual transmission, the clutch is just about the most inconvenient part of the driveline to get at. It's up in the bellhousing, sandwiched between the flywheel and the transmission. To make matters worse, it rides on the clutch shaft of the transmission, so you can't take it out unless you remove the transmission first. That's why it is recommended that you rebuild the clutch when you have the engine out. However, if your engine doesn't need an overhaul, but your clutch isn't so good, here's what to do.

HOW IT WORKS

Before we get into removal and repair, here is a brief explanation of how a typical older car's single-plate, dry clutch works. (Some early cars had cone clutches with leather facings. Hudson and a few others had clutches that spun in fluid, and still other cars had multi-disc clutches, but these are fairly rare exceptions that are beyond the scope of a general book.)

When you depress the clutch pedal, you cause the clutch release, or *throwout bearing,* to go forward into a set of levers or diaphragm, depending on the design, that pull(s) the clutch pressure plate away from the asbestos-lined clutch disc. Without the clutch disc pressing against

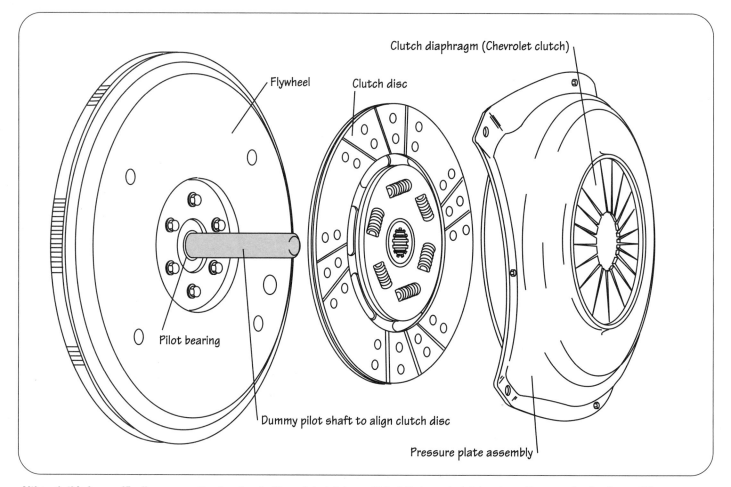

Clutch diaphragm (Chevrolet clutch)

Flywheel

Clutch disc

Pilot bearing

Dummy pilot shaft to align clutch disc

Pressure plate assembly

Although this is specifically an example of a classic Chevrolet clutch, you'll find that most clutches have the same basic pieces. When you reassemble your clutch, be sure to use a wooden or plastic dummy pilot shaft to align the clutch disk so the transmission will slip into place properly.

Before attempting to work on your clutch, put your car up on sturdy jackstands and make sure it is stable. Even with your car on jack - stands you will need to exercise caution. Some of the bolts you will need to loosen are pretty tight. Just tap the end of your wrench with your free hand rather than jerking on the wrench.

Things you'll need:
- GOOD QUALITY PARTICLE OR DUST MASK
- TRANSMISSION JACK
- WRENCHES
- STURDY JACKSTANDS
- WHEEL BEARING GREASE
- HIGH TEMPERATURE GREASE
- FLASHLIGHT
- WOODEN OR PLASTIC DUMMY PILOT SHAFT
- 4" TO 6" BOLTS (2) SAME DIAMETER AND THREAD AS TRANSMISSION TO BELLHOUSING BOLTS
- FINE WIRE

This is what your clutch looks like from behind. In the center of the clutch disc beyond the pressure plate assembly is the pilot bearing. Make sure it is in good shape while you have everything apart. Loosen bolts holding pressure plate assembly evenly a little at a time until tension is released.

the flywheel, the transmission will stop turning. When you take your foot off the clutch, the strong springs in the pressure plate push the clutch disc firmly up against the flywheel, and you start rolling again.

TROUBLESHOOTING

The clutch will make weird noises, along with other symptoms, to let you know it is tired and worn. To determine what your noise problem might be, try these tests. With the car stopped and the transmission in neutral, depress the clutch. If you hear a squealing noise only when the clutch is fully depressed, you probably have a dry pilot bushing (or bearing) in the flywheel. If you hear a noise as soon as your foot takes up the play in the clutch linkage, you may have a bad throwout bearing or worn pressure plate levers. If, as you engage the clutch, you hear a grinding, but it stops when the clutch is fully engaged, your clutch lining may be worn out.

This clutch lining is almost worn down to the rivets. Time to replace it.

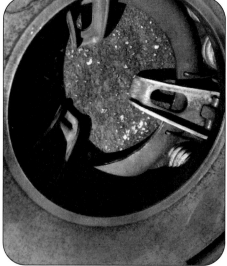

This pressure plate stuck to the clutch disc because of long idleness in storage. Sometimes such clutches can be freed by spraying with brake cleaning fluid and tapping them with a soft hammer.

Grabbing & Shuddering

Clutch lining, like brake lining, is damaged by oil or grease, and because the clutch rides between two reservoirs of oil, namely the engine and the transmission, lining contamination is a common problem. A leaky rear main bearing in the engine, or a poor seal on the front bearing of the transmission, will spray the clutch with oil and cause it to slip, shudder and burn. The easiest way to check for this problem on most cars is to remove the clutch inspection pan on the bottom of the bellhousing. Put on a good particle mask when you do this, because the dust inside the pan is asbestos, a known cancer-causing substance. The clutch and its housing should be completely free of oil. If it isn't, you will need to deal with the source of the oil leak as well as repair the clutch.

Slipping or Failing to Disengage

These problems are usually a result of wear or the clutch linkage being out of adjustment. To begin with, there should be about 7/8" to 1-1/4" of travel in the clutch pedal before it makes contact with the throwout bearing. As clutches wear, the free play decreases, because as the asbestos lining of the clutch disc gets thinner, the fingers (or the diaphragm of the pressure plate) are allowed to move toward the throwout bearing. The clutch begins to slip after a certain point.

Dragging clutches have the opposite problem. The throwout bearing cannot move far enough toward the clutch release levers to free the clutch disc from contact with the flywheel. Set the free play on your clutch according to the diagram on page 59 and try it again.

Pulsing Clutch Pedal

This problem can be caused by a misaligned flywheel, which may be due to a bent crankshaft flange. The trouble may also be a bent clutch shaft on the transmission, or the transmission itself may be out of alignment. Some of these problems may have been caused by badly done clutch work in the past. On many cars there are shims between the bellhousing and the engine that align everything. If a person neglects to put these back where they belong during reassembly, clutch and transmission misalignment will be the result. If you suspect this problem, you can check the

Check fingers of pressure plate assembly for wear. If they are as badly worn as these are, they will need to be replaced when the clutch is rebuilt.

run-out on your flywheel using a machinist's dial indicator attached to a magnetic base.

CLUTCH REMOVAL & REPAIR

Unless your car has a very small transmission and you are a weight lifter, rent a transmission jack. It will help you avoid ruining your clutch and your back. To get the clutch out of the car, you will have to disconnect the driveshaft, then remove the transmission. Put the car on sturdy jackstands high enough off the floor for you to work comfortably. Some transmissions have long pilot shafts that aren't removable, so the car will have to be up high enough for you to slide the transmission back, then pull it down and out.

Removal & Disassembly

The following instructions refer to front-engine, rear-drive cars with con-ventional drivelines. Most cars made 20 years ago or earlier are set up this way, but the Volkswagen Beetle and early Renaults, Fiats and Subarus are notable exceptions. In any case, make sure you carefully read the section in your car's shop manual on clutches before proceeding. No general book such as this can tell you everything you need to know.

With that caveat in mind, let's get started. Begin by removing one of the upper bolts that hold the transmission to the bellhousing. Find a couple of bolts 4" to 6" long that are the same diameter and thread size, then saw off their heads. Now file a screwdriver slot in the cut-off end of each bolt. These are to be used as locator pins when you remove the transmission. They will allow you to slide the transmission back safely, and will help prevent damage to your clutch disc.

Split the front universal joint, then wire the bearing caps together to keep from losing the bearings. Move the driveshaft

Flywheel and crankshaft flange should be marked with a punch if there is any possibility of putting them back together out of sync with each other.

out of your way. Drain the transmission. Disconnect the shift linkage. If your car has the rear motor mounts attached to the transmission, brace the motor carefully before going further. Don't try to brace it under the pan, because the weight of the engine will likely crush it. Instead, brace the engine at the flanges using jackstands or a cradle made of large pieces of scrap wood.

Remove the upper bolts that attach the transmission to the bellhousing, then install your locator pins. Slip the transmission jack under the transmission, run it up until it touches, then strap the transmission in place. Pull the transmission back until it clears the pins. Now lower the jack and slide the transmission forward and out.

Remove the Bellhousing—On some cars, the bellhousing is cast integrally to the transmission. On others, the clutch can be removed without taking off the bellhousing. Check a shop manual to see how things should be done on your car. Disconnect the spring attaching it, then slip the throwout bearing out of its yoke.

This is a typical older Chevrolet clutch with a diaphragm instead of actuating fingers. Its flywheel will need to be resurfaced when the clutch is rebuilt.

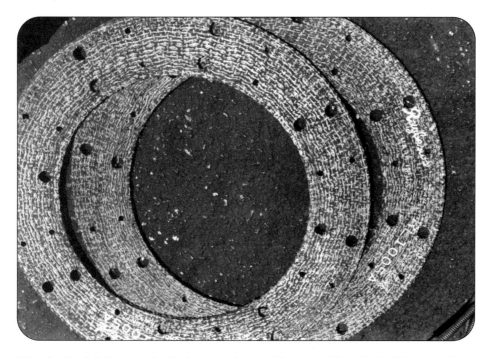

Old-style clutch lining is made of asbestos so be careful when working with it. Wear a mask when cleaning out the clutch inspection pan. This is new lining yet to be riveted in place.

Wipe up any asbestos dust with a damp cloth, wear a mask, and don't try to blow things out with compressed air. When you unbolt the housing, save any shims that helped align it, and note their locations. If you don't put them back where they are supposed to go, you will have clutch troubles later.

Unbolt the Pressure Plate—Use a punch to mark the clutch and flywheel in relation to one another. They are usually balanced as a unit, so it is important to get them back together right. Loosen each of the attaching bolts a half turn at a time, working in a crisscross pattern, so you release the spring tension evenly. When all of the pressure is relieved, unscrew the bolts, but be ready to catch the clutch disc as it slips out. Note which way it faces in the clutch. It is possible to put the disc in backwards during reassembly, but the clutch won't work right if you do.

Remove the Flywheel—Flywheels get glazed, grooved, warped, and sometimes cracked in operation and must be resurfaced at the same time the clutch is overhauled. Most flywheels can only go back on the crankshaft flange the same way, but some years of Ford will allow

you to put it on rotated 180 degrees. If you have such a car, mark the flywheel and crankshaft flange with a punch before removing the flywheel.

Have It Rebuilt—Special tools and skills are required to rebuild a clutch successfully, and even professional

mechanics leave clutch overhaul to other pros. You will want the disc relined, the springs replaced in the pressure plate, and the pressure plate and flywheel reground. Sometimes you can exchange your disc and pressure plate for one that is already rebuilt. If you do that, look each part over carefully to make sure it matches. A replacement clutch will also need to be mated with the flywheel and the whole unit balanced at a machine shop.

Replace or Repack Pilot Bushing—The darned things are impossible to get at when the car is back together, so install a fresh one if you can.

Clean Throwout Bearing—Wash the bearing clean with solvent and inspect it carefully. Don't spin it with compressed air to dry it, because you may damage the bearing in the process. Check the balls for pitting. Also check whether the races are smooth and shiny. Put a little clean grease on the bearing and turn it slowly. If it binds, or if it doesn't pass the other tests, replace it.

Reassembly

Install the Flywheel—On cars where

Drilled spots indicate where flywheel and clutch were balanced at the factory. If you install a new clutch assembly you may have to balance everything again. Check teeth of ring gear for starter. If they are damaged, have the clutch rebuilder replace the gear.

Wash the throwout bearing in solvent, then turn it slowly. It should be smooth and without excessive looseness or play. If it catches or is sloppy, replace it.

the flywheel can be installed more than one way, make sure you align the flywheel using the punch marks you put in the crankshaft flange and the flywheel before disassembly. It is wise to replace the heat-treated bolts that held the flywheel in place with new ones of the correct hardness. But never use ordinary hardware store bolts for this purpose. They could shear during operation with disastrous results. Be sure to use new lock washers or locking devices under them.

Attach the Clutch—At your local auto supply, pick up a wooden dummy pilot shaft to hold the clutch disc in place while you attach the pressure plate to the flywheel. Use new lock washers under the bolts, and tighten them down evenly a half turn at a time in a crisscross pattern. Now attach the bellhousing, being careful to put any shims back where they belong.

Install the Transmission—Place the transmission back on its jack, then jockey it into position. Put the transmission in high gear, which is direct drive, and turn the tail shaft slightly to get the clutch shaft to line up with the clutch disc. Slide it home on the locator pins. If it doesn't slip in all the way, try turning the tail shaft a little, but don't tighten the bolts that hold the transmission in place to get it to mate up. You could damage the clutch disc if you do. Now install the driveshaft. If your universal joints are sloppy or worn now is the time to replace them. Otherwise, pack them with wheel bearing grease before putting them back together. Make sure you use new locking devices on the bolts.

Hook Up Shift Linkage—Make sure the transmission is in neutral, then hook up the links and install new cotter keys and washers. Finally, fill the transmission with the correct gear lube as specified in your car's shop manual. Your shop manual will also tell you how to adjust the shift linkage to its optimum setting. Make sure the clutch freeplay is adjusted as shown in the illustration below. Look the job over carefully before taking your car out for a test drive. ∎

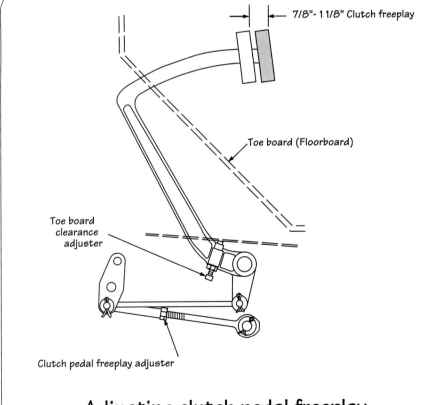

Adjusting clutch pedal freeplay

It is important to adjust clutch freeplay to correct specs after installing a new one or when clutch drags or slips. These dimensions are typical for most older American cars, but check a shop manual to determine what yours should be.

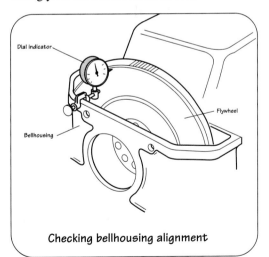

Checking bellhousing alignment

Flywheel-to-bellhousing alignment can be checked using a clamp base and a dial indicator. Shims are often used between the bellhousing and engine to correct alignment problems. If you find any when you disassemble your clutch, note where they go and put them back in place when you put things back together.

TRANSMISSION OVERHAULING

6

Early crash-box transmissions, such as those in Model A Fords, had straight-cut gears and no synchromesh. They were noisy, and they were more difficult to shift, but they were rugged and simple to work on. Then Cadillac introduced synchromesh in 1929, and things got complicated. More modern gearboxes are complex mostly because of their synchromesh system and their constant mesh, helical gears. Because of these factors, many garages send transmission work to a specialist and confine themselves to removing and installing the unit.

A capable amateur restorer can rebuild a synchromesh transmission, provided he can find the parts and has the specialized tools that are sometimes necessary, but the job should not be undertaken lightly. Every transmission shop has stories about guys who bring their transmissions to them in a basket—guys who just get in too deep. That's because if you aren't very careful and organized when you take your tranny apart, you will lose track of how it is supposed to go back together. If you do decide to tackle rebuilding your car's standard transmission, read up on

This is all there is to a Model A Ford transmission. Later ones aren't this simple. If you want to learn the fundamentals, these early crash-boxes are a great place to start.

how it works, then study a shop manual, or find an old *MoToRs* manual that includes your year and make. Also, before you tear your old gearbox apart, check on the availability of replacement parts.

Automatic transmissions are definitely beyond all but the most gifted and resourceful hobbyist restorer. They are exceedingly complicated, and require special equipment to do them correctly. The best most of us can do is locate a good rebuilder and trust the job to him.

DIAGNOSING STANDARD TRANSMISSION TROUBLES

Before you take your gearbox apart, or before you take it—and your checkbook—to the nearest transmission shop, look things over carefully. There are a number of problems that can easily

be remedied without tearing your transmission completely down and overhauling it. Here are some possibilities.

Difficult to Shift

If your car is equipped with the old "three on the tree" column shift, the linkage may be worn or out of adjustment. Also, the detents (little balls and springs usually located in the side or top plate of the transmission) may be worn. These problems can be fixed without removing the gearbox.

To adjust the linkage on a column shift, put the transmission into neutral, then pin the two shift levers on the steering column together. There are usually holes in them that make it easy. Now adjust the slack out of the linkage. Replace any worn grommets or washers.

Worn detent mechanisms usually only require new springs and balls. Check a shop manual for your car to see how these assemblies are used in your gearbox.

These are the shifting detents that are in the top, or sideplate of your transmission. Sometimes they get worn out and the springs that hold the balls out against the shifting forks lose their tension. Poor shifting is the result.

Transmission Locks Up

If when you shift gears your transmission locks up and kills the engine, you may have a bent shifting fork, or worn detent mechanisms. Depress the clutch and restart the engine. If the engine will start and run with the clutch depressed, your transmission is in two gears at once. Don't try to push the car to break it loose. Instead, climb under it and move the shifting forks to unlock it. Bent shifting forks and worn detents are easy to repair.

Transmission Whines

Before you take out your car's gearbox, make sure it isn't *supposed* to be noisy. Try to get a ride in other cars of the same make and year as yours. Some gearboxes in cars of the late '20s and early '30s were just naturally noisy, especially when they were cold.

Leaks

Transmissions often leak as a result of overfilling. The rule of thumb is: If your transmission is warm, the fluid should just be level with the access plug on the side. None should run out. If your transmission is cold, the level should be about 1/4"

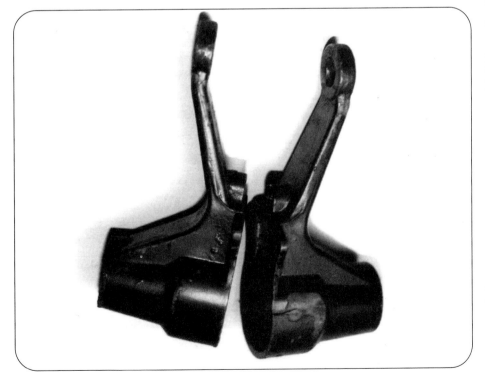

If your old "three on the tree" transmission is shifting badly, take a look at the shift levers on the other end of the shift mechanism on the steering column under the hood. Slack can usually be adjusted out of the system. Put your transmission in neutral, then slip a pin through the holes in the sides of these levers to hold them straight. Now adjust the threaded rods that go down to the transmission so there is no slack in them. If your shift levers are badly worn, a machine shop can drill out the holes and bush them back to specs with bronze sleeves.

Notches on the shifting forks ride on balls of detent mechanism and provide crisp shifting if detents are not worn or forks bent.

If you were to see your transmission out of your car, you might think the shaft sticking out the front and the shaft sticking out the rear were all one piece. They are not. The front one is the clutch shaft, and the rear one the output shaft. However, when your car is in high gear, they are linked together and do function as a unit. The car is in direct drive. On the other hand, when the car is in low or second gears, the clutch shaft and the output shaft are turning at different speeds. There is a bearing at the rear of the clutch shaft that turns in every gear but high, so it's probably the problem. To replace it the transmission will have to be disassembled.

Transmission Pops Out of Gear

This could be because of linkage that is out of adjustment, or because of a bent shifting fork. It may also be a result of worn gears or bearings. And it may be that the transmission is out of alignment because its mating surface on the bellhousing isn't absolutely parallel to the flywheel. To check for this condition you will have to remove the gearbox and check the flywheel and bellhousing with a dial indicator.

lower than the plug. The best way to verify it is to stick your finger in the hole and check it. If the front and rear bearing seals are leaking, the transmission will have to be removed and the seal replaced.

Gearbox Growls in All Gears

When your car is in gear and the clutch is released, the cluster gear assembly is spinning on the countershaft even when the car is in high gear. So if you hear growling in all gears, chances are the problem is in the bearings between the countershaft and the cluster gear. To repair this problem you will need to remove and disassemble the transmission. The problem could also be the front bearing on the clutch shaft.

Modern clutch shafts and gears such as these are helical rather than straight cut as they were in early crash-box transmissions.

Automatic transmissions are best left to the pros. They are complex, require special tools, and are unforgiving of novice efforts to repair them.

When you take a universal joint apart to remove the driveshaft, wire its bearing caps in place to prevent loss of small needle bearings. Pack the bearings with wheel bearing grease and use new locking devices when you put U-joints back together.

drained and flushed to remove metal particles, because they can destroy it in short order. If you drive the car for very long with a stripped gear, a strain will be put on that gear's surviving teeth and they will eventually fail too.

REBUILDING A FORD MODEL A TRANNY

One classic car transmission that is simple, and for which there are plenty of replacement parts, is the Model A Ford's. In fact, the A transmission is so simple that it is probably as much work to get it out of the car as it is to rebuild it. Here's what is involved.

Disassembly

Wash the gearbox so dirt won't fall down inside when you open up the case. Now unbolt the shift tower. Automotive parts cleaning solvent or kerosene will do the job, or just use a strong mixture of dishwasher detergent and water. Wear neoprene gloves to protect your hands.

Clicking in One or More Gears

This condition could be a result of worn gears, or teeth missing on one or more gears. Pull the side (or top) plate off of the transmission and inspect each gear carefully. If there are any broken teeth, the transmission needs to be disassembled and the bad gears replaced. If you know you have broken a tooth off of a gear out on the road, the transmission should be

Countershaft gear assembly, otherwise known as the cluster gear, is cast in one piece on Model A, as it is on many later cars. Note pitting and damage to gears in center of shaft.

If shifting forks aren't bent or shafts worn, they can be cleaned, greased, and put back in service. Otherwise, replace them.

Remove Bellhousing—Unscrew the four bolts holding the housing to the transmission. On a Model A, the bellhousing holds the front bearing of the transmission in place. On many later cars, it is held in by a retainer or snap ring.

Pull Out Clutch Shaft—Peel away the old gasket, then pull the clutch shaft out the front of the gearbox.

Remove Main Shaft—On the back end of the transmission, remove the four bolts holding the bearing retainer/universal joint cover in place and lift it off. Peel off its gasket. The mainshaft can now be pulled out from the back of the transmission. The low/reverse gear, and the second/high gear can now be lifted out of the gearbox.

Remove Countershaft—At the rear of the gearbox case is a retainer that holds the countershaft and reverse idler shaft in place. Unbolt it. Now use a hammer and a brass drift to tap the countershaft out, working from the rear of the case. The hole for the countershaft at the front of the transmission is .001" larger in diameter than the one at the rear to facilitate its removal, so don't try to drive the countershaft from the front out the back.

Pull Cluster Gear—Just as on many later transmissions, the cluster gear, or more properly, the countershaft gear assembly, is all cast in one piece. With the countershaft removed, the cluster gear just lifts out. Remove the two roller bearings in either end of it. Also remove the thrust washers.

Remove Reverse Idler Gear—Pull the shaft for the reverse idler gear out the rear of the case. Lift out the reverse gear.

On Model A, bellhousing holds front bearing in place. Once bellhousing is removed, peel the old gasket away, then pull out the clutch shaft.

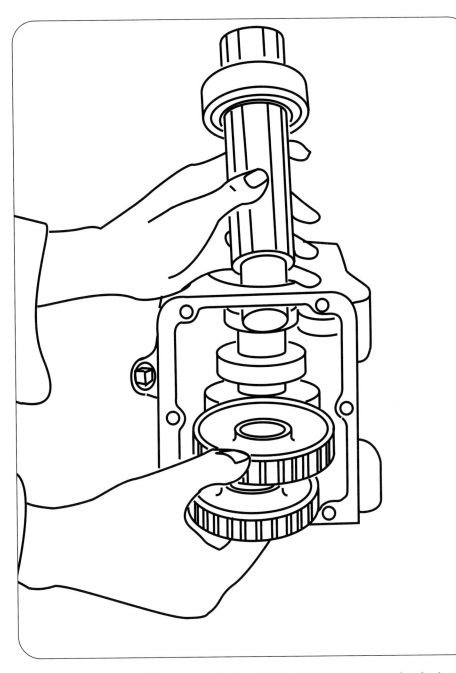

their own weight, or require a slight nudging. If they flop down easily, they're too loose.

Bearings—If the bearings are pitted, galled or discolored, replace them. If they look okay, put a little light oil on them and turn the bearing slowly. If you feel a catch, or the bearings are not perfectly smooth, get new ones. If you need to replace the bearings on the clutch shaft or mainshaft, have the old ones pressed off at a local machine shop with a bearing press, then have new ones pressed on.

Thrust Washers—If the washers are rough, deformed, or thin, replace them with washers of exactly the same thickness. Also look at the shafts. If they are grooved or worn, replace them too.

Shift Tower—Are the shifting forks bent? Are their shafts smooth? Is the detent assembly worn? Is the tension spring sound? Replace any defective parts.

On the back of the transmission, remove the four bolts holding the bearing retainer in place and lift it off. Peel off the gasket. You can now pull the main shaft out of the transmission from the rear. The low/reverse and second/high gears can now be lifted from the transmission case.

Rebuilding

Wash everything with solvent before doing an inspection. Check each component carefully. Are any of the gears pitted or grooved? Do they have teeth missing? Are the ends of the teeth ground off, chipped, or bent? If so, you will need to replace the bad gears. But if a gear only has a few minor burrs, it can sometimes be cleaned up with a stone or fine file.

Gears—If you need to replace the low/reverse, or the second/high gears you will need to buy them together with a new mainshaft because they are selectively matched to each other and are machined to very close tolerances. The clearance between the gears and the shaft should be no more than .002". A rough check can be made by lubricating the parts, then holding the shaft vertically and sliding the gears onto it. They should just slide of

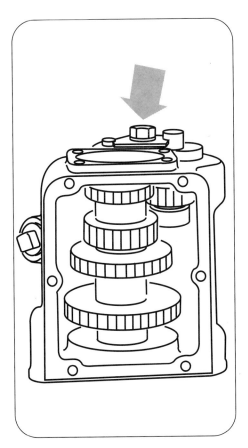

At the rear of the gearbox a retainer holds the countershaft and reverse idler shaft in place. Unbolt it.

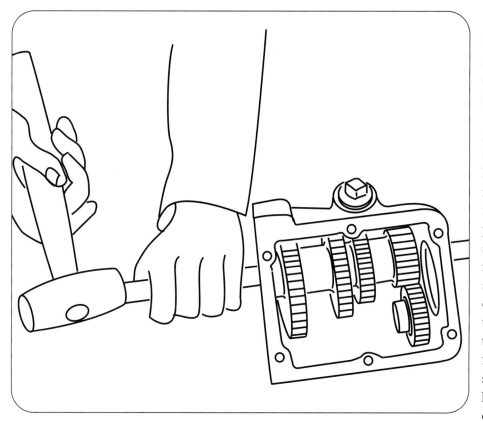

Install Reverse Idler Gear—Place the reverse idler gear in the case with the flush side of the gear facing the rear of the case. Now insert its shaft so that its flat side faces the countershaft hole.

Install Countershaft—Put a little grease on the cluster gear thrust washers, and paste them in place, aligned with the holes in the case. Slip in the cluster gear roller bearings. The longer bearing goes into the end with the small gear. Now place the cluster gear in the transmission so its small gear is at the rear, and is meshed with the reverse idler gear. Next, slip the countershaft in through the front of the transmission case, through the thrust washers and cluster gear and into the back of the case. Make sure its flat face is turned toward the reverse idler shaft. Tap the shaft home with a soft hammer. Now install the retainer for the countershaft and reverse idler shaft.

Install Mainshaft—Place the transmission on your bench front end down. Now place the second/high slider gear in the case so its shifting collar faces up. Align it with the mainshaft hole. Now place the low/reverse slider gear in on top of it, shifting collar down, or facing

Use a hammer and brass drift to drive the countershaft out from the rear of the case. Don't try it from the front, because the back end of the shaft is tapered and smaller than the front end.

ASSEMBLY

Thoroughly clean your workbench, tools and hands. One tiny bit of grit can ruin a bearing. Now coat all of your transmission's internal parts with gear lube. Make sure the case is thoroughly clean and its holes are deburred and smooth.

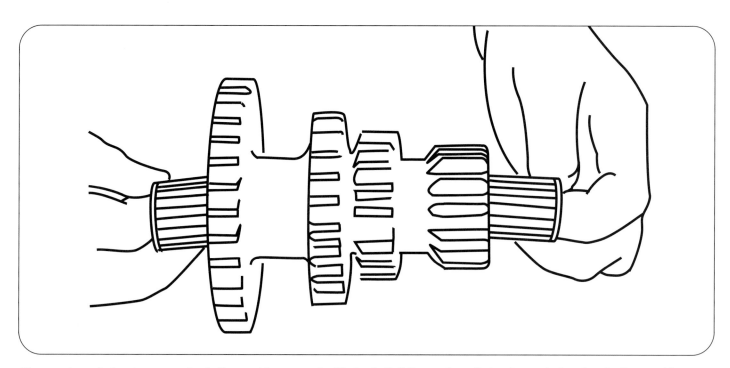

The one-piece cluster gear or countershaft assembly can now be lifted out. Pull the small needle bearings out of each end. Clean and inspect them. If they are worn, pitted or discolored, replace them.

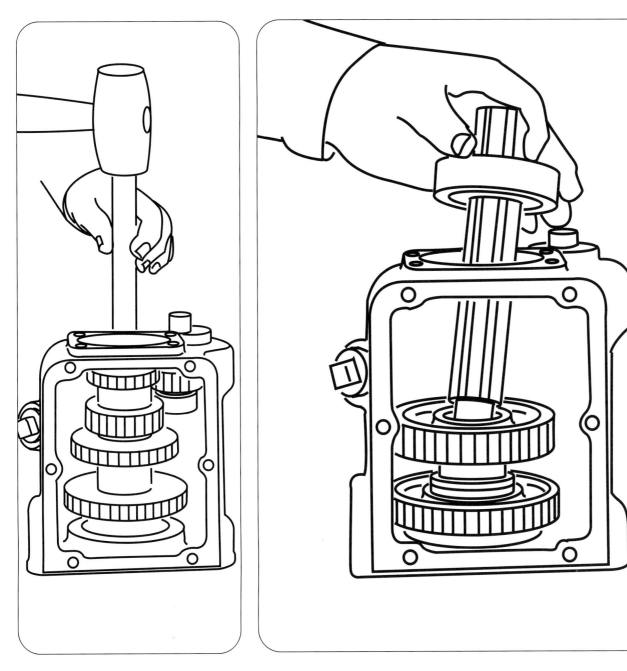

Put a little grease on the cluster gear thrust washers and paste them in place at the proper holes in the case. Slip in the roller bearings. Now slip in the cluster gear so the small gear is at the rear and is meshed with the reverse idler gear. Slide in the countershaft.

Put the transmission on your bench front end down. Now place the second/high gear in the case so its shifting collar is face up. Align it with the mainshaft hole. Now place the low/reverse gear on top of it with its shifting collar down. Slide the mainshaft in from the rear until its bearing seats.

the low /reverse gear. Make sure its spline teeth are aligned with those on the second/high slider gear.

Slide the mainshaft in from the rear of the case until its bearing seats. Next, coat the U-joint cover/bearing retainer gasket with a little silicone sealer or Gaskacinch, and put it in place. Attach the U-joint cover/bearing retainer with its lubricator

fitting facing downward. Tighten the bolts, and wire them into place.

Install Clutch Shaft—Flip the transmission over. Place the pilot bearing over the end of the mainshaft and collar assembly. Now slide the clutch shaft and main drive gear assembly down over the mainshaft until its bearing seats in the transmission case.

Attach Bellhousing—Coat the gasket and set it in place. Now position the bellhousing on the front of the case and bolt it down evenly. That's all there is to it. Fill the transmission with fresh lube, put on a new gasket and install the shift tower. Make sure the shifting forks are in the gear collars, then tighten the bolts down evenly. ■

DIFFERENTIAL OVERHAULING

7

Probably the longest lasting part of any car's driveline is the differential. Engines take a beating because of the heat they produce and the reciprocating motion of their pistons and rods. Transmissions get abused by frequent shifting of the gears in normal operation. Universal joints are exposed to the elements on most cars, and they have to endure a lot of twisting and turning. But differentials, though they operate under tremendous pressure,

have it comparatively easy, so they usually endure much longer than other components.

In fact, if you hear a funny noise reverberating from your car's driveline as you drive along, chances are it is not the rear end. Such noises are much more likely to come from the clutch, transmission, universal joints or even the tires, rather than the differential. But, because the various components of a car's driveline are all connected, sound telegraphs through them, making it

difficult to isolate problems merely by listening. Even experienced mechanics sometimes misdiagnose running gear problems. So before leaping to conclusions, check things out thoroughly. Start with the simple things first.

DIAGNOSIS

Check Lubricant—Remove the inspection plug in the differential carrier assembly, then stick in an extended finger horizontally and check the fluid

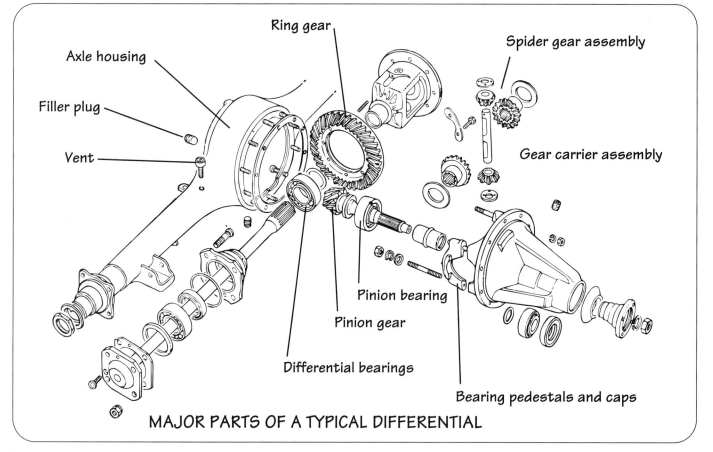

MAJOR PARTS OF A TYPICAL DIFFERENTIAL

This is an exploded view of a typical differential. It differs a little from the one we used for our photographs but shows most of the major components. The rear end in your car may be similar or quite different. Read the differential section in your shop manual before taking it apart.

Things you'll need:

- Gasket material
- Silicone sealer
- Hammer, punch and drift
- Bearing puller
- Magnetic base and dial indicator
- Access to a bearing press
- Cleaning solvent and brush
- Sharp putty knife
- New axle bearing seals
- White lead or methylene blue grease
- Fine wire
- Brake tubing wrench
- Jackstands
- Bearings and gears as required

level. If the car has been sitting, the level should be about 1/4" below the opening, and if the car has been in use and is warm, the fluid should be up to the fill plug, but none should spill out. A differential that is low on lubricant will be noisy, and will fail fairly quickly. Inspect the seals around the differential and axle housings. Are they leaking? If so, you will need to replace them regardless of other problems.

Check Tires—Are they inflated to the correct pressure? Are they properly balanced and aligned? If not, they may be causing your noise problem. Have you put new tires on the car recently? Sometimes radial tires will make a drumming noise when installed on cars that were not designed to be equipped

with them. Even if you installed the original types of tires on your old car, it is likely that the tread on them is deeper than on the ones you took off, and it may have a different pattern than your previous tires. Both of these factors could change the sounds emanating from your car as you drive along.

Try over-inflating all of your tires to about 40 pounds, then drive slowly around the block. If the sound goes away, or diminishes considerably, tires are probably the source of the sound. When doing this comparative test, it helps to roll the back windows down, and if your car is a sedan, have a passenger listen from the back seat.

Check Other Related Parts—Read the troubleshooting sections in the clutch and transmission chapters. Make sure you have eliminated the possibilities presented in them before pointing an accusing finger at the differential. Transmissions can make noises that will even fool a professional. Worn bearings in the mainshaft assembly make a constant noise that sounds much the same as a worn differential.

Check U-Joints—On a typical, conventional, Hotchkiss, open driveline, you can see them readily when you roll under the car. But if your car is an earlier one equipped with a closed, torque tube type driveline (early Fords, Buicks and Chevrolets had these) read up in your shop manual as to how you go about inspecting its universal joint. On most closed driveline cars, there is only one, and it is usually situated in a housing just behind the transmission. There should be no side play in your car's universal joints and they should rotate and swivel freely and effortlessly. If your U-joints have zerk fittings, shoot a little grease into them at low pressure, so you don't rupture their seals. If, after injecting fresh lubricant into them, your U-joints aren't absolutely free and smooth, with no play, replace them.

Universal joints often fail because they have been neglected. They don't need to

be serviced every time a car gets a lube job, so some people neglect to service them at all. If your car has a lot of miles on it, and U-joints are readily available for it, play it safe and replace them. You just might be surprised at how smooth and quiet your car will become. And you may prevent a U-joint failure that, on an open driveline car, could be dangerous.

Rebuild or Replace?—Many seasoned mechanics hesitate to work on differentials because they can end up worse than when a person started if he isn't extremely careful and exacting in his work. On the other hand, there is no magic involved. Read up on your particular car's differential to see how it is designed, and to learn the exact procedure you'll need to follow to rebuild it. A general book such as this can warn you of pitfalls, and give you tips on easy ways to do things, but it cannot cover every type of rear end for every car. The one shown in the photographs is typical of many open driveline differentials, but may differ considerably from the one in your particular car.

If your car is a common make for which a good replacement differential is available, it may be much easier, and not much more expensive, to put in a replacement rather than rebuilding your old one. Depending on your mechanical skill, the availability of parts and how much you value your time, replacement may well be the wisest solution. If you do decide to rebuild your old unit, and you are doing it for the first time, get an experienced friend to help and coach you. Differentials are not at all forgiving of even slight mistakes made during their assembly, and will fail quickly if they are not adjusted properly.

REMOVAL

The disassembly and reassembly of drivelines can vary significantly from brand to brand. However, once you have the differential gear carrier assembly out of the car, the overhaul procedure is usually pretty similar. Our example is a typical Hotchkiss open driveline design with two universal joints of the type used on virtually all front-engine, rear-drive cars made in the last 30 years, and on most cars made before that.

Be Safe—Before you attempt to remove your car's rear end, slightly loosen the lug nuts on the back wheels, loosen the axle nuts if there are any, then jack your car up at all four corners and put sturdy jackstands under it. Next, put a piece of 2"x 4" between the brake pedal and the floorboard to keep the pedal from being depressed unintentionally. Finally, release the parking brake. While you are working, always keep in mind that cars can be pulled off of jackstands by overzealous mechanics, so be careful.

Disconnect Driveshaft—Gently pry the locking clips loose, then remove the bolts holding one differential yoke of the universal joint assembly to the bearing caps. Split the universal joint, then wire the bearing caps together so you won't lose the bearings inside them. Slide the driveshaft out of the way. Disconnect the emergency brake at the equalizer link in the center, underneath the car.

Remove Brake Drums—Remove the back wheels, then tap around the rim of the brake drum with a rubber mallet or block of wood to help loosen it from the brake shoes. Remove the axle nut if there is one, then attach the correct type of drum puller to the brake drum and tighten it to pop the drum loose.

There are two types of drum pullers. Which one you need depends on the brand of car you have. Some cars, such as early Fords, Packards and Chrysler products, have axle nuts that hold the drums on. Such cars require a puller that attaches to the studs on the drum, and tightens in the middle on the axle. Never pound on the end of this type of puller in order to remove the drum. You'll damage the differential if you do.

The other type of puller attaches to the rim of the drum and tightens against the center of the axle. It's okay to tap on the end of this type of puller to help pop the drum loose. In either case, work with caution because drums can come off with a lot of force.

Remove Brake Backing Plates—Put newspaper under them, then clean the brake assemblies with a brush. Wear a mask while doing this, because old brake linings are made of asbestos. Next, using a brake tubing wrench, disconnect the hydraulic lines to the rear brakes. Now loosen and remove the bolts holding the backing plates to the axle housing. Pull off the backing plates, with the brake assemblies attached, and lay them aside on clean newspaper. Save any shims you find between the backing plates and axle housings, and don't mix them up.

Remove Axles—On some cars, the axles slip out with a firm tug, but other cars require an axle puller. Check the rear wheel bearings and races for wear once you have the axles out. Replace them if they are loose, pitted or worn.

Drop the Gear Carrier—Before removing the gear carrier from the axle housing, get a sharp putty knife, some solvent and a stiff brush and clean the carrier casting thoroughly. You don't want any dirt or grit falling into the gears as you slide the differential out. Now drain the rear end and check the gear lube for metal particles, burning or contamination. If none of these signs of problems are in evidence, you're in luck. Metal particles could mean gear wear; burned fluid usually means ruined bearings.

Remove one of the bolts from the differential housing and find two longer bolts with the same types of threads. Cut the heads off of the two longer bolts so you can thread them into the differential housing as locator pins and supports. Remove two bolts from the differential at the 3 o'clock and 9 o'clock positions on the housing, then thread in the two longer studs for support.

Next, slide a transmission jack under the rear end to support the differential when you pull it loose. A transmission jack can be rented at most tool rental yards, or large blocks of wood can be used. Don't try to manhandle the rear end assembly without support unless you're an Olympic class weight lifter; they are surprisingly heavy and awkward to handle.

Remove the rest of the bolts holding the gear carrier to the axle housing, then pull it forward onto your waiting transmission jack. Slide it out from under the car and mount it on an engine stand or put it in a large smooth-jawed vise to keep it from rolling while you are working on it.

INSPECTION & DISASSEMBLY

Before you start taking things apart, look your differential over carefully. The teeth on the ring and pinion gears should be smooth and shiny with no signs of pitting, discoloration or grooves. Chipped teeth and sharp edges indicate wear problems too.

Move things around with your fingers. A lot of side-to-side or end play usually means worn bearings. Close inspection will often yield the answer to your problem.

Bearing Caps

With a hammer and punch, mark the bearing caps and pedestals so you will be able to get the caps back on the same side and facing the same way as they came off. Also mark the big bearing adjusting nuts in relation to the pedestals so you can get the bearings back into approximate adjustment.

Remove the Nuts & Caps—Carefully bend back the metal tabs that keep the cap bolts from turning, so you can get a socket on the bolt heads. Loosen the bolts to allow the bearing adjusting nuts to turn easily. Unscrew the adjusting nuts, counting the number of

Before you begin disassembly, mark the differential bearing carriers and their caps using a hammer and punch. It is crucial that you get the caps back on their original pedestals facing the right way.

Count the number of turns required to remove each adjusting nut. You will have to put them back as they were when you put the differential back together.

Also mark the bearing adjusting nuts as to their positions in relationship to the pedestals or caps before loosening them.

turns it takes to remove them. Note the number of turns on each nut using tape or tags. Now remove the bearing caps.

Disassemble

Lift the differential case and ring gear out of the main casting. Use a bearing puller to remove the differential bearings. Inspect the bearings and races for pitting, discoloration and ridges or grooves. The bearings should ride smoothly in their cages without slop or binding. If they

don't, replace them.

To remove the pinion shaft bearings, remove the pinion nut and universal joint yoke, then slide the pinion shaft out the rear of the main casting. On some makes, the rear pinion bearing is pressed onto the shaft and comes out with it. Your car may be different; check your shop manual for details.

Next, pry the pinion seal out of the front of the casting. The front bearing and adjusting cone can now be removed by

simply lifting them out. Drive the inner bearing races out of the main casting with a hammer and drift. Use a bearing puller to get the bearing off of the pinion shaft.

Ring & Pinion Gears

If they are discolored, grooved, worn to a sharp edge or chipped, you will need to replace them. Ring and pinion gears only come in matched sets, so don't attempt to replace one without the other. If you do, they will be noisy and wear out quickly. On our example, the ring gear was bolted to the differential case, then wired in place to keep it from coming loose. If you need to replace the ring gear, unbolt it evenly a little at a time. When you reinstall it, tighten it in a cross pattern, evenly, in three stages, to about 45 ft-lbs. with a torque wrench. (This torque specification is correct for most cars, but check your manual to make sure.) Rewire the bolts into place or reinstall new locking devices as required.

Replacement—If you must replace the ring and pinion gears, you may want to consider changing the ratio. A manual for your make and year of car will tell you which ratios were available for it. As an example, on many cars of the '30s and '40s, six-cylinder models often came with very low gears in their differentials. That was because hills weren't as well ramped in those days and could be quite steep. But for modern highways, use of such gearing makes your car's engine work too hard at normal speeds. The solution is to get a ring and pinion set from an eight-cylinder model of the same year and make, because they are generally a better ratio for modern needs. Usually they will fit. Another reason you might want to change ratios is because some models of '50s and '60s cars had tall gearing that made off-the-line acceleration rather leisurely. A differential from a station wagon might give such a car the bottom-end torque you're looking for.

There are some side-effects to changing rear end ratios though. For instance, your speedometer will read correctly only with the gearing that came in the car. So if you change the differential gears, you will need to change the speedometer gear also. If you are installing a replacement differential, try to get the speedometer gear out of the car from which it was removed, or try to find a speedometer gear that will be correct for your new rear end gearing.

Another side effect of changing differential gear ratios is that doing so will affect your fuel economy. On older cars, if you go from low gearing such as 4.56:1, to higher gearing, such as a 3.96:1 ratio, your fuel economy should improve dramatically, but you will loose some of your ability to accelerate quickly, and you will have to downshift to climb steep hills. Conversely, with big-engined cars from the '60s, where you install lower gearing to increase your acceleration, you will no longer be able loaf along at low rpm while the car is doing 80 miles an hour.

If you are interested in pursuing gear ratio changes further, and want to determine exactly what effect they will have on your particular car, pick up a copy of HPBooks' *Auto Math Handbook*.

Pinion gear bearing must be pressed into place with a hydraulic press. Your local machine shop should be able to help you with this task.

It is an invaluable source of information on many aspects of automotive engineering, and will help you forecast the effect such modifications will have on your car.

Spider Gears

The little pinion and side gears (spider gears) in the differential case seldom wear out unless the car has been abused or driven extensively in icy, slippery conditions. In straightline driving, they don't turn at all. If there is slop in the gears, replacing the spacers in between them will often correct the problem.

ASSEMBLY

Most of the time, all that needs replacing in a differential are the bearings. Take your old bearings to a supplier and match them up. Or, if you have trouble finding bearings to fit, try: OlCar Bearing Company, 455 Lakes Edge Dr., Oxford, MI 48371. (313) 969-2628.

Install Pinion Shaft—Slip the inner bearing races into the differential assembly casting and make sure they are properly seated. In the pictured example above, a new bearing had to be pressed on

the pinion shaft at the local machine shop. Your make may have differing requirements or use shims to establish this tolerance. Slide the pinion shaft into the casting, then slide the preload adjusting cone in from the front. (Your differential may use some other method of adjusting preload.) Now install the front bearing and then the pinion seal using a seal-

Sometimes it pays to change ring and pinion gears to taller ratios so your classic can cruise at highway speeds without over-revving. Another reason for changing differential gearing is for better acceleration at the bottom end. For that you would want lower gearing. This set fits a mid-fifties Chevy.

This Chevy limited slip differential drops right in and can be a good addition if your car pumps out lots of power from a big V8, causing you to break the rear tires loose in the wet or when going around corners under acceleration.

installing tool or a hammer and a socket that matches the outer diameter of the seal. Tap the seal squarely into place, free side out, being careful not to damage or deform it. Finally, slip the universal joint yoke into place and put the castle nut on finger-tight.

Install Differential Case—Have new bearings pressed onto the differential case assembly at a local machine shop. Place the differential case and ring gear assembly back in its journals, then install the bearing caps, locking devices and bolts; but leave the bolts finger-tight. Make sure the punch marks on the caps line up with those on the pedestals. Install the bearing caps and tighten them within a turn or two of the original setting.

Adjustments

Set Preload—Before adjusting the backlash on the ring gear, you must preload the differential bearings. Our rear end was designed to be adjusted using a large bull caliper and a .010" feeler

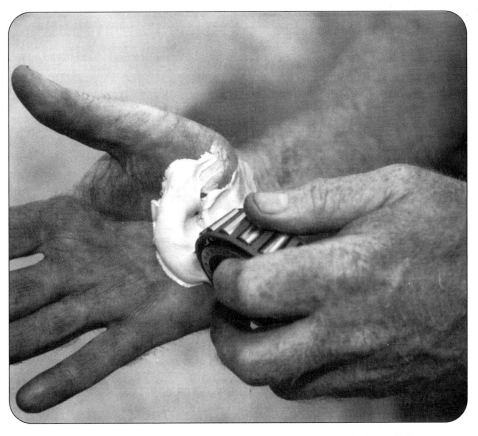

Wash old bearings thoroughly in solvent, then turn them slowly to check them. If they are sound, or if you have new replacement bearings, pack them with grease before installing them. Put a little grease on the heel of your hand and work it well into each bearing.

New differential bearings had to be pressed on at the machine shop. Never try to hammer such bearings into place—you'll ruin the bearing if you do.

Place a machinist's magnetic base on the gasket mating surface of the differential casting and attach a dial indicator to the base. Situate the dial indicator so its pin is against a tooth of the ring gear. Now move the pinion gear back and forth. The latitude of movement, or backlash, should be .003" to .005". If it is greater than .005", back off the right-hand adjusting nut and tighten the left one the same amount until the backlash is correct. By adjusting the nuts exactly the same amount on both sides, you will not disturb the bearing preload. (The tolerances may differ on your differential. Check a shop manual for the right dimension.) Recheck the bearing preload just to make sure you haven't disturbed it.

Smear a light coating of white lead, or methylene blue, on the pinion gear teeth and slowly turn the ring and pinion gear assembly. Look carefully at the footprints the teeth of the pinion gear leave on the ring gear. Consult the illustrations nearby to determine if the gears are meshing properly. The gears should mesh evenly from heel to toe, and over their full faces. If they don't, readjust them until they do.

gauge. To do it, place a feeler gauge against one finished boss of a bearing cap, then measure from it to the other bearing cap boss with the feeler gauge interposed between the boss and the caliper. Lock the caliper at this setting. Now tighten the differential bearing adjusting nuts equally until the caliper will just slip over the bearing cap bosses. The bearings are now correctly preloaded.

Adjust Backlash—This is the critical part. If it isn't right, your rear end could be noisy and wear out in a hurry. When adjusted properly, the pinion gear will be in just the right place on its fore and aft axis, and the ring gear will be in its place from left to right. Some types of differentials use shims to obtain the correct fore and aft placement of the pinion shaft. Check your shop manual to see how it's done on your make.

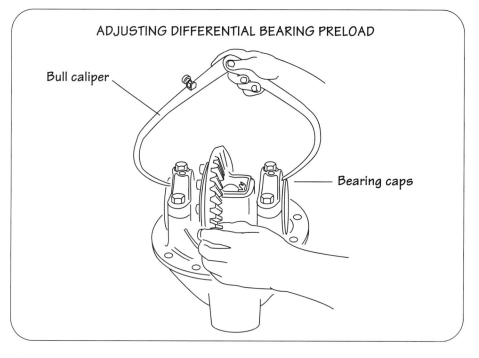

ADJUSTING DIFFERENTIAL BEARING PRELOAD

Bull caliper

Bearing caps

Differential bearings usually require a certain amount of preload. A large bull caliper and a feeler gauge are used to make the adjustment.

Otherwise, you will end up with a noisy differential that will wear out in a hurry.

INSTALLATION

Lightly coat the mating surfaces of the differential casting and the axle housing with silicone sealer, let it skin over, then put the gasket in place. Now, using the same locator pins you used to remove it, slide the differential home against the axle housing. Put the bolts in finger-tight, then remove the locator pins and install the remaining two bolts. Tighten them evenly in a cross pattern to the correct torque specification. Some cars use a cork gasket in this application. If yours does, don't over-tighten the bolts. You will crush the cork and force it out from between the mating surfaces if you do.

Install Axles

Push them back into the housing. Pack, or replace, the outer bearings and install a fresh seal. Now reinstall the brake backing plates. Make sure you include any shims you found when you removed them originally. Connect the brake hydraulic lines to the wheel cylinders.

Check End Play—On some cars, such as vintage Chrysler products, you will need to check the end play, or the distance the axles move in and out when you tug on them. Use the same dial indicator and magnetic base you used to check the backlash. A typical tolerance would be .004" to .007", but check a shop manual for your car to verify the dimension. If the axle play is too little, subtract shims; if it is to great, add them.

Install Brake Drums—Slide the drums onto the axle splines, install the thrust washers, then tighten the axle nuts into place. Bleed the wheel cylinders to remove any air bubbles. Now install the back wheels and lower the car down off of the jackstands. Set the brake, then use a long extension to tighten the axle nuts to somewhere in the neighborhood of 200 ft-lbs. Failure to tighten axle nuts sufficiently will result in sheared axle splines and ruined drums. Install new cotter keys.

Tighten U-joint Yoke—The differential pictured was designed to have the pinion bearing preloaded by tightening the nut that holds the universal joint yoke in place until the adjusting cone in the carrier case just starts to buckle. It takes a bit of muscle to make this happen. Consult your manual for instructions on your make. Install a fresh cotter key.

Repack U-joints—While you have your driveline apart, pack or replace the universal joints. Don't forget to install new nut locks. Finally, fill your differential with fresh hypoid gear oil and take the car for a test drive. ∎

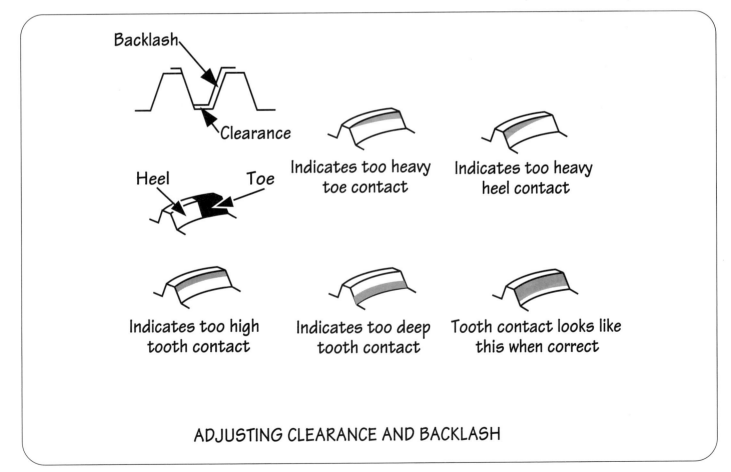

ADJUSTING CLEARANCE AND BACKLASH

Backlash

Clearance

Heel   Toe

Indicates too heavy toe contact

Indicates too heavy heel contact

Indicates too high tooth contact

Indicates too deep tooth contact

Tooth contact looks like this when correct

Correct backlash and gear contact are crucial to silent and dependable operation. Use white lead or methylene blue dye to verify gear teeth footprint.

ELECTRICAL WIRING

8

Most cars 30 years old or older should be rewired. Insulation gets stiff and brittle with time and eventually cracks and crumbles, leaving wires bare. Shorts and fires are a common result. Neglecting wiring is a recipe for disaster. Fortunately, replacing it isn't difficult.

CIRCUITRY BASICS

Before rewiring a car, you need a basic understanding of how automotive electrical systems work. They're kind of like the plumbing in a house, but with some important differences. Electricity flows through wires much like water flows through pipes. Switches are like faucets or valves. They can stop the flow of current through wires, just as valves can stop the flow of water in plumbing. (Current is measured in *amperes,* or amps for short.)

Voltage is like pressure. Higher voltage allows the same amount of current to flow through a smaller wire, just as higher pressure can push more water through a pipe. That's why the wires for 12-volt systems can be smaller

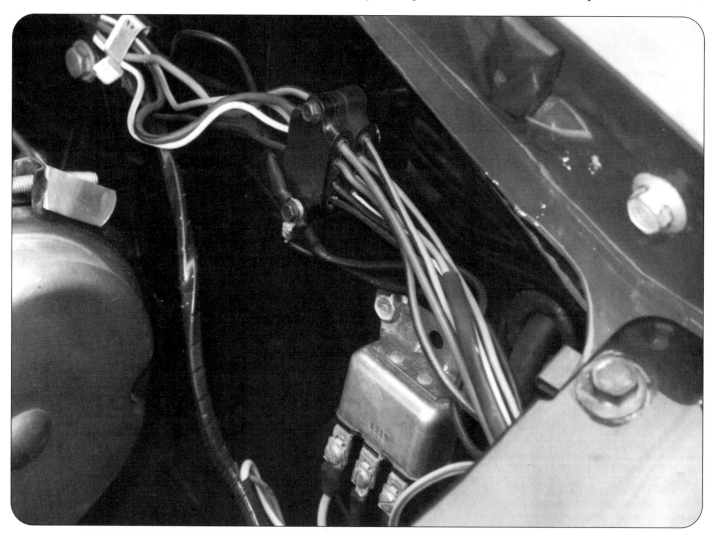

Clean, neat wiring in excellent condition not only looks sharp, but it is safer and your vehicle will run more reliably. Replacing your harness isn't as difficult as you might think. Photo by Michael Lutfy.

Before you begin work on your car, remove its battery. You won't want a short to start a fire or burn you.

A few inexpensive tools are all that are required to rewire most cars. However, you also need a basic understanding of electrical systems and how your car is wired. If you can locate a schematic of your car, you'll be far ahead. Also, I recommend that you read up on the subject with sources like HPBooks' *Auto Electrical Handbook*.

Old wiring like this is a fire hazard even when wrapped with electrical tape. Its insulation is brittle and prone to shorts. Pick up a new terminal block at your local auto supply if yours is crusted and corroded.

in diameter than 6-volt systems.

The big difference between an electrical system and plumbing is that plumbing only goes one way, but an electrical system must be a loop, or circuit. A circuit must also have *resistance* in the form of a light bulb or appliance. If there is no resistance in the loop, a short circuit occurs that can destroy the system and the battery and possibly start a fire. (Resistance is measured in ohms.)

A typical automotive circuit would be one for lighting. Current flows through a wire from the positive (on some older cars the polarity is reversed) pole of your battery, through a switch, and then to a light socket and bulb. From there it goes through the bulb's filament (which provides resistance) then back through your car's sheet metal and frame, through the battery's ground strap and into the negative pole of your battery. The metal of your car acts as the return leg of the circuit.

That's why, when bare wires in your car touch metal, a short develops. And that's why it is important that lights and accessories be grounded to your car's frame or body. A bulb or motor that isn't grounded won't work because its circuit isn't complete.

Things you'll need:

- Wire harness for your car's year and model
- Wiring diagram
- Soldering iron
- Flux and electronics solder
- Multimeter or circuit tester
- Pocket knife
- Wire stripper & crimper
- Screwdrivers
- Fine sandpaper
- Heat-shrink insulation tubing
- Extra wire, grommets, fuse holders, contacts
- Dow Corning insulating compound or white lithium grease

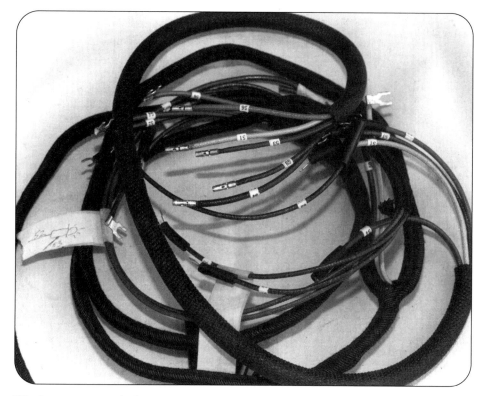

Wire harnesses come in the correct types and colors of wire and with the correct connectors. All you have to do is follow the little number tags to hook it up.

WIRE HARNESS

Replacement wire harnesses are available for most cars that were ever made, from Model T Fords to '69 Cadillacs. They come from the manufacturer in the correct colors and types of wires and are tagged with numbers so you can hook them up simply by following a list. Order your new harness, then wait until it arrives before tearing into your car's electrical system. That way you can use your car while you're waiting. There are several good sources for wire harnesses which are listed in the sidebar nearby.

Of course, there are a few cars out there for which you will not be able to get a new harness already made up. In that case, HPBooks' *Automotive Electrical Handbook* by Jim Horner can advise you on how to make one. It is a book worth having for anyone planning to rewire a car because it covers the subject much more completely than is possible in a general restoration book such as this one.

Cut wires behind instruments to make removal easier.

Removing Your Wiring Harness

The first thing to remove from your car is the battery. That's so you won't be faced with inadvertent shorts or a fire. Next, climb under the instrument panel and note how things are arranged. Make sketches of the light switch, ignition switch and ammeter showing the numbers, colors and types of wires

WIRING HARNESS SOURCES

Y and Z's Yesterday's Parts
333 E. Stuart Ave A
Redlands, CA 92374
909/798-1498
Catalog $2

Harnesses Unlimited
P.O. Box 435
Wayne, PA 19087
215/688-3998
Catalog $2

Narragansett Reproductions
P.O. Box 51
Wood River Junction, RI 02894
401/364-3839

Egge Machine Co.
8403 Allport Ave. #C
Santa Fe Springs, CA 90670
800/866-EGGE

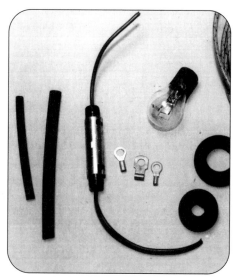

Items you will have to buy separately. You may find burned out bulbs that need replacing, and you may have aftermarket accessories that need new wires too. Grommets are necessary to prevent chaffing wherever wires go through metal bulkheads. Extra inline fuses are a good idea for early cars with inadequate fusing. Heat-shrink insulation is also a good idea.

	YEAR/MAKE	1941 PACKARD
	MODELS	110 120
	BODY TYPES	ALL EXCEPT CLIPPER
	HARNESS TYPE	HEADLIGHT EXTENSIONS PG 3

NO.	NO.	COLOR	FUNCTION
			LEFT HEADLIGHT EXTENSION
23	23	B	FROM HEADLIGHT JCT. BLK. TO SEALED BEAM SOC. GRD
14	18	R	FROM HEADLIGHT JCT. BLK. TO SEALED BEAM SOC. LO
16	19	G	FROM HEADLIGHT JCT. BLK. TO SEALED BEAM SOC. HI
17	21	B-R	FROM HEADLIGHT JCT. BLK. TO FENDER LT. CONN.
	29	G-B	FROM PLUG ON COWL WIRE #29 TO LEFT SIGNAL
			RIGHT HEADLIGHT EXTENSION
23	23	B	FROM HEADLIGHT JCT. BLK. TO SEALED BEAM SOC. GRD.
14	18	R	FROM HEADLIGHT JCT. BLK. TO SEALED BEAM SOC. LO
16	19	G	FROM HEADLIGHT JCT. BLK. TO SEALED BEAM SOC. HI
17	21	B-R	FROM HEADLIGHT JCT. BLK. TO FENDER LT. CONN.
	31	Y-B	FROM PLUG ON COWL WIRE #31 TO RIGHT SIGNAL
			FRONT EXTENSIONS TO FOG OR TRIPPE LIGHTS
	28A	B	FROM TWIN CONN. ON #28 TO LEFT FOG LIGHT
	28B	B	FROM TWIN CONN. ON #28 TO RIGHT FOG LIGHT
	28C	B	FROM LIGHT SWITCH FUSED TERM. TO HOT SIDE OF FOG LIGHT SWITCH
	28D	B	FROM FOG LIGHT SW. COLD SIDE TO LIGHT SW TERM #3 WITH WIRE #10 TO LIGHT TAIL LIGHTS WHEN FOG LIGHTS ARE USED ALONE

Putting in a new wire harness is easy. Just follow the list. The only places you are likely to find confusing are light switches, ammeters and ignition switches. Make sketches or take Polaroids of these items before you remove the old wires.

switch under the floorboard. Take out the horn button and remove the horn wire. Then open the trunk and remove wiring to the taillights. Now crawl under the car and remove the wire to the gas tank sending unit. You may have to lower the tank to get at it. If so, disconnect the filler hose, then lower the tank onto supports. But be careful, work outdoors, and don't smoke. A stray spark could cause an explosion. For more on gas tank electrical connections and how to test your gas gauge sending unit, see Chapter 3.

Now that your old harness has been disconnected, cut it where necessary in order to remove it, such as behind the dash and in the trunk, then gently pull it out through the firewall. Cut any branches going to lights and accessories in other areas of your car, then pull the rest of the wiring out.

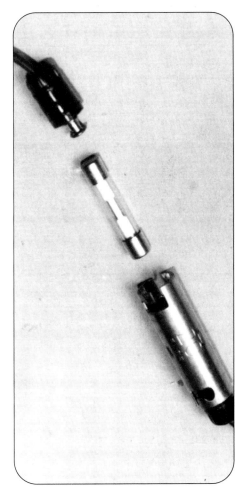

Inline fuse holders come in various sizes. It is a good idea to add them to cars from the '20s and early '30s as a safety precaution.

connected to their terminals. These are the devices that are most likely to confuse you when installing your new harness.

Now start disconnecting the old harness under the dash. To gain access, take off any panels that can be removed. Also, remove the glove compartment box and lid. Disconnect all the wires and save any fuse blocks or holders. Cut accessory light wires just behind their sockets unless you will be making up your own harness, in which case you should try to remove the old harness in as complete a state as possible so you can use it as a template.

Engine compartment wiring is next. Everything but the ignition system wiring must go. If the ignition wiring needs replacing, it will have to be done separately, because it will not be included with your new wire harness. Save any connectors, fuse holders, clamps or other items you might need when you reinstall your wire loom.

Disconnect wiring from the dimmer

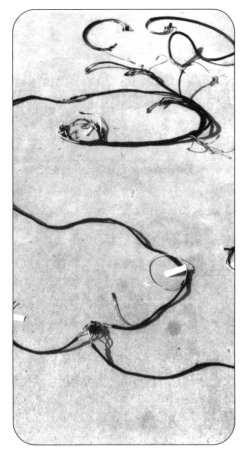

Lay your new wire harness out on your driveway or garage floor so you can see how it is arranged before attempting to install it.

Wiring for cars with 6-volt systems must be much heavier than on 12-volt cars. If you use wire intended for 12-volt applications on 6-volt systems, there will be too much resistance. Things won't work properly, fuses will blow and wiring will burn.

Connectors just snap together at junctions. Make sure you attach things correctly. Double check each junction before going on to the next.

Installing a New Harness

Replace any grommets in sheet metal where the new harness passes through. Then starting under the dash, feed the harness out through the firewall. Don't hook anything up yet. Extend the new harness out to each accessory to make sure it can reach every item. Loosely clamp it into place along the frame and fenders.

Hook Up—Grab your sandpaper, pocket knife, insulating compound and the harness manufacturer's instructions, then climb back under the dash. Clean and brighten each terminal and contact before attaching wiring. Smear a little insulating compound or lithium-based white grease on each connection to keep it from corroding. Follow the harness maker's list and diagrams while hooking things up, then double check to make sure you've got everything right.

Solder the Sockets—If your car is a later model with a 12-volt system, you can buy new light sockets at the auto supply and simply install them. All you have to do is attach the wiring with a solderless connector and cover the connection with heat-shrink insulation.

If your car has a 6-volt system, you will have to unsolder the little contacts in your old sockets and solder them to the new wiring. Sockets and wire intended for 12-volt systems will not be adequate for 6-volt applications. Modern 12-volt systems use 18 to 20 gauge wire, which is lighter than the 14 to 16 gauge wire used on 6-volt systems. If you need heavier

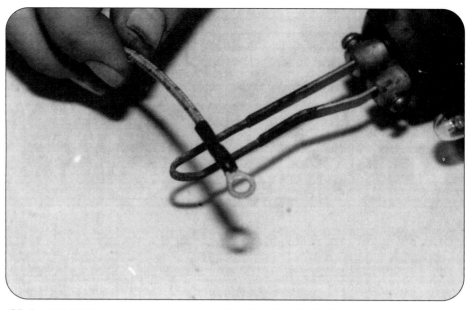
Slip heat-shrink down over end of connector, then heat the plastic, being careful not to burn through it, to shrink it into place.

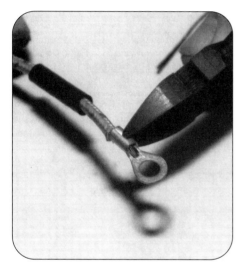
To attach a new connector, first slip a length of heat-shrink material onto the wire, then crimp connector in place.

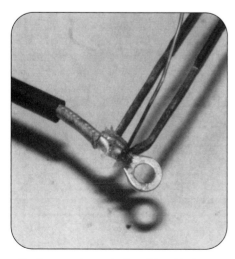
Heat connector and wire with soldering gun, then let solder flow into joint by capillary action.

wire for your car, call the sources listed in the sidebar on page 78.

Make the Connection—Wires for such accessories as heaters, radios and dome lights may not be included in your harness. Make wiring for them out of the correct, or heavier gauge wire, and use correct colors if possible. Solderless connectors can be used on 12-volt systems, but it is advisable to solder connections on 6-volt wiring because of the low voltage.

Install Fuses—If your car is an oldie, it may not have enough fuse blocks for adequate protection. Install them where they can't be seen, then make a list of where the fuses are. Keep the list in the glove compartment of your car, along with spare fuses.

Add Lights—Finish the installation by hooking up the headlights, taillights, gas tank unit and dimmer switch.

Testing

Before installing the battery, go down the numbered installation list that came with your harness and make sure each item is connected correctly. When you're satisfied everything is the way it should be, set the battery back in place, hook up its ground strap, then check to make sure

all lights and accessories are off. Also, disconnect the electric clock if your car is so equipped.

Now darken your shop as much as possible, then briefly touch the positive lead to your battery's terminal. (Negative lead if your car is positive ground). If you see a spark, you either have a short, or there is a light or accessory left on somewhere. Find and fix the problem before attaching the cable to the battery.

If you don't see a flash, re-attach the clock wire, then attach the cable to the battery. Next, try each light and appliance in turn. If anything fails to work, chances are the problem is a loose connection or faulty ground. A multimeter can be used to check whether a wire is conducting current. A socket with a bulb in it, and alligator clips on its wires, can do the same job.

Polarize It—If your car has an old-fashioned charging system with a generator and voltage regulator you will need to polarize it. This is usually accomplished by touching a short length of wire momentarily from the GEN to the BAT terminals on the voltage regulator. Check a shop manual for your make to determine if this is correct procedure for your car. ∎

9

BRAKES

The first item that should get attention on any collector car are the brakes. It is the most neglected system on most older cars, and the most dangerous if it is left that way.

BASIC OPERATION

Old cars with single-bore master cylinders (most cars made before the mid-sixties) are subject to total brake failure if a leak develops in their hydraulic systems. The results can obviously be catastrophic. That's why routine inspection and regular adjustments are a must. But before we tear into your classic's brakes, let's go over how a typical older system works.

Each wheel has two asbestos- or synthetic-lined shoes that are attached to a backing plate. These shoes expand against the inner surfaces of the brake drums to provide stopping power. The forward shoes are called the *primaries* and the rears the *secondaries*. Brake shoes are held in fixed relationship at the top of the backing plate by the anchor pin. They are movable at the bottom and are held against the adjuster mechanism by springs.

When you step on your brakes, you actuate the master cylinder (usually

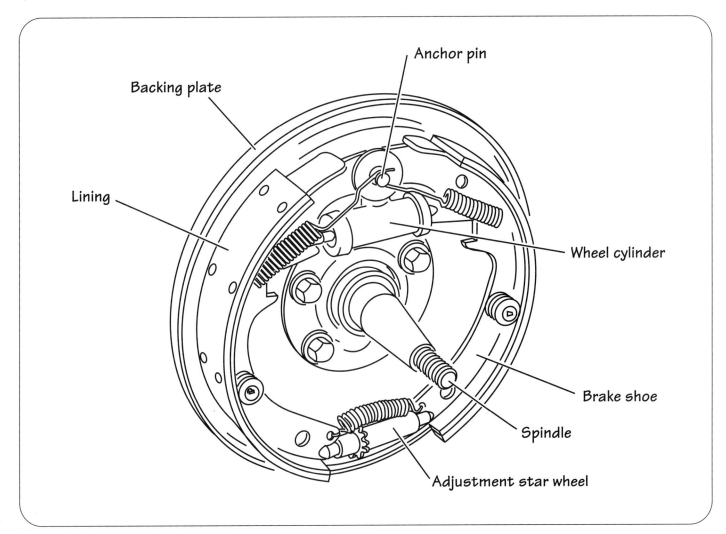

Parts of a typical hydraulic brake assembly.

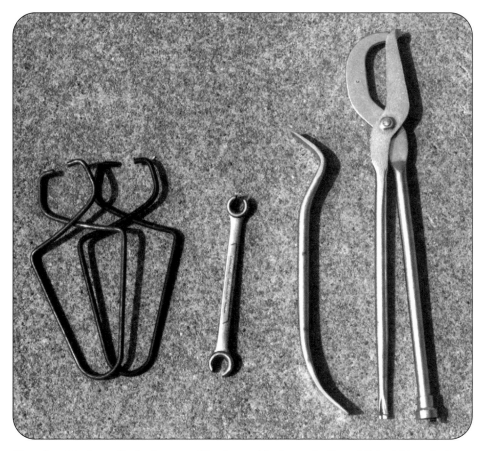

These hand tools are the basic necessities for most brake work. From left to right are brake cylinder clamps, tubing wrench, adjusting spoon and brake pliers. Cylinder clamps hold wheel cylinders together when you remove brake shoes. If you don't use them, the cylinders may pop apart and allow air into the hydraulic system. You'll need a tubing wrench to remove wheel cylinders because loosening the tubing attached to them can be tricky. Ordinary wrenches will ruin the attaching fittings. An adjusting spoon is indispensable for any kind of brake work. It is difficult to adjust brakes without one. Brake pliers make it possible to release tension on the many springs involved in brake work. They allow you to reattach springs easily too.

Inspect wheel bearings and races. Bearings should be smooth, polished and tight in their cages. Races should be shiny with no traces of pitting, scoring or discoloration.

mounted on the firewall or frame), which exerts hydraulic pressure through steel tubing to the wheel cylinders (they're near the tops of the backing plates), which force the shoes out against the drums. The primary shoes hit the drums first, then they energize the secondary shoes, which do most of the braking.

Because of a car's momentum and its suspension system, weight is transferred forward when the brakes are applied, putting most of the load on the front brakes. Consequently, they tend to wear quicker.

TROUBLESHOOTING

Clean the master cylinder and especially the area around the master cylinder filler cap, then loosen it and top up the brake fluid. Don't fill past the bottom of the filler neck. After you have worked the brakes a few times, check the cleaned area around the cylinder as well as the fluid level. If it has dropped, or there is fluid around the outside of the cylinder, you have a leak. We'll talk about how to fix it later in this chapter.

Jack up your car and put jackstands at each corner. Take the car out of gear and release the hand brake. Remove the wheel covers at all four wheels, then pop the small axle-nut covers loose on the front wheels. Usually the axle-nut covers can be pulled off with a pair of channel-lock pliers. (On early Fords they twist off.) Place clean newspaper on the floor below each wheel to catch any loose bearings or parts. Now, working one wheel at a time, pull out the cotter key that keeps the castle nut from turning on the spindle. Remove the castle nut and thrust washer and put them aside. Remove the outer wheel bearing and put it in a Ziploc bag to keep it clean. Next, grasp the tire and pull the wheel, hub and all, off of the spindle.

Disconnect Emergency Brake— Roll under the car and pull out the pin holding the equalizer line of the parking brake to the cables going to the rear

THINGS YOU'LL NEED:
- Cylinder clamps
- Tubing wrench
- Adjusting spoon
- Brake pliers
- Drum puller
- Hydraulic brake cleaner
- Brake fluid
- Wheel bearing grease

wheels. This assembly is normally located about mid-frame just behind the transmission.

Remove Rear Drums—On most cars, you'll need a drum puller to get at the rear brakes. They can be rented from tool rental yards or obtained at automotive tool outlets. Be sure you get the right one for your car. Older General Motors cars require the kind that attaches to the rim of the drum and exerts pressure on the axle hub plate. Other makes, such as old Chryslers and Packards, need a puller that attaches to the studs for the wheels. On GM cars, you can rap on the end of the puller to pop the drums loose, but don't try it on the Chrysler-type hub. You'll damage the differential if you do. Instead, try tapping the rim of the drum with a rubber mallet.

Inspect the Hydraulics—Start at the master cylinder. Are there any signs of leaks? If so, overhaul it. (We'll tell you how later.) Is the tubing from the master cylinder to the wheel cylinders rusty or kinked? If it is, replace it. Now take a look at the wheel cylinders. Are the rubber end-cups swollen and cracked? Are there signs of leaks? If so, rebuild them. Also look for brake fluid contamination on the linings. If the

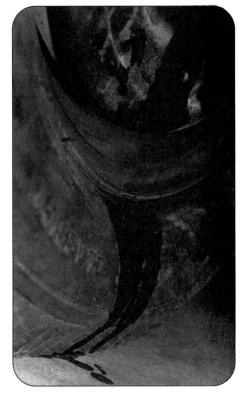

If your old car has been sitting in storage there is a good chance its hydraulic brakes may leak. Top up the master cylinder with brake fluid (don't fill past the neck of the master cylinder), then pump the brakes slowly. Examine around each wheel and at the back of the master cylinder for leaks.

contamination is only minor, clean it off with alcohol-based brake cleaning fluid. Otherwise, the lining will need to be replaced.

To inspect your brakes you will need to remove the front wheels and drums. Now is a good time to inspect and repack your front wheel bearings too. Be sure to put newspaper on the floor where you are working so you can keep everything clean. Pop the small nut cover off of the drum. (On early Fords they twist off.) Pull the cotter key, remove the axle nut, then slip the washer, bearing race and bearing out of the hub. Now pull the front wheel off of the spindle.

Make sure wheel cylinders are leak-free and that rubber cups at each end are not swollen or cracked. If they are, rebuild the cylinders.

If your brake drums are in good shape you can clean them up with a little #360-grit emery cloth. This drum is too deeply grooved for that treatment. It will have to be turned at a machine shop.

Make sure brake springs are not stretched, rusted or broken. If they are, replace them with new ones of the correct tension. They are usually color coded so you won't mix them up.

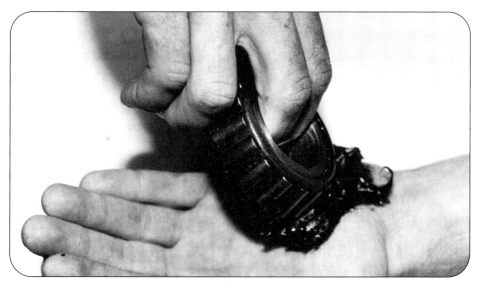

It is best to grease wheel bearings the old-fashioned way. Put a gob of grease on the heel of your hand, then drag and push the bearing into it and through it making sure that grease is forced up around all of the rollers or balls.

This completed brake assembly is ready to go back on the car. It was removed for a complete front end rebuild. Everything has been cleaned, new lining has been installed, the wheel cylinder rebuilt and new springs attached. All that remains is to smear a little white grease on the contact points of the moving parts.

Linings & Drums—Are they black, hard, and shiny indicating that they have been burned and glazed? Are they worn down close to the rivets or below 1/8" thick? If so, you need to reline them. Also have a look at the drums. Are they deeply grooved or scored and discolored? Minor grooves can be removed with fine emery cloth, but deep ones will require that the drums be *turned* or machined, replaced or built up and reground.

ASSEMBLY & ADJUSTMENT

Unless you're performing a total restoration, a little cleaning and an adjustment may be all your brakes need. Here's what to do.

Assembly

Brush all dirt, rust and grease from the backing plates and shoes, but be careful not to get any of the above on the linings. Wear a good particle or spray painter's mask while working, and don't use compressed air to blow the dust away. Until recently, brake linings were made of asbestos, which is a known carcinogen.

Smear a little motor oil around leather or neoprene rear axle seals before installing them to prevent chaffing.

Note slot in brake drum through which a feeler gauge can be inserted to measure lining to drum clearance. Rubber inserts should be replaced in these holes when you finish the job so water and dirt can't contaminate brake linings.

Lubricate Mechanism—Put a little Lubriplate or white grease on all metal-to-metal contact areas, such as anchor pins, adjusting screws and eccentrics. Apply it sparingly, and don't get any on the linings.

Now roll under the car and shoot a little penetrating oil on the emergency brake assembly. Make sure you coat the cables and guides. And while you're under there, smear a little grease on the moving parts.

Tighten Backing Plates—Look each of the springs over to make sure it isn't rusted or stretched. Replace any that are. Finally, tighten the bolts holding the backing plates to the hubs.

Reconnect Emergency Brake—Use a new cotter key of the correct thickness in the pin that holds the cable to the equalizer.

Reinstall Drums & Wheels—Now is a good time to pack the front wheel bearings. Get new seals at the auto parts store. Wash bearings out in solvent, dry them, then work new grease into them. To install them, use a wrench with an eight-inch handle and with one hand, tighten the castle nuts until tight, then back off approximately one quarter turn so the nut aligns with the hole in the spindle. Grab each wheel and work it back and forth to check for slop in the bearings. If you discover any, reset the pre-load on the bearings using the same eight-inch wrench, but set it just a little tighter. When you've got it right, install a new cotter key of the correct size.

Adjustment

When your old car's brakes are in good repair and proper adjustment, you'll enjoy driving it, and you'll know you're

Master cylinder actuating rod needs to be adjusted so there is 1-1/4 to 1-1/2 inches of freeplay before cylinder is actuated. On most old cars, the master cylinder is bolted to the frame just in front of the brake pedal.

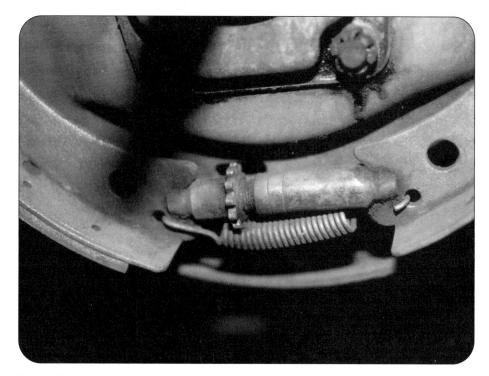

Most of the adjusting done on a hydraulic brake system is done on this star wheel at the bottom of each brake backing plate. Adjusting spoon is inserted from behind.

not likely to have a problem stopping it.

Check Shop Manual—Most older American car hydraulic brakes are very similar in design, but check a shop manual for your make to learn the details of your particular system. There can be minor differences in the way they should be adjusted. Also, your car may be equipped with self-adjusting brakes which may entail some extra steps.

Adjust Master Cylinder—Set the master cylinder actuating rod so there is about 1-1/4" to 1-1/2" of free movement in it before it starts to actuate the piston in the master cylinder. There is a threaded portion on the rear end of the rod that has an adjusting nut and a lock-nut. Loosen the lock-nut, then adjust in, or out, to get the correct clearance. Be sure to tighten the lock-nut when you've finished setting the movement.

Adjust Shoes—On many older cars, there is an eccentric with a lock-nut and adjusting screw that allows you to adjust the lower shoe clearance. If your car is so equipped, you'll find the eccentrics on the back of each backing plate about midway

up and to the rear.

To adjust brakes with eccentrics, loosen the lock-nut, then rotate the drum so its adjusting slot is adjacent to where the bottom of the secondary shoe meets the drum. Place a .010" feeler gauge in the slot, then adjust the eccentric in the

direction of forward wheel rotation until the gauge is held snugly in place by the lining and drum. Now tighten the eccentric lock-nut.

Next, loosen the anchor pin lock-nut (at the top center of the backing plate) one complete turn and insert the .010" feeler gauge at the upper end of the secondary shoe. If the clearance is too great, turn the anchor pin in the direction the wheel turns as the car moves forward.

When you have it right, hold the anchor pin in adjustment and tighten its lock-nut with a wrench. Check the clearance at both ends of the secondary shoe; if it is incorrect, adjust the eccentric and anchor pin again.

Fine adjustment can be done with the star-wheel at the bottom of the backing plate. Grab a brake adjusting spoon and use it to turn the star wheel down to expand the brakes, or up to contract them. You're finished when the difference at the ends of the secondary shoes is within .002" of each other.

Adjust Emergency Brake—Use your brake spoon to adjust the star wheels downward on the rear wheels until there is heavy drag when you try to turn them. Now pull the brake cable toward the

This brake cylinder is so corroded and full of dirt that its pistons are stuck in their bores.

equalizer link. Remove any slack and adjust the clevis pins (the U-shaped clips at the ends of the cables) so the pin will just enter both clevis pins at the equalizer link when the equalizer link is parallel with the driveshaft. Always install clevis pins with the head at the top. Back off two turns on the clevis pins, then tighten the clevis lock-nuts and install new cotter keys. Finally, back the star wheels off (adjust upward) on the rear brakes until they check out correctly with your feeler gauge (usually about 20 turns).

Put rubber plugs in the adjusting slots on the drums, put the wheels back on, then top up the master cylinder one more time. Take the car out for a road test and check the adjustment. If the brakes grab or have too much slop, then correct the adjustment until you have it right.

OVERHAULING HYDRAULICS

If you discover during your brake inspection that the hydraulic system is leaking or in need of an overhaul here's what to do.

Jack your car up, put jackstands under it, then remove the wheels and drums as outlined in the adjustment section. Next,

Shine a light from behind into each cylinder's bore so you can observe any pitting of the cylinder walls. Brake cylinders can be cleaned up using a brake cylinder hone attached to an electric drill if their bores are not too badly pitted. If pitting is excessive, cylinders will have to be replaced or sleeved.

using the end of your brake pliers, undo the springs holding the shoes in place. Remove the hold-down pins that attach the shoes to the backing plates. Set the brake shoe assembly aside where it is not liable to be splashed with brake fluid.

Master & Wheel Cylinders

Place clean newspaper on the floor, wash your hands, then carefully pull each wheel cylinder apart. Check the bores of the cylinders for pitting. If there is only

slight damage, it can be ground out with a brake cylinder hone. If pitting is deep, the cylinder will have to be replaced or machined out and sleeved to the correct inner diameter.

The master cylinder will need to be removed from the car if it needs rebuilding. The hydraulic lines going from it to the wheel cylinders can sometimes be a challenge to disconnect. Use a tubing or flare nut wrench. It looks like a box wrench with a slot cut in it. Gently tap on the connections to loosen corrosion before attempting to take them apart, but never attempt to use heat to loosen them.

Honing — While you have the cylinders apart, keep a rag pulled through the bores that you are not currently working on. It will help keep dirt out. Tighten the hone into an electric drill and check to make sure it is centered in the chuck. Now lubricate the stones of the bit with a little brake fluid, then slide them into the bore of the cylinder. Start the drill. Move it in and out slowly and evenly to remove the pits. Be careful not to let the stones slip out the end of the cylinder. If, after a few passes, the pits still persist, they are probably too deep to

Master cylinders are as prone to corrosion and pitting as wheel cylinders. You may need to unscrew a plug at the end of the cylinder opposite the actuating rod in order to clearly see its bore.

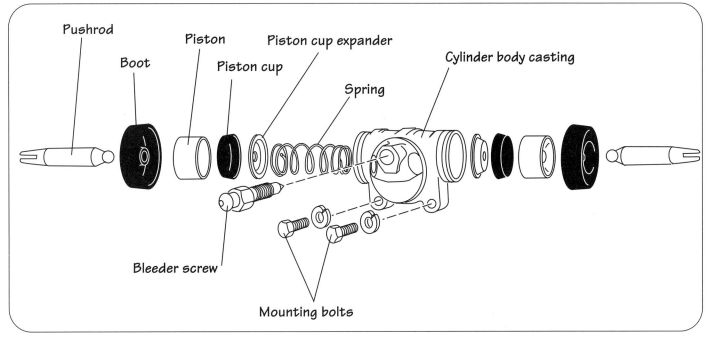

Pushrod

Boot

Piston

Piston cup

Piston cup expander

Spring

Cylinder body casting

Bleeder screw

Mounting bolts

Parts of a wheel cylinder.

safely be removed by a hone. You will need to buy replacement cylinders or have yours sleeved.

Sleeving—If a wheel or master cylinder is too pitted to be cleaned up with a hone, it will need to be machined out and sleeved. That's because if you hone cylinders out too far, a standard rebuild kit won't work in them, and even if it would, you would dramatically increase the pedal pressure needed to stop the car. There are several mail order services that sleeve master and wheel cylinders. Here's one that does an excellent job: White Post Restorations, 1 Old Car Drive, P.O. Drawer D, White Post, VA 22663. (703) 837-1140. White Post will return your cylinders clean and with fresh new brass sleeves installed.

Install New Kits—Buy new cylinder rebuild kits from your local auto supply, or order them from such mail-order sources as: Egge Machine, 8403 Allport Ave. #C, Santa Fe Springs, CA 90670. (800) 866-EGGE.

Before you begin reassembling your master and wheel cylinders, thoroughly clean your work area and your hands. One tiny bit of grit in a cylinder can cause scoring and leaking. Have plenty of clean,

lint-free rags on hand to wipe up spills. Reinstall the wheel cylinders on the backing plates before installing new kits. The front and back wheel cylinders are usually different in diameter. Don't mix them up when you reinstall them. Never use Teflon tape to stop leaks at the tubing connections.

Work one cylinder at a time. Place all the items from the rebuild kit in a cup of brake fluid, then lightly coat the bore of

the wheel cylinder as well. Follow the instructions and diagram with the rebuild kit for reassembly. Use brake cylinder clamps to hold the wheel cylinders together until you're ready to reinstall the linings. If you are rebuilding the master cylinder, make sure the bypass port is clear before beginning reassembly.

Brake Bleeding

Top off the master cylinder with brake

Cylinders that are too worn or damaged to be rebuilt can be resleeved with brass or stainless steel, either of which will last nearly forever.

fluid, then attach about two feet of clear plastic tubing to the bleeder nipple on the cylinder at the rear wheel on the passenger side of your car. Place the other end of the hose in a glass jar with about an inch of brake fluid in it.

Get a friend to pump up the brake pedal several times. Then have him hold it down as you open the nipple. Let fluid run into the jar, then tighten the nipple and have your friend pump up again. Release fluid, repeating this process, until all air bubbles are gone from the fluid. Let the fluid run until it is clear of bubbles, then tighten the nipple. Do this at each wheel finishing at the wheel closest to the master cylinder. (Usually the front wheel on the driver's side.) Check and refill the master cylinder as needed. Watch carefully for leaks.

When you've finished the process, if the brake pedal is firm, take the car out for a test drive and adjust the shoe-to-drum clearance as required to get them right. If the pedal is still spongy, check for leaks, repeat the bleeding process to get any air out of the lines, then road test again.

RELINING BRAKE SHOES

If your brake linings are getting thin (below an eighth of an inch thick) it's time to reline them. If they are neglected until the rivets holding the linings on, or the steel backing, cuts into the drums, the drums will be destroyed. And brake drums can be very difficult to find for many older cars.

Remove Shoes — Follow the instructions in the previous sections for removing wheels and drums. Use brake pliers to remove the springs holding the shoes to the cylinders. Hold the cylinder assemblies together with brake cylinder clamps. Disconnect and remove the hold-down pins attaching the shoes to the backing plates.

Remove Grooves — Deep grooves in the brake drums will have to be removed by turning them at a brake or machine shop. While they're at it, they can arc the shoes to match. If the grooves in the drum are shallow and smooth to the touch however, they can be taken out with emery paper. Drums can only be turned or machined a few times before they must be replaced.

Assembly

Mount the relined shoes on the cylinders and backing plates using new springs and hold-down pins. Springs that appear the same but are different colors

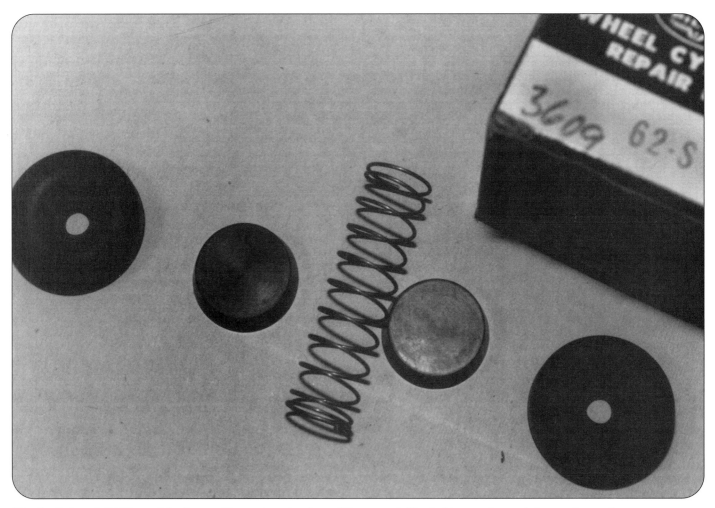

Wheel cylinder rebuild kit consists of new rubber parts and springs. Kits are available at old car parts supply houses for nearly every car ever made.

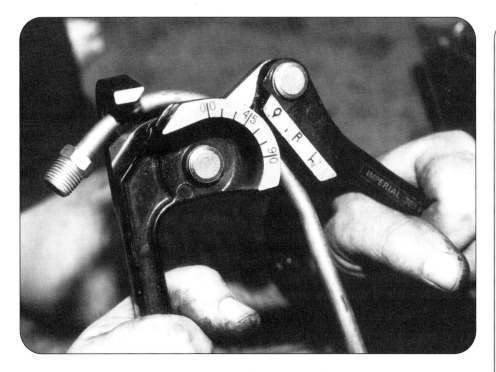

If you need to replace brake tubing, purchase it in the correct diameter at an auto supply. Use only steel tubing. Copper is too fragile for brake applications and will soon fail. Make any required bends using a tube bender, also available at auto supply stores.

usually have different tensions. Use only springs that are correct for the application. Check a shop manual to determine what you need.

Your new linings will be much thicker than the old ones, so you will need to adjust your brakes following the instructions at the beginning of this chapter. You may also need to bleed them if any air seeped into the hydraulic system. ■

Cut tubing to length as necessary using a small pipe cutter, then dress end with a fine file. Be sure to double-flare all connecting nipples for added strength using a flaring tool.

SILICONE BRAKE FLUID

Hydraulic brakes on vintage cars were a major improvement over most mechanical systems, but there was one problem with them that always surfaced eventually, and that was internal corrosion. Because the systems were filled with polyglycol (DOT 3) brake fluid, which attracted moisture like a sponge, sooner or later their cylinders got rusty, pitted and rough, and as a result, finally failed. Moisture in brake systems also heated up and caused vapor lock in heavy downhill braking, often with disastrous results. Of course, one could change the brake fluid every year to minimize the problem, but few people ever did.

The U.S. Postal Service had especially big problems when brakes failed on their trucks, so they asked Dow Corning to solve the problem. The solution they came up with was silicone brake fluid (DOT 5). It does not attract moisture, so it virtually eliminates the need for brake hydraulic overhauls.

However, you must first purge your system of all the old fluid, and that includes getting out all residual fluid in the cylinders and lines. You can't just drain the old fluid and add new. The best time to do it is when you have the system apart. If you have your system apart for overhaul, shoot brake cleaner down the hydraulic tubing to clean out the old polyglycol. When you rebuild your cylinders, soak all the internal and rubber parts in clean silicone fluid during assembly. Bleed your system the conventional way, as outlined earlier. Discard the fluid that you bleed out of the system. Even though silicone brake fluid is expensive, it is unwise and unsafe to use the fluid that came out when the system was bled.

REMOVING & PREPARING SHEET METAL 10

There are several reasons for removing the exterior sheet metal on a car. First, if you're doing a ground-up restoration, you'll need to remove all sheet metal to get at the frame underneath. Second, you may need to remove body panels for repair, fine metal finishing and painting. The most important aspects of a show-winning restoration are the quality of the chrome and the bodywork. These are the details everyone sees and judges most critically. Cars that barely run sometimes win at prestigious concours events because their paint, chrome and upholstery are done beautifully. So if you are planning to go for the gold, you will need to do super-quality metal finishing and painting. To do that you must first take your car's body all apart. It is a task that must be done carefully and in an organized fashion.

PREPARATION

A cosmetic restoration takes a long time and a lot of work. You will need at least a two-car garage, and you will need to build or buy some shelves. A source of electrical power (preferably 220 volts) is necessary to power conventional spray equipment. Good lighting is also essential. So get things set up properly and comfortably before going to work. It may be a long time before your car leaves your shop again.

Take Pictures—Before you begin the disassembly of your car's bodywork, pick up a cheap auto-focus camera with a

Most of the time it is not necessary or wise for a hobbyist restorer to lift the body from the frame when restoring his car. It is a lot of work, and if you don't get it back on right, with all of the shims in the correct places and properly aligned, nothing will fit right. The body on the Model A Ford is an exception. It is small and light, and can be removed with relative ease.

To remove sheet metal and work on it, you'll need at minimum a space like this one. Plenty of walkaround room, lots of light, and workbenches big enough to support body panels to work on. Photo by Michael Lutfy.

job means taking the body of your car all apart, stripping it to clean, bright, rust-free bare metal, then fixing any dents or imperfections before priming and painting it. At that point you're half done, because you still have to color-sand and rub out your work and reassemble the car. It's a big project, but the end result will be a magnificent-looking machine.

THINGS YOU'LL NEED:
- **Professional paint stripper**
- **Degreaser**
- **Metal prep**
- **Enamel primer**
- **Putty knives, small wire brushes, string**
- **Paint brushes**
- **Newspaper**
- **#80-grit sandpaper**
- **Neoprene gloves, painting mask and goggles**

built-in flash and keep it on hand during the restoration process. Also, purchase a supply of Ziploc bags and a notebook. You will need to keep fasteners sorted and labeled and you should keep a journal of your progress. You will want to note, or sketch, how certain items went together too.

Before you begin disassembly, take pictures of your car from every angle. Get close and shoot all of the details. It will be a long time before you see your car together again. It's easy to forget how things were put together.

DISASSEMBLY

A fairly decent paint job can be done on a car simply by fixing the dents, loosening the fenders, scuffing the old finish, then masking trim items off and shooting the car with enamel. But fairly decent paint jobs don't win shows. Only spectacular paint jobs do that. And a spectacular paint

Trim

The first step is to remove decorative items and mirrors. You must work carefully. It's easy to find parts like U-joints or rod bearings for most old cars, but scavenging for lost or broken trim pieces can be very time consuming and difficult. Often, many of the ornamental items on a car are appropriate to only one year and model. So be very careful when you remove your car's chrome. Look behind it to see how it is fastened. If it is fastened with clips, or screws and nuts, you will obviously have to undo them. But on most cars, expansion fasteners are used on emblems and trim and they can be popped loose from the outside. However, pry very gently on things that

When disassembling your car, look things over carefully to see how they should come out. This Mustang windwing lifted out as a unit.

must be pried. Try not to break any fasteners, and save them in labeled baggies. Use penetrating oil on rusty nuts and bolts, and let them soak overnight before trying to loosen them. If required, tap gently but rapidly on fasteners (but not on the parts that show) with a small ballpeen hammer.

Don't use heat on any cast metal parts. You may only succeed in ruining them if you do. Wrap fragile items in newspaper to protect them, then label and store them in an orderly fashion. Tape delicate chrome or stainless strips and castings to pieces of wood so they won't get crumpled or broken. Attach baggies containing their fasteners to the planks too. Finally, remove bumpers and bumper guards and store them.

Body Panels

Remove the fenders, hood and decklid. Make careful notes as to where any shims or washers were used for aligning of the sheet metal, and trace around the hinges with a scribe so you will know where to position them during reassembly. If you don't get these items back where they are supposed to go, your hood and your trunk lid won't fit properly, or close correctly. Stubborn fasteners will sometimes yield to the WD-40 treatment, but often you have to resort to heating them with a propane or acetylene torch to get them to break loose. Keep a fire extinguisher handy in case you ignite more than your passion to loosen the recalcitrant fastener.

Only remove doors if it is necessary in order to repair them. Getting doors back on a car so they hang properly is a job that is best left to a pro. If you are restoring a small, simple car like a Model A Ford, you can remove the body from the frame without much difficulty, but bigger, heavier cars should only have their bodies removed if it is absolutely necessary. If you decide to do it, make careful measurements of exactly where your car's body sat on its frame, and save any shims that were used to align it. You will need to put them back exactly as they were when you reinstall the body. Also, get several friends to help, and lift the body evenly so you don't distort or warp it.

Glass—To paint your car properly, you will need to take out all of its glass. Refer to Chapter 13 on how to do it. Rust often forms under rubber gaskets and eats away at your car's body. You will want to paint under the lip of the windshield and rear window seals to prevent further deterioration and leaks. And if you are doing a complete restoration, you will most likely want to replace your car's glass anyway.

Gaskets & Weatherstripping—Pull out all of the old rubber gaskets around the doors, hood and trunk lid and anywhere else you find them. Very old rubber can be difficult to remove. Using a torch to heat the back side of metal to which it is bonded will allow you to scrape it off easily, but be careful not to start a fire.

Clear the Firewall—Show winners are pristine and fresh from every angle. There can't be any holidays ("painter talk" for places missed in the refinishing process) even in the engine compartment. Everything will have to be removed from

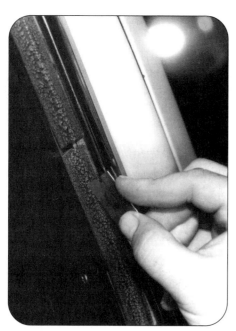

To paint your car properly, you will have to remove all of its glass. Use a utility knife or single-edge razor blades to cut rubber gaskets. A propane torch can help remove recalcitrant rubber from sheet metal. If you need to use a torch, be careful; keep a fire extinguisher close by. For more details on glass, see Chapter 13.

Use good quality automotive paint stripper, available from automotive paint stores, to strip your car's body of old paint. Apply stripper with a cheap bristle brush, then let it bubble. Scrape it off with a sharp putty knife. Be sure to wear a paint mask, gloves, eye protection and long-sleeved clothing. Paint stripper is volatile stuff, and can be absorbed into your bloodstream through the skin and it can damage your lungs. Dispose of the residue properly according to regulations in your community.

Stripping a car is a nasty process, but it is necessary if the paint job is to be first rate and is to last. In this case, windows were left in place at owner's request, but it is better to remove them if possible. Care must be taken handling big curved windshields because they are difficult to find and expensive to replace.

Rust along this fender bead will have to be cut out and replaced with sound metal. Note deteriorated body filler under hole. It too will have to come out.

the firewall, then it too will have to be stripped to bare metal and refinished. On some cars you can take all of the accessories off of the engine, then cover it with a heavy tarp while you work. But on many cars you will have to loosen the engine and pull it forward in order to do the job right. Of course, if you are doing a complete restoration anyway, you'll want to take it out of the car completely.

STRIPPING THE PAINT

Stripping the paint off of old cars can be done in several ways, but there are only a couple that an amateur restorer should consider. I do not recommend sand blasting. It peens, pits and warps sheet metal, and in the wrong hands, sand blasting equipment can cut right through your car's irreplaceable tin. A relatively new process called *bead blasting* is a possibility, but a very messy proposition if you are trying to do a car body. Glass beads are sharp, so they will imbed in your skin and will get into your clothing. Of course, if there is someone in your area who does bead blasting professionally, you may wish to take removable parts to him. A high speed surface grinder is sometimes used in production shops to remove paint, but in inexperienced hands grinders can do irreparable damage.

Chemical Stripping

The best way for a hobbyist to get paint off of a car is to strip it off chemically, and that's also the way most reputable pros do it. Whether you take your car's sheet metal to a commercial stripper, or do it yourself at home using automotive paint remover, you can't go too far wrong. Another way to get paint off of sheet metal is to mix up a vat of Drano and hot water and submerse your parts. They'll come out clean as a whistle. But be careful. Drano is deadly stuff and can damage your skin and eyes. Also, don't let kids or pets anywhere near your work.

Preparation—If you are going to strip your car chemically, work outdoors if possible. Otherwise, work only in a place where there is plenty of ventilation. Wash the car to remove any loose dirt, then spread dampened newspapers on the ground where you plan to work. Aircraft paint stripper is evil stuff indeed. It can

Stripping an old car can sometimes reveal a multitude of problems. Note extensive rust along rocker panels. Also note poorly done previous bodywork in rear area of fenderwell. Old body filler will have to be removed, as will any deteriorated lead.

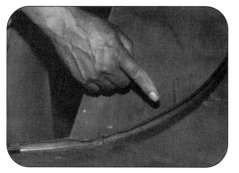

Old bodywork is evident along seam where fender was welded at factory. Also, fender bead will need to be carefully straightened with a picking hammer.

To paint wheels properly, tires will have to be demounted and wheels bead blasted. Rust around inside of wheel and valve stem opening is common.

cause painful burns if it gets on your skin. Before you begin work, put on a painter's mask, goggles, neoprene gloves and coveralls.

Application—Pour a little stripper into a metal container. (Stripper will dissolve plastic.) Using a paint brush and starting from the top and working down, slop on a heavy coat of stripper over an area about two feet square. Don't brush back through it, because you will hasten the evaporation of key ingredients in the stripper. Give the stripper a few minutes to do its work (you'll see the paint start to lift and bubble) then scrape it off with a putty knife.

Keep old newspaper in one hand and your putty knife in the other. Use the newspaper to clean the putty knife. Chances are, unless your car is a fairly recent model with only its original coat of paint, you will have to go over it two or three times before you get to bare metal. Be patient and keep at it until all of the old

finish is removed. Small wire brushes are good for getting paint out of tight places such as drip moldings. String can be pulled through grooves to clean them.

You will no doubt uncover old repairs and rust as you work. Stripper softens and ruins plastic filler, so you will have to remove it completely. Use #80-grit sandpaper for this job. If you are experienced with surface grinders, you can make short work of the task, but if you don't know how to use one, remove body filler by hand. A grinder will take off a lot of metal in a hurry and make already work-thinned metal thinner.

Lead filler, commonly used on older cars, deteriorates too, and usually needs to be replaced. Dig it out of cracks and sand it off of parts. Keep your mask on while you work, because lead is toxic.

Clean It—When every piece of your car's body has been stripped bare, wash it down with dishwasher soap and water, then dry it thoroughly with towels. Use compressed air to get in holes and grooves. Now go over the whole car with #80-grit sandpaper to remove any pitting or rust, and to give the metal "tooth" so the primer will adhere properly. Be sure you clean and sand every last crack and groove, and don't leave even a tiny bit of stripper anywhere, because it will cause your new paint to bubble if you do.

Protect It—Unprotected sheet metal will begin to rust in a matter of hours, so you will need to protect it until you are ready to make the necessary repairs and paint it. Red oxide enamel primer is what most pros use for this purpose. Lacquer primer is what you'll use later, when it's time to paint, but it is not waterproof. Unless you are going to repair and paint each part immediately, you risk the possibility of rust forming before you can spray on a protective coat of color. Wipe the parts down with a degreaser like Dupont's Prep-Sol, then wash them with Metal Prep to etch the metal. Shoot a coat of enamel primer on everything, then store your parts on shelves in a dry place until you are ready to take them to the next step.

Some restorers will tell you that an enamel primer undercoating will lift and ruin lacquer primer and paint. And, if it has not had enough time to cure properly, they are absolutely right. At least a week is needed for the enamel primer undercoat to dry before any new paint can be put over it. Two weeks are even better. If you are a hobbyist working at home, this isn't usually a problem, because it will generally take at least that long to fix all of the dents, rusted-out areas and other imperfections before beginning to apply primer surfacer. ■

After car is stripped and washed, it should be given a coat of red oxide enamel primer to keep it from rusting until you can finish the project with final paint.

BASIC BODYWORK

Some cars just aren't worth restoring. If they are badly dented, rusted, damaged and incomplete, the work and money involved to do them right is usually too great to make the task worthwhile, unless they also happen to be Clark Gable's Duesenberg roadster. On the other hand, most cars, even if they were commercial failures when built originally, are worth doing if you love them and can make them new again, given your resources. The preservation of a piece of automotive history is always a worthy enough goal.

BASIC SKILLS & EQUIPMENT

Benny Goodman once was asked how he came to play at Carnegie Hall. "Practice, man. . . practice" was his reply. Likewise, there are a lot of skills and arts involved in doing show-winning paint work that cannot be learned on the fly, unless you are willing to run the very real risk of ruining your classic's precious tin. Don't do any pounding on your car until you've learned some basic skills. The easiest way to acquire the needed knowledge and tender touch is to take evening classes in welding and body repair at your local junior college or trade school. If there are no classes nearby, work from a book. HPBooks publishes a number of bodywork and painting handbooks that cover the subject in great detail. Then practice, man. . . practice.

Using a hammer and dolly requires a bit of practice. Develop such skills as "hammer-on" and "hammer-off" on a scrap fender before attacking your classic's precious sheet metal.

97

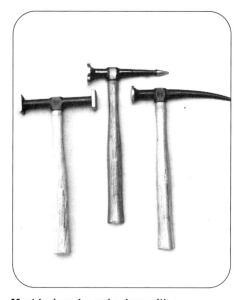

Most bodywork can be done with a combination hammer and picking hammers. Combination hammers are used to take out broad dents. Picking hammers are used for smaller dents and to get into tight places.

Dollies are used like small anvils to back hammer blows directly or indirectly. You will need a combination, a heel and a toe as shown here. If you buy used hammers and dollies, make sure their heads are smooth so you won't be hammering dents into your car's sheet metal instead of out of it.

In addition to these recommendations you can use the following tips to help get you started. Pick up a couple of terminally dented fenders at your local body shop or salvage yard and hone your skills on them. Don't get parts from modern Japanese imports because they are made of thin, high-carbon steel that is virtually unworkable. Also, to further your education, try to cozy up to someone who knows how to do bodywork so he can answer any questions you might have. To learn painting techniques, practice on your junk fenders, big tin cans and other round rubbish. Don't start on your classic until you can apply even, wet coats of paint, without runs or sags, over curved surfaces.

If there is much rust or dent repair work to be done on your vintage vehicle, you will need to know how to use a torch. Welding sheet metal requires a fair amount of skill. Take the time to master the techniques, or take your welding and cutting work to a pro. Don't be tempted to try to learn as you go. You can easily warp, melt and ruin thin sheet metal if you don't know what you are doing. Another, easier alternative to fixing badly dented or rusted fenders, hoods or doors is to get better ones from parts cars. If such items are available, they will be well worth the investment, because even properly repaired parts are rarely as good as originals. Check such automotive publications as *Hemmings Motor News* and *Classic Auto Restorer* for these items. Swap meets are a good source of new tin too.

Tools

Most body and fender work can be accomplished with just three basic hammers, three dollies, a spoon, and a vixen file. You may also need a slide hammer and some dent pullers. All of these tools can be purchased inexpensively at your local automotive paint store, or you can order them from: The Eastwood Company, 580 Lancaster Ave. Box 3014, Malvern, PA 19355-0714, 1-800-345-1178. You can also pick up good quality used tools at swap meets.

However, if you buy used equipment, make sure the heads and tips of the hammers, and the surfaces of the dollies, are perfectly smooth; otherwise you will create new dents when you try to use them.

Hammers—Body hammers are specialized for different tasks. For starters, you will need a combination hammer with a flat head on one end and a rounded head on the other. You will also need a long picking hammer for hard-to-get places, and a short picking hammer for taking out dings.

Dollies & Spoons—Dollies are small, hand-held anvils made in different shapes for different jobs. The dollies you want are: a general purpose, a *heel,* and a *toe.* A spoon is a necessity too. Spoons are long, heavy strips of steel used to back up hammer blows in tight places, and are sometimes employed to spank out broad, shallow dents. Body and fender men often make them out of pieces of broken leaf-springs. A vixen file is another required tool. Vixen files are very coarse and remove a lot of metal fast.

Hammering Techniques

Hammer-On—This is the most obvious way to smooth out bumpy sheet metal but not the only way. It works well to raise low spots and flatten high spots. With this method, the dolly is truly used as an anvil. Place the dolly behind the dent and tap the area that is backed by it. It takes some practice, in hammer-on work, to find the dolly and strike it squarely. You'll be able to tell by the sound when you are doing it right. The hammer-on technique is most useful for small dents.

Use the hammer-on technique with a shrinking dolly. The cross-hatching gathers the metal, after which it is filed and finished with body filler as required.

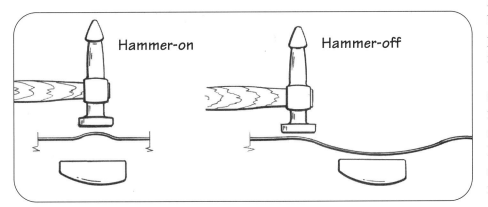

Hammer-on technique is used for smaller dents. Hammer-off is used for broad, shallow dents.

Always tap on dents rather than pounding on them. Your hammer stroke should be no more than a couple of inches in most cases, and the hammer should bounce only slightly after each blow. If you strike the metal too hard you will stretch and harden it, and you may succeed only in making more dents rather than a repair.

Hammer-Off—The point of the hammer-off approach is to use the dolly to push the dent out from behind by tapping on the raised area next to it with the hammer. The force of your tapping is transferred to the dolly. The larger the dent is in diameter, the further the hammer must be from the dolly to do the job. On small dents, the blow should fall right next to the dolly. On larger dents, the dolly may need to be as far as two inches away.

Spooning—Spoons are good for spanking broad shallow dents into shape from behind. They can also be used as dollies in hard to reach places. It is not always possible to get your hand and a dolly in behind a kick panel that has braces around it. A spoon is the obvious alternative.

Picking Hammers—Picking hammers are used, without dollies behind them, to take out small dents and dings. Place an old bastard file behind the ding to determine if your blows are connecting with the dent. The crosshatch file teeth leave small marks when struck. It takes a bit of practice to develop an accurate picking technique. File away small imperfections.

If you have trouble learning to pick out small dents, try a *Bullseye Pick* available from The Eastwood Company and automotive paint stores. They are sort of like old-fashioned ice tongs, except they are pointed on one end, and have a small, flat dolly on the other. You just sandwich

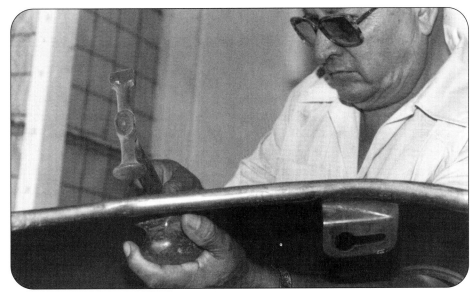

Hammer-off technique (striking next to the dolly rather than directly on it) is used to remove broad shallow dents. Don't pound on vintage tin; just tap it to shape. Your hammer only needs to swing a couple of inches in most instances.

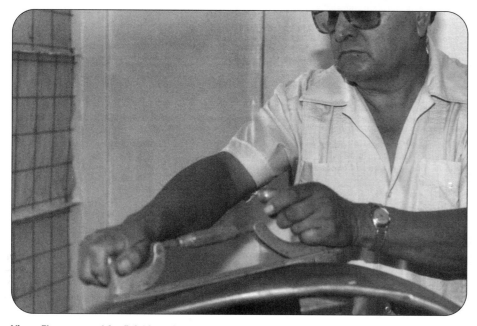

Vixen files are used for finishing after hammer work. They take a lot of metal off quickly, so be careful when using them.

protect them from rust, you can shoot on a thin mist of a light, contrasting color, then sand it off with a sanding block and #360-grit dry sandpaper. High spots will appear right away, because the speckles of paint will be removed from them first. Keep sanding. Low spots will become evident as you remove the paint from the higher surfaces surrounding them.

Metal Shrinking

Dents stretch sheet metal. Small dings can often be fixed by picking and filing, but a dent of any size usually requires shrinking as well as shaping. In fact, the best bodywork professionals can usually repair dents without the use of body filler or lead, simply by tapping them out, then shrinking the stretched metal back into

the dent in question between the ends of the pick, then tap it flat by working the rod-shaped picking tong up and down. You are guaranteed a direct hit every time. Bullseye Picks are expensive ($60 to $70) but they work beautifully.

Slide Hammers & Pullers—Use these devices as a last resort. They are usually employed to remove dents that can't be accessed from behind. If you must use a slide hammer, drill holes in the dent, then screw in a sheet metal screw. Attach the slide hammer to the screw then slap the dent flat, a hole at a time. Dent pullers are another alternative. They look like small meat hooks, and are inserted into holes to pull out dents. Tap on the high spots with a hammer to help the puller do its job. When the dent is pulled out, the metal is shrunk as needed and high spots are filed down, then the holes are filled with plastic filler or lead. Dent pullers and slide hammers should only be used when no other approach will work, because the process weakens panels considerably.

Finding Faults

To do a winning paint job, you will have to remove every nick, ding and

Small dings can be tapped gently to shape without the use of a dolly. Practice makes perfect. You need to know how hard to tap in order to remove dents without making new ones.

imperfection in your car's sheet metal. And small dings can be hard to find. Experienced pros close their eyes, then run the palms of their hands slowly over all of the surfaces to find those little, hard-to-spot dents that will only stand out after one has spent many hours painting and color-sanding his chariot.

Another good way to find small imperfections in your car's tin is to use a guide coat. Assuming you have given your parts a coat of red oxide enamel to

shape. All that is needed after these guys work their magic is a little filing and some paint. One method of shrinking involves heating the metal with a torch, then quenching it to cool it rapidly. The other requires the use of special hammers and dollies with crosshatch patterns.

Cold Shrinking—If a dent is small and shallow, it probably needs only minimal shrinking. You can do that with a shrinking hammer or a shrinking dolly. But don't try cold shrinking on larger

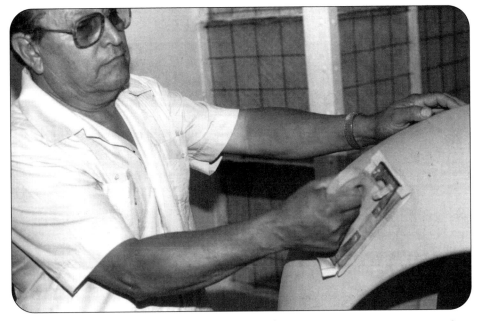

Sanding over protective primer using a sanding block will tell you where slight unevenness is present. Remove all primer and other paint before applying body filler to a specific area.

dents because you will overwork and harden the metal if you do. A shrinking hammer crumples and gathers the metal to shrink it. A shrinking dolly does the same thing, but from behind. Don't use a shrinking hammer and a shrinking dolly together.

Heat It Up—The most effective way to shrink stretched metal is with an oxyacetylene torch. This is the technique: Adjust the torch to a neutral flame, then heat a spot about the size of a dime until it is bright red. The metal will expand into a bulge as it is heated. Quickly place a dolly behind the spot, then strike the hot spot with a body hammer. You don't need to hit it very hard, because the metal is soft and pliable when it is hot. Next, quench the spot by placing a soaking wet rag on it, or better, shoot it with compressed air, from about an inch away, to cool it. You will have to do this many times on a large dent to get it back to its proper contour.

CUTTING & WELDING

Unless your classic chariot was hermetically sealed in a vault in the Arizona desert for the last 30 years, it probably has some rust in the bodywork. Most of it can be stripped and sanded away, but holes and serious deterioration will have to be cut out, or the panel will have to be replaced with a new one.

If you are not an expert welder, the best way to deal with damaged panels is to replace them. Parts can be found for most American production cars made in quantity in the last 50 years. And if you are restoring a Model A Ford, a mid-fifties Chevy, or a VW Bug, your task is easy. Replacement parts are still being made for these vehicles. And even if you are doing a '51 Plymouth, there are plenty of parts cars around with pristine panels that can be had for less than the cost of getting your old ones repaired.

But some parts can't be replaced, and some panels are impossible to find. In such cases, the bad spots will have to be cut out, and new pieces welded in to replace them. Body shop pros call this *sectioning*.

Cut It Out—Mark with masking tape the lines where the cuts are to be made. Make sure you are cutting into sound metal, not more rust. Now cut the bad area out using a hacksaw, tin snips or nibblers. Don't try to cut your car's sheet metal with a cutting torch. You will warp it and produce ragged edges in the process. Also, don't throw away the old piece of metal, because you will need it as a template.

Make a Patch—Cut your replacement patch out of mild steel of the same gauge (thickness) as the metal it is replacing. Make it slightly larger than the original so you can hold it in place and trim it to fit exactly. If you need to shape it, you will need a sand bag or *shot bag*. Professionals use a leather bag filled with buckshot as a backing, and work the metal with a body hammer. You can make an adequate alternative by filling a canvas sack with sand. Make templates for checking your work by cutting pieces of cardboard to shape, then holding them perpendicular to the original panel to verify their contour. When you have the correct shape, use the template to check your replacement piece.

Weld It In—When you are happy with your patch, clamp it into place with vise grips or welder's clamps, or attach it with magnets. Tack-weld the patch in place at each end, then once in the middle. Now tack a spot about every inch or so, alternating back and forth until you meet in the middle again. Pause between each spot weld to let the metal cool so you minimize warping and distortion.

Hammer-Weld It—The secret to good sectioning is *hammer-welding*. This is a technique employed by the pros that accomplishes several important things. It flattens the bead of the weld, making finishing work easier, and it helps shrink the metal back to its correct shape. Weld about an inch, then slip a dolly behind the weld and tap the bead flat with a body hammer. Have a friend pass the torch over your weld while you work, to keep it red hot. Your blows will also strengthen the weld by driving the welding rod into the split for better penetration. Keep working until the seam is completely welded and flattened. Finish it off with a vixen file.

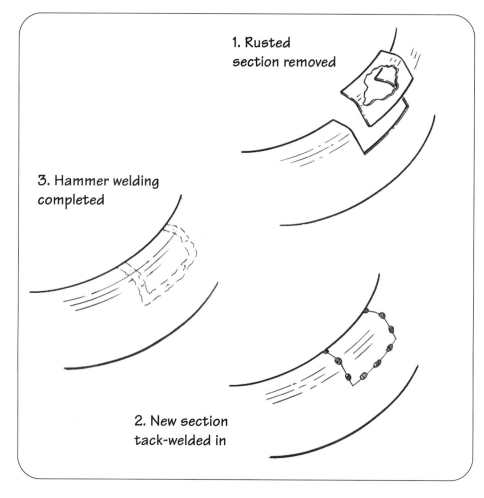

1. Rusted
section removed

3. Hammer welding
completed

2. New section
tack-welded in

Badly rusted sheet metal must be cut out and replaced. Cut bad metal away with sheet metal nibblers or a hacksaw, but not a torch. Attempting to use a cutting torch will warp and ruin your car's panels. Cut a patch from the same gauge mild steel your car is made of and tack-weld it into place to prevent warping and misalignment. Now hammer-weld the rest of the seam to drive in welding rod and cut down on necessary finishing.

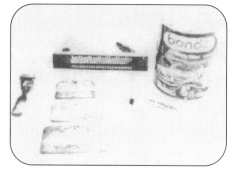

Believe it or not, there really is a filler called Bondo! So many manufacturers have plastic body filler that we tend to view them all as Bondo—which is one manufacturer's tradename. Accompanying gallon of body filler is hardener (catalyst), plastic spreaders, a Surform file and a body filler file.

BODY FILLERS

It is very likely that you will have to use filler in order to fix minor unevenness in your car's panels. Some purists in the restoration hobby insist that lead is the best choice. I asked an old pro in the restoration business, who has been painting cars since the '30s, what he thought about this. He said he felt plastic filler, commonly known as *Bondo,* was much superior to lead. He pointed out that the reason lead was used years ago was because it was all they had, but that it is difficult to apply, the acid used to tin the sheet metal causes paintwork to bubble, and it is toxic.

So unless you are a glutton for trouble, why not do as most pros do, and use modern plastic filler? Such work is well within the grasp of novice restorers, and mistakes are fairly easy to correct. Plastic filler is easy to apply, stable, and holds up well if it is done properly. Here are some tips on how to use it.

Buy the Right Stuff—Buy your plastic filler at an automotive paint store. The materials they sell are better quality and fresher than what you can find at an auto supply or hardware store. And while you are there, pick up some plastic spreaders, a "cheese grater" or shaver tool, a can of lacquer thinner and some #80-grit sandpaper for rough shaping.

Application—Make sure you remove every bit of rust, paint and oil before attempting to apply filler. You can do this with #80-grit sandpaper to remove rust and paint and a little lacquer thinner to remove the oil or grease contamination. Body filler should never be more than 1/8" thick when it is finished, and it can only successfully be applied over clean, rust-free, bare metal. If your panels need more filler than that to make them smooth, do more metal shaping rather than using thicker filler. Mix only what you can easily work in a few minutes, because plastic filler sets up pretty quickly. Follow the mixing instructions precisely. If you don't, when you spread on a second application, it may be harder or softer than the last, so your shaping and sanding will be very uneven.

Keep a can of lacquer thinner on hand to clean your spreaders and mixing board, and clean them frequently. Otherwise, you will pick up little bits of contamination which will make grooves in your work. Spread on a coat of filler in long sweeping strokes, then let it set up until it gets to the consistency of cheese. Now get out your shaver tool and rough your work into shape. Once the filler hardens, you can finish shaping it with the #80-grit sandpaper. For more details, see the sidebar on the next page.

Protect It—Shoot on a coat of red oxide enamel primer to protect your work until you are ready to begin painting. Plastic filler is not waterproof, and will actually absorb moisture, which will attack the unprotected metal beneath it. ∎

APPLYING BODY FILLER

Text and Photos by Michael Lutfy

Follow these simple steps for applying body filler. Make sure surface is clean, and that you only do small panels at a time. Also, only work with small batches of filler, and apply it quickly. It tends to set up and harden fast if you followed the mixing instructions correctly. Generally, you need at least enough filler to cover the area to no more than 1/4-inch thick.

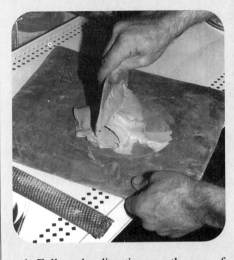

1. Follow the directions on the can of filler to get the right ratio of catalyst to filler. Work the catalyst into the filler with your plastic spreader, overlapping and blending it evenly until filler is a uniform color. Be careful not to get any air bubbles trapped in the filler—you'll create pinholes if you do.

2. Apply over dented area with smooth, even strokes going in one direction only. Changing directions will lift the filler underneath. Overlap the area to be filled, to a depth of no more than 1/4-inch. If you mixed the filler correctly, you'll have about 3-5 minutes before it becomes too hard to work properly. Try not to build it up too high—you'll increase your sanding time if you do.

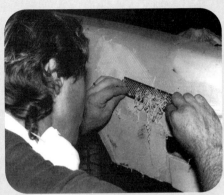

3. After filler sets up to the consistency of a hard cheese-like texture, use a Surform file to scrape off high spots and excess. Filler should come out of the file like you see here—like shredded cheese.

4. Put on your paper mask and start sanding with #80-grit sandpaper. Sand until it is flat and smooth. If you don't have a power sander, use a long board. Sand in 45° angles to get a crosshatch pattern.

5. When you think you have it smooth, use the "feel" method to check for high spots. You can also use a light guide coat at this stage, like many pros do. You may have to apply another, lighter coat of filler to get that "perfect panel."

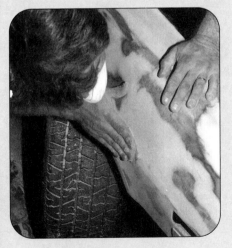

6. Do final sanding with #100-grit, then #220-grit. If you're not a pro, you should use a block or board to prevent grooving the filler with the pressure of your fingers.

PAINT TIPS

Your panels are rust-free, dent-free, straight and clean. But after all that work, your car still doesn't look like much. Now the fun begins. Your automotive toad will be transformed into a prince of the highway. There is still more spraying and sanding ahead, but when you are done, you will be amazed at how beautiful it looks. However, there are a few things you should consider before unholstering your spray gun.

CHOOSING PAINT

It's the most important step. You can easily undo all of your hard work by painting your car with an inappropriate color. Car companies pay designers a lot of money to come up with colors that will best suit their cars. They consider things like size, shape, highlight patterns, interior colors and how much brightwork is on the car. You should too. If you are unsure about what you want, get a paint chip chart for your year and make and consider the choices it offers.

Now that you have gone to the work of producing a mechanically correct restoration, you won't want to spoil it by picking a color that is not appropriate. A 1930s Rolls Royce formal sedan would look horrible in bright red, but a '58 Ferrari Testa Rossa is magnificent in that color. Likewise, a Model A Ford painted metallic lime green would be laughed off of the judging field, but the same color on a late 1960s Dodge Charger looks great. Every classic car is an artifact of a

This 1923 photo shows Charles Jeffrey, an instructor at Master Motor Coach Refinishing of Detroit, using the latest technology in automotive refinishing—paint brushes! Cars were sanded with gasoline between brush painted coats, and then finally polished with emery cloth. The slow drying of the cottonseed or linseed oil-based paints meant cars took about a week to paint, and the final paint job was lucky to last one year out in the sun. But in 1924, all of that changed with a dramatic development in auto refinishing—the spray painting of nitrocellulose lacquers. Photo courtesy John Jeffrey of PPG.

THINGS YOU'LL NEED:

- Prepsol or Pre-Kleeno degreaser
- Sandpaper (#360-grit open coat dry, #400, #1000, #1500, and #2000 wet and dry)
- Rubber sanding block
- Lacquer primer-surfacer
- Acrylic lacquer paint
- Acrylic lacquer thinner
- Sanding sealer
- Tack rags, stirring sticks, paint filters, masking tape, masking paper and a large bucket
- I recommend: 3M's Imperial Microfinishing Compound, Finesse-it II, Imperial Hand Glaze

A show-quality paint job can be done by even a first timer who is willing to spend the time and energy to do it. Long hours of hard work are involved, but the results are spectacular and worth the extra effort. This is the author's 1936 Packard 120 touring sedan, painted in lacquer using the techniques outlined in this chapter.

bygone era. It should be kept that way.

If you don't have much experience shooting paint, you may want to do your car in a light, non-metallic color. Lighter shades are more forgiving of imperfections in bodywork. On the other hand, metallic colors require an experienced touch. The paint must go on uniformly so the metal flakes in it lie flat for maximum luminosity. An inexperienced painter will have dull bands along the car where the paint went on too heavily. The problem only gets worse when he tries to rub it out.

Types of Paint

It is beyond the scope of this book to go into detail on the types of automotive paint currently available. For in-depth information, you should purchase a good paint book, such as HPBooks' *Automotive Paint Handbook*. However, I can give you some background on the two basic types: lacquers and enamels.

Lacquers were the first paints sprayed on cars, beginning in 1924. Several years later, enamels were also introduced in a form which could be sprayed on cars and trucks. Lacquer and enamels differ in their consistency and application. Enamels are thicker than lacquers when mixed for spraying and are applied with thicker but fewer coats. Enamels cure when they dry, by evaporation to some extent, but they also harden by the cross-linking of their molecules. Lacquers dry primarily by evaporation, and therefore lacquers remain more susceptible to damage by solvents.

Lacquer—Lacquer paint became more popular in the fifties, when a tougher acrylic lacquer made it more durable for automotive use. General Motors used acrylic lacquer for their more glamorous models and colors. Lacquer's image as the premium paint is still a common public perception, largely due to its use on custom cars with exotic paint jobs featured in auto shows and magazines.

PAINTING FRAME-OFF RESTORATIONS

by John Pfanstiehl, author of the *Automotive Paint Handbook*

Although car aficionados universally agree that a collector car should be painted the original color, the type of paint is open to a little more debate. Some purists call for repainting with nitrocellulose lacquers on those cars which originally were painted with nitrocellulose lacquers. However, as mentioned in the text, the types of paint applied at the factory are different than the types of paint available to body shops and restorers, so exact originality isn't possible in any case.

From a practical standpoint, on a high-quality paint job, it's not easy to tell the chemical composition of an automotive paint just by looking at it. I've never seen it proven that a judge, no matter how experienced, can be certain whether a paint is nitrocellulose or acrylic lacquer, or even if it is urethane. In some cases it is questionable whether an observer can tell for certain if a car is clear coated.

Other factors, such as *orange peel,* can be more easily judged. The factory paint jobs on production cars were never perfectly smooth. If judging at this level is important to you, research the subject with your car club or judging authority beforehand. It is harder to put orange peel back on a paint job than it is to take it off.

Considerations such as matching the orange peel and the defects of factory paint jobs are relatively new to the field of automotive restoration. Perfection in restoration used to mean perfection in paint and detail. The paint on the insides of hoods and fenders is often flawless in finish and gloss. Although the cars were often not finished to this detail when they were first made, it certainly makes them more exciting and impressive to look at today.

Up into the '80s, the common philosophy of restoration was that the cars should be restored or rebuilt to the degree of paint finish the factory would have *wanted* them to have. Frames and engine compartments were treated to dazzling perfect paint. At some point, a group of car enthusiasts took a new look at this and decided that restoring means restoring the cars to the way they actually were, flaws and all. Corvette restorers, in particular the Bloomington Gold Certification and the National Corvette Restorers Society (NCRS), were among the first to put this new philosophy of restoration into systematic use.

At national meets, classes are held to discuss the details of each part of the process—from frame restoration to platings.

Detailed judging manuals strive to describe what types of finish should be on each part. The types of subjects discussed range from how many runs should be in bumper brackets which were dip coated, and where overspray should be on engine compartment components.

Restorations that adhere to this philosophy are much more expensive and take more time to complete. It is much faster and easier to do a cosmetically flawless restoration than an authentic one. In addition, preserving these types of restorations is much more difficult because many of the steel parts were not painted at all, and steps must be taken to prevent the bare metal from getting surface rust. Only you can decide the type of restoration you want for your car, and to what degree you'll go for authenticity.

The term *frame-off restoration* is popular in car collector circles and it refers to a restoration in which the car's body is lifted off the frame to permit a thorough cleaning, reconditioning, restoring and painting of the underside of the body and the frame. It's also used to describe restorations of cars that don't have frames, such as Mustangs. Frame-off, at the least, should mean that all suspension, brake, drivetrain and all other parts that are bolted to the body are removed and restored to their original condition.

This level of restoration presents a problem because it is nearly impossible to keep overspray and dirt off a restored chassis, drivetrain and engine compartment through the whole process of restoring and repainting the body. One of the techniques that has evolved is restoration and repainting of the body before the chassis restoration is completed.

In this procedure, the body is raised to permit installation of new body mounts where appropriate. If a different frame is going to be used, the body will be installed onto it at this stage. After the body is tightened down and secured to the frame, the bodywork begins. The alignment of doors, hoods and trunk lids is made perfect by adjustment or by trimming or building of the adjacent body panels. Then all the remaining bodywork and repainting is done. Only after painting and buffing is completed, is the body removed.

Then the chassis and drivetrain get their full restoration and repainting. When the body is once again united with the frame, hopefully the only extra work the paint on the car will need is a quick polish or buff in any areas chafed or marked by the straps used to hoist the body.

However, lacquer's glory days are numbered due to environmental concerns and the superior performance of the new two-part enamels. But, it is still available, and there are advantages and disadvantages to its use. Lacquer is the easiest paint to spray, and that's one reason why it is the choice of many beginning painters and hobbyists. Lacquer also dries quickly, which decreases the problem of dirt and bugs in a paint job. Such contamination happens even in the best paint booth and it is much more of a problem for cars sprayed without a booth, such as in the home garage. If something falls, flies or walks into the car during painting, the intruder can be easily brushed off or lightly sanded out because lacquer dries so quickly.

Lacquer can be applied in thinner, drier coats which helps avoid the problem of massive drips or sags. A novice painter has to be very careful with the variation in the wetness of the paint because it will affect how metallics settle out and can easily make the paint look blotchy.

Lacquer facilitates some of the more advanced painting techniques and therefore lends itself to certain types of custom painting. In the past, some custom auto paints only came in lacquer.

Another reason some people choose lacquer is that it was the original paint on many cars produced from the mid-twenties into the seventies, and in particular the popular GM cars of the fifties and sixties. When people restore these cars, they often choose lacquer so that the car will have the original type of paint. Actually, the lacquer they're buying today is not chemically identical to the stuff the factory applied. Another advantage of lacquer is that it is easy to do spot repairs and blending in a repaired area.

On the down side, lacquer can be a fragile paint. Even after months of drying in the sun, if a bird gets a direct hit on your car, you'll have problems. Not only bird droppings, but hard water,

People bent on restoring a car to absolute original condition will attempt to match the exact paint type and color originally sprayed by the factory. But paints applied at the factory, in the past as well as present, are chemically different than those available to body shops and home painters. Most factory paints are thermoset formulations to cure in hot ovens, so it is virtually impossible to reapply "original" paint to a restored car. Photo by Michael Lutfy.

gasoline spills, acid rain, and just about anything else will actually eat down into the paint. This may not be a problem for a show-car or collector car which is usually kept garaged and covered, however lacquer is a relatively delicate finish for cars which are driven daily.

Lacquer is already outlawed in several states, and may be outlawed in other states in the near future. The reason: More of lacquer paint goes into the atmosphere than any other type of paint. Most of the paint which is poured into the gun does not end up on the car.

Another disadvantage is that lacquer dulls down when it dries. That means you should wait a week before wet-sanding and buffing a lacquer paint job, which is what happens with most heavy-volume collision repair shops. As lacquer continues to dry, over a period of weeks, it will continue to sink and lose its gloss as the solvent evaporates. With the best custom paint jobs, professionals recommend that you wait as long as two months before buffing a new lacquer paint job.

Enamels—In comparison to lacquers, enamels have a much smaller portion of their chemistry evaporating into the atmosphere. They cure and chemically change from the liquid state in which they are sprayed to a hard solid film of paint. The newest enamels and spray systems are aiming for paints which will have less than 35% of their weight comprised of solvents which evaporate into the atmosphere. Regular one-part enamels are among the least expensive paints to apply. The labor of the paint job also costs less than lacquer painting because enamels don't require the labor costs for hours of wet-sanding and buffing. Enamels dry glossy.

The durability of good one-part enamels, particularly alkyd enamels, is usually not as good as two-part enamels but they hold up better than most lacquers when subjected to the same conditions. Acrylic enamels, particularly

when used with hardeners, can be quite durable under many conditions.

Alkyd enamels are often called synthetic enamels, because they were the first enamels to be made with a resin which was modified by synthesizing with petroleum products. The label synthetic has stuck although it isn't really appropriate today because all modern paint resins are synthesized.

Some bargain-priced enamels don't last long. Some really poor enamels have problems after just a few months in the sun. It is also much more difficult to apply than lacquer.

The spraying of enamel requires a little more practice because enamel is sprayed on wetter than lacquer. Also, shortly after it is sprayed on the car, the enamel flows out, which reduces surface texture problems like orange peel and increases the shine. However, when enamel flows out improperly it can run or sag. The painter has to anticipate what it will do after it is sprayed on—it's a fine line

between ending up glossy or ending up runny.

A charcoal filter mask is recommended during spraying. Also look around the room and cover everything which you don't want to receive a color change. Enamel overspray is difficult to remove. As always, ventilate the area and use a fresh air hood system if the enamel is catalyzed.

Although technically an enamel, two-part enamels have enough special qualities to warrant their own category. Their best quality is that they are extremely durable. Dupont's IMRON brand polyurethane enamel, introduced in 1970, is one of the most well known of these extraordinarily tough new enamels. These are also called *two-pack enamels* or *two-component enamels* because they require the addition of a second component, an activator or hardener. Without the hardener, they won't dry, but with it they quickly undergo a chemical change. They'll even solidify inside the

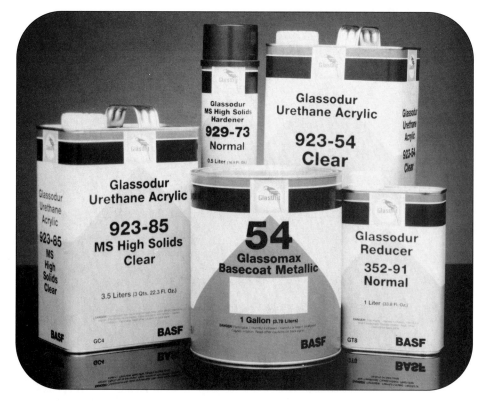

Using a paint system refers to using compatible paints of the same brand for all layers in the paint job: primer, color and clear. Today's paints are so chemically complex that mixing brands is risky business, and can lead to problems such as delamination and peeling. Don't mix and match.

paint gun before they are sprayed if the painter waits too long.

In addition to the fast setup times, they also have strong advantages in durability. Many custom shops that used to paint exclusively in lacquer have switched to the new two-part enamels because of their ability to resist cracking and because they retain their gloss longer. Some are so tough that chemical paint strippers can be poured on them with no effect. One proof of their superiority is that paint manufacturers only give written warranties to car owners on two-part enamels.

Another advantage is the speed of drying. This reduces the time the car is susceptible to dust contamination while it's wet. This also allows cars to be removed from the paint booth sooner.

Two-part enamels can be buffed very soon after painting. Many are buffed the next day. In fact, it will be a lot harder to buff them if you wait much longer than twenty-four hours. Unlike lacquers, two-

If you can't remove all body parts and/or trim, then careful masking is necessary. A masking machine helps make the process quicker and more efficient. Photo by Michael Lutfy.

part enamels will retain their gloss for years, even without waxing.

The main drawbacks are price and difficulty of application. Two-part enamels are costly. Just the cost of the basic materials, including the paint, primer, reducers, catalysts and special

additives can run over $500 for some cars.

Two-part paints have become much easier to paint, but their application requires special breathing apparatus for the painter. At the very least, experienced painters will use a face mask with new charcoal elements. However, a fresh air hood system (a pump delivering fresh air to the painter's hood by means of a hose) is strongly recommended, particularly when spraying paints which contain *isocyanates*. Isocyanates are about the most toxic chemicals a painter will encounter. Always make sure the spray area is properly ventilated for your health and to improve vision.

Paint Systems—In addition to the final top coat of paint, you'll need to purchase undercoats (primers) intermediate coats (primer sealers or primer surfacers) and perhaps a clear coat. This can make the decision complicated. However, it isn't if you stick with a single manufacturer's "paint system." Martin Senour, Dupont, PPG and BASF all offer top quality paint systems that are designed to be chemically compatible. Purchase all of the paint you are going to need for your car at the same time to insure uniformity of color. How much you need depends on the size of the car and the number of coats you intend to apply.

MASKING

If you're short of time or a trim piece simply can not be removed for some reason or another, then it must be masked off. The subject of masking could probably be stretched out into a chapter but a few basic tips are all most people will need to get started. Masking is one of those skills that seems awkward and difficult at first but proficiency comes quickly with experience, and masking can almost be fun at times. There is much more to masking than simply covering a piece of trim or a part with tape or paper.

You will need sturdy shelves to store your car's parts while you are involved in the various stages of painting them and rubbing them out. Don't be tempted to shorten the drying time between coats of paint. You'll get checking, blistering and cracking if you do.

Proper masking entails covering items with clean, even edges. Some people are blindingly fast (and good) at masking. However, this is certainly a part of repainting where rushing will cost you time. A trim part that takes a minute to thoroughly mask could take an hour or more to clean overspray from. In the case of vinyl or convertible tops, a masking mistake that allowed overspray through could cause damage which would be almost impossible to remedy.

In haste, one of the simplest things is often overlooked: cleaning the surface being masked. Tape is generally the first barrier to paint overspray and tape can't stick to a dusty surface. Wipe the surface which is to be taped with Prepsol or Prekleeno.

Masking Materials—Masking tape and masking papers come in many widths. The narrower the tape, the easier it will form around curves. Use expensive tape unless you can afford the time to test less expensive brands. 3M is always a safe choice. Good quality masking tape will not allow paint to seep through, it will stick uniformly to the surface and it will be easy to remove later. The wider the tape, the greater the coverage. Paper comes in several widths. Never use newspaper for masking because it is too porous, and the wet paint can bleed through. Furthermore, the black ink can bleed and contaminate the surface with an oily film.

Masking Procedure—Use 1/4-inch tape for tight curves or hard-to-tape areas. Small items such as door handles and emblems can be masked off with tape only. On large areas to be covered with paper, run a strip of tape around the trim or edges of the area. Add the masking paper, folding the edges of the paper under to match the contour of the item being masked. When the paper is shaped to the item, apply another strip of tape to the paper edges. This makes an effective seal to prevent overspray from blowing underneath. If you need to use more than one piece of paper to cover an area, make sure you tape the seam. A word of advice is to use a double layer of paper at first until you're sure the paint you're using won't seep through one layer.

Mask engine compartments thoroughly. This is important because the overspray goes much farther than you would expect. This is particularly important with paints whose overspray is extremely difficult to remove, such as enamels and urethanes. Lay a drop cloth over the entire compartment and tape paper to the inside of the fenders and cowl. Headlamps, wheels and tires and bumpers need to be masked off as well.

Be generous with masking until you learn about spray paint's tendency to penetrate the slightest tape gaps or overlapping papered areas. Extra caution is also advised when spraying enamels because its overspray can bond very tightly to almost anything it falls on. And in particular, be concerned about masking parts of the car which can be extremely difficult to remove overspray from, such as fabric tops.

LACQUER PAINTING TIPS

The following information consists of a few tips to help you apply lacquer paint. As I mentioned before, you'd be well advised to purchase a separate book that covers painting in greater detail.

Sawhorses with pieces of clean carpeting tacked to them are ideal for supporting your car's parts while you color sand and rub them out. Make sure you cover the carpet with plastic when you aren't using the sawhorses so grit won't get into it.

This is what many professional painters wear—body suits, fresh-air face mask and neoprene gloves—especially when spraying catalyzed enamels. You must cover up and at the very least wear a charcoal-filtered mask. Photo by Don Taylor.

SPRAY GUNS

A revolution in auto painting technology has taken place in the last few years as a result of environmental laws. The newest equipment is not only less contaminating, it is also less expensive, and less trouble to use. Old timers will insist that the air compressor and Binks spray gun can't be beat. And for them it is true. That's because those guys are as facile with such equipment as Al Unser Jr. is with an Indy car. But if you are a novice, or a hobbyist with limited experience and a limited budget, I highly recommend you choose one of the new, high-volume, low-pressure (HVLP) guns to paint your classic. It takes the same amount of time and effort to master either type of equipment, but the newer systems have some big advantages.

The old conventional systems typically consisted of a compressor with at least a 2 horsepower motor, fifty feet of hose, two water traps and a Binks model 2001 or similar spray gun. But this description is a simplification. If you want to acquire such equipment, go to your local automotive paint shop and ask them to help you configure your system.

If you decide to try one of the new spray systems, consider the Accuspray. A complete setup costs about $800 at this writing and includes everything you need to do the job. It is available from The Eastwood Company and includes a portable compressor, 30' of hose and a gun. No water filter is needed. It operates on standard household current too.

You may not have much choice if you want to stay on the right side of the law, because high-volume, low-pressure (HVLP) equipment is all that many localities will permit. The old, high-pressure outfits throw off a great deal of over-spray that pollutes the atmosphere. The new systems are easier on your wallet too, because they use less paint. Most of what you spray goes on the car. But a good job can be done with either type of setup, provided you take the time to master the art of spray painting.

However, these tips should get you in the ballpark. The following procedures apply only to the spraying of lacquer. I've chosen this type because it is the easiest for the novice to apply.

Prepare Your Shop—Check with local environmental authorities as to whether it is acceptable to paint your car at home in your area. If it isn't, see if you can rent a spray booth, or sign up for a body shop class at your local trade school. If you decide to work at home, you will need a clean, well-lighted place with plenty of ventilation. Make sure that all pilot lights from water heaters and gas dryers are extinguished prior to painting.

Clean your shop thoroughly. Dust, grit and cobwebs will be drawn to your wet paint like a magnet. If you are working in a garage, you may want to staple heavy plastic tarps to the studs and rafters to keep dust from sifting off of them. Wet the floor to minimize contamination from that direction prior to spraying paint.

You will need a large table to place parts while working, and you will need shelves to store painted items while they are curing. Large hooks made of wire and hung from the ceiling are handy for painting some parts. Sawhorses with carpet remnants tacked on their tops are good to have when you are color sanding.

Prepare Yourself—Painting cars can be dangerous! Fumes and particles generated from sanding and paint are highly flammable and toxic. They can destroy your lungs or blow up the garage (and you along with it). If you inhale particles of fiberglass while sanding, they will be permanently lodged in your lungs. They do not "cough" out. Therefore, always wear a particle mask when sanding.

The fumes from the paint and solvents you'll be working with are also highly toxic. Therefore, never spray paint near an open flame such as an appliance with an active pilot light and don't smoke. It

Spray guns come in all sizes and prices. At left is a cheap but adequate knockoff of a more expensive product. At right is a Binks spray gun. This is a high quality professional product that will give excellent results and years of service. In the center is a small touchup gun which is handy for tight spaces and small items.

sounds like common sense, but many people forget that the water heater located in the garage, or the gas dryer, have pilot lights going all the time. They fill the garage with paint fumes and BOOM!, their garage becomes the world's largest combustion chamber. Furthermore, any electrical equipment you operate must have a "fire safe" motor. If you're thinking of using the cooling fans used in the bedroom—don't. The motors on these fans can produce sparks, which of course is not in your best interest. Get special exhaust fans for ventilating your garage.

Always wear eye protection and particle or ventilated air masks. Do not, under any circumstances, paint without a ventilated paint mask of some sort. When painting, the best system is a fresh air hood. If that's too sophisticated for your budget, then at the very least use a face mask with disposable charcoal filters. Do not, however, use Imron with anything other than a fresh air hood. Furthermore, make sure that you cover your skin by wearing long-sleeved shirts and long pants—the harmful byproducts of paint can be absorbed through your skin into your bloodstream. The chemicals of today's automotive paints, especially with the two-part enamels, can cause irreparable damage to vital organs, and in many cases, even death. Safety must always be your primary consideration.

Material Safety Data Sheets (MSDS) are specific, detailed listings of the components of products. In the automotive paint field, products that require MSDSs range from the hazardous catalysts used to cure paint to the relatively benign bottles of touch-up paint sold to consumers. Whether you are a professional painter or an office worker, you now have the ability to learn about the nature of products used in the workplace. Ask the manufacturers or suppliers for the MSDS for any product which concerns you. It's important to know what chemicals your lungs and skin are coming in contact with!

Prepare Surface—Whether dealing with painted or unpainted surfaces, you should begin surface preparation by wiping the entire surface with a wax/grease remover, such as Pre-Kleeno. If the body panels were stripped of paint, they should be sanded with #100-grit sandpaper to remove any remaining materials, smooth out high spots and to give the primer a textured surface to "bite" into. Unpainted steel panels should be primered soon after stripping to prevent surface rusting.

If body panels weren't stripped, the old paint or primer should be sanded with #100-grit paper. Any nicks, chips or other defects in the surface should be filled with polyester glazing putty and then block-sanded smooth with #180-grit paper.

If the old paint has been sanded down to the point where the body panel is exposed, those areas should be spot-primed. Although it is not always necessary, it may be safer to apply primer over all areas which are to be painted, even those which are covered with old paint. This provides a more uniform base for the top coats and it makes an evenly colored background. It also provides some isolation of the new top

Catalyzed polyester primer-surfacer is an excellent product. It doesn't shrink, which eliminates the need for multiple coats and sanding.

coats from the older paints underneath.

Sealers go one step farther to help isolate potential problems caused by the fresh paint reacting badly to the underlying older finish. Adhesion promoters are another option, and are generally employed when repainting over clear coats or other slick surfaces which the new paint might have difficulty sticking to. If sanding scratches, feather-edges or other surface defects have to be covered, primer-surfacers are the next step. They are high-build, sandable primers that are meant to go on heavy and fill any surface defects. They are meant to be easily sanded so that a smooth surface is left for the top coats.

Final Wipe-Down—Before priming, it is wise to quickly go over the hard-to-reach areas with a scuffing pad, such as a fine Scotch pad. Like sandpaper, it helps to degloss the paint, remove dirt or wax and make the surface rough to help paint adhesion. Plus, the flexible pad enables the user to get into more difficult-to-reach areas and crevices.

Immediately before any painting, from the initial priming to the final top coats, the car should be wiped with a fresh *tack rag*. The sticky fibers of the tack rag pick up any remaining loose dirt and dust on the surface. Wad the tack rag up into a ball and gently wipe—or tack—the surface to be painted. Never let the tack rag sit on the car. The varnish in the rag will quickly adhere to the paint. You can find tack rags at paint supply stores.

One other piece of advice, it never hurts to recheck the body for any remaining dents or defects before the top coats are applied. It is well worth the effort to make a diagram of the car and mark every chip or ding before the work begins, and then to check those areas closely after the prep work is finished. Every painter has at one time or another looked at a freshly sprayed car and said, "How did I ever miss that?" Protect yourself so it doesn't happen on your car.

Spraying Primer—Lacquer primer-

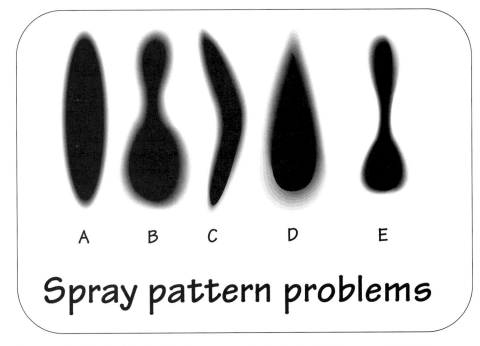

Spray pattern problems

You can tell a lot about the health of your spray gun by looking at the spray pattern it produces. **(A)** This is the way the spray pattern should look. **(B)** A pattern that is fat, irregular and spattery indicates that atomizing pressure is too low. Increase pressure at gun or compressor. **(C)** If you see this shape either to the right or left, it is because a wing port on the air cap is clogged. Remove the air cap and soak it in lacquer, then clean the little orifices with a toothpick soaked in thinner. Don't use a paper clip or wire, you'll damage the port. **(D)** If your spray pattern is big at the top or bottom as shown here, it's because there is an obstruction around the fluid tip. Wash the air cap and fluid tip in lacquer thinner, then reinstall them. **(E)** A pattern that is squeezed in the middle and fat at the ends indicates too high atomizing pressure.

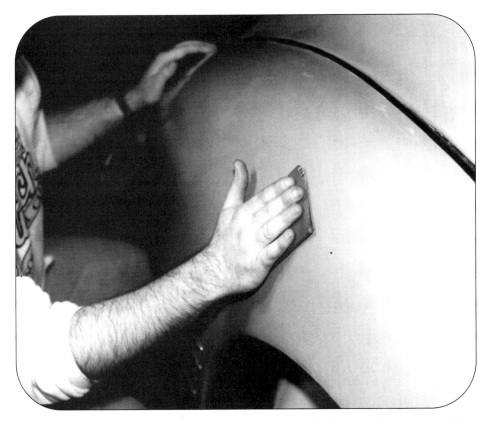

Use a rubber sanding pad and color sand in a cross-hatch pattern (opposing 45° angles) rather than in one consistent direction so you won't make grooves in your paintwork. Don't use a lot of pressure. Let the sandpaper do the work for you.

surfacer comes in concentrated form, so it must be thinned with about 1.5 times as much lacquer thinner. In other words you need to dilute it by 150%. Stir the paint thoroughly before, and after, thinning it.

Wash down a part to be painted with degreaser to remove any oil or fingerprints, then go over it very lightly with a tack rag. Spray on three coats of primer, starting on the underside and edges, and finishing up on the broad surfaces. Let each coat flash over (dry to a dull finish) before shooting on the next. When you have finished spraying every part, put them away on shelves and let them cure for at least five days before going on to the next step. If you try to shorten this time, you will run the risk of having your finished job crack and craze from escaping gases later.

Block Sand—After your part has cured, do your sanding outdoors, away from your painting area. Spray on another light, guide coat. A fine mist of cheap aerosol enamel is fine. We'll be sanding it all off anyway. Now put on a particle mask and begin sanding with a block and #360-grit, open coat dry sandpaper. If your parts still have imperfections they will soon show up. Raised bumps will appear first, and dips will stand out later as the guide coat is removed. Fix any dings you might have missed, then re-shoot as necessary.

Sand in long, diagonal strokes across the part. Work in one direction, then the other in a crisscross pattern. That's so you won't sand ridges or ripples into your finish. Don't apply a lot of pressure; let the paper do the work. Slap the dust out of your sandpaper frequently. When the paper gets dull or clogged, discard it. Do not sand edges or sharp corners. The paint is always very thin in such areas because it tends to be blown away from them during spraying. If you break through to bare metal anywhere, you will need to re-shoot with primer.

Hold up each part to a good light

TIPS FOR BEGINNING SPRAY PAINTERS

1. Carefully follow the mixing instructions on paint cans. Sloppy measuring can result in nightmarish problems when you spray.

2. Always wear a professional quality painting mask and long sleeve coveralls while spraying.

3. Lacquer is usually shot at about 35 lbs psi. through conventional guns, and at the full five pounds pressure with HVLP equipment. The pattern adjustment knob (usually the upper one) should be opened fully for the broadest possible pattern. Try 3-1/2 turns open on the fluid control knob (usually the lower one).

4. Keep your gun perpendicular to the surface you are spraying at all times. The width of your hand from tip of thumb to tip of pinkie (about 8") is the distance you will want to maintain between the surface to be painted and the nozzle of the spray gun while spraying.

5. Move at a constant rate in long horizontal sweeps. Maintain about a 30% overlap from one pass to the next.

6. Don't try to wipe off runs or sags. You'll just create a bigger mess. It is easy to sand runs out of lacquer after it has dried.

7. Keep your spray gun surgically clean. Most equipment malfunctions are due to dirty equipment. When you finish shooting paint for the day, clean the paint cup, then put a little lacquer thinner in it and shoot it with your finger over the nozzle to back flush the gun. Disassemble the gun and clean the nozzle orifices with a toothpick. (Never use wire, as it will ruin tightly machined surfaces.) Run pipe cleaners soaked in lacquer thinner down the siphon and vent tubes to clean them. Pull out the fluid control needle valve and clean it. Grease its shaft with a little Vaseline where it goes through the packing gland.

source and inspect it for imperfections. Look for any unevenness or ripples. Wash your hands to get any oil or grease off of them, then run your hand over the surfaces to feel for unseen problems. If you find any, re-spray the part, sand it, and inspect it again. But don't shoot any more paint on the car than is necessary to produce a good surface. There is no advantage to a thick coat of primer. It will only make it easier for the color coat to chip off and shatter when struck or bumped.

Apply Primer Sealer—When you are satisfied that you have your car as pristine as you can make it, shoot on a coat of sanding or primer sealer. Follow the directions on the can. Sanding sealer prevents sand scratches from swelling and showing through on color coats. Let your parts cure for another five days before applying the final top coat.

Applying Final Lacquer Top Coat

Clean your shop once again. Contaminants will show in your final finish. Now open each can of paint and stir it completely, then pour all of the paint into a large clean bucket. Stir it together thoroughly. Pour it back into its original cans and seal them carefully. The reason for this ritual is to insure that each gallon of paint is the exact same color as the others. As good as paint systems are, no two cans of paint are precisely the same shade. If you don't mix your paint together, your hood might not match your fenders when you get the car back together.

Check the Weather—A perfect day for painting would be one that was clear, dry and 70 degrees F. But life is less than perfect. As a rule of thumb, the further the weather deviates from the above, the greater the possibility of problems with painting. The speed, or drying time, of the thinner you use with your color coat will depend on climatic conditions too. A fast drying thinner on a hot day will cause the paint to dry on its way to the surface you are trying to cover. In other words, you'll be shooting dust. A slow drying thinner on a cold, damp day will allow sand scratches to swell and show through, and the paint may blush with trapped moisture. Blushing refers to dull grayish patches that form in the finish.

Spraying—Usually you thin acrylic lacquer approximately 125% to 150%. In other words, each gallon of paint should be thinned with about a gallon and a half of thinner, but follow the manufacturer's directions, printed on the paint can. Stir it thoroughly, then pour it through a filter before pouring it into the paint cup of your spray gun. Go over the surfaces to be painted lightly with a tack rag.

Shoot such things as door jambs and the undersides of fenders first. Give parts 3 or 4 coats, letting each coat dry at least 20 minutes before spraying the next one. Let everything dry at least a week before going on to the next step.

Color Sand—Fill a small bucket

with water, then add a little dish detergent. Put 3 or 4 pieces of sandpaper in the water to soak. Wrap your block-sanding pad and sand your parts in diagonal strokes, first one way, then the other to avoid making grooves. Keep the surface you are sanding wet at all times. Dip your paper in the bucket frequently. Discard paper as it gets clogged. Keep working until the last hint of orange peel or unevenness is removed. Again, don't sand the edges or corners.

Apply More Coats—Wash your parts with Prepsol, go over them with a tack rag, then shoot on three more coats of color. Let everything dry another 5 to 7 days. Color sand again with #400-grit paper and water, then shoot on two or three final coats of color thinned 200% so it will melt into the coats below and produce a smooth surface that won't require a great deal of rubbing. Let things dry another week. (Now you know why the pros charge so much for show quality work.)

BUFFING

The moment has arrived. You're about to get your first peek at the splendor that your restored classic will have. All the hard work begins to pay off. But you must be careful. Keep everything clean while you are working, because one tiny bit of grit will put a deep scratch in your new paint.

Color Sand Some More—This time, use #1000-grit paper, dipped frequently in your water bucket. Once again, use a sanding block and work in a crisscross pattern. Keep working until all orange peel is gone. Stay away from edges. Now go over the car again with #1500-grit paper to get rid of the fine scratches made by the #1000 grit. Finish with #2000-grit, only this time, sand with the direction of the highlights and lines of the car. When you've finished the car will have an almost shiny satin finish.

Rubbing Compound—You'll need plenty of soft rags for the next step. Make sure they are free of snaps, buttons and zippers. Dampen a cloth, fold it into a pad, put a little 3M Imperial Microfinishing compound on it, then start rubbing. Work in an area about two square feet until it shines. Keep going until you have done the whole car.

Now repeat the process with 3M Finesse-it II. This is to remove the fine spider-web-like scratches that the previous compound left. When you have done your entire car to your satisfaction, go over it with 3M Imperial Hand Glaze.

REASSEMBLY

By now you have a garage full of jewels. Each piece of your chariot glows with a spectacular finish. The final challenge is to put it back together without damaging things. Take your time, work carefully and follow these suggestions:

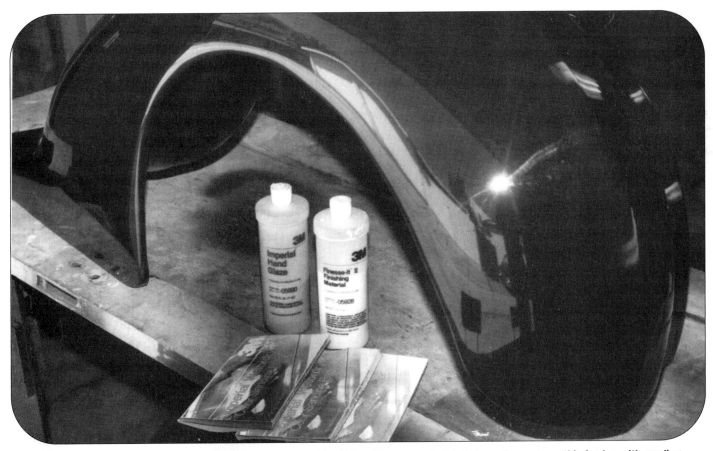

Here are the stunning results of 3-stage color sanding and careful rubbing. There are a total of nine color coats on this fender, with sanding between every three coats, then final color sanding and buffing.

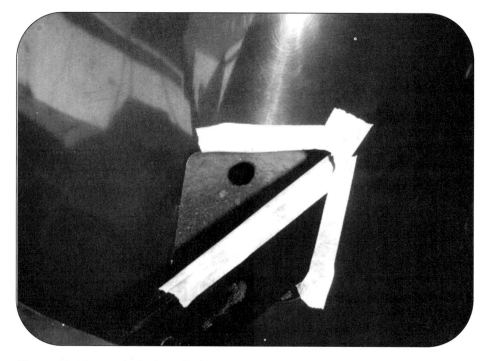

Use masking tape around edges of painted parts to minimize chipping during reassembly. If you do make a little chip (everybody does at some point), retouch it using a small artist's brush until nick is slightly over-filled, let it dry for a week, then color sand.

Protect Parts with Blankets—Put carpet remnants under your parts when you set them on the floor, and wrap them in blankets or furniture pads when moving them.

Mask Edges—Tape around edges that could get bumped during assembly.

Use Extra Manpower—It is almost impossible to man-handle hoods and trunk lids into place without help. You risk damaging their finish if you try to do it all by yourself.

Fix Nicks—Nobody gets a car back together without making a few little nicks and chips in the paint. Go to an art supply and pick up a small artist's brush. Dab in tiny drops of paint until the nick is slightly over-filled. Let your touch-ups dry thoroughly, then sand and rub them out. For more details, see the sidebar on p. 114. ■

Here is the author's '36 Packard as it was being reassembled. There are several months of weekend work in the paint job at this point. Fitting the hood is next and is a delicate process. Everything must be lined up carefully. A good steel measuring tape is a must for this job. Measure length of opening at top and bottom and on left and right to make sure everything lines up properly.

The next task after a show-winning paint job is glass. You had to take it out to paint the car, so why not replace it now? Or, if the glass in your restored collector car is pitted, cracked or de-laminating, and the whisker moldings on your roll-up windows are worn out, they need to be replaced.

The first thing to do is to order the rubber seals and the whisker channels you'll need for the job. Unless you are restoring a fairly recently made car, you won't be able buy the rubber parts for it from a local source. The sidebar nearby lists several sources of good rubber stripping.

If your windshield glass is in good shape, then all it may need is a minor touchup. The Eastwood Company offers a glass polishing kit that includes everything but the drill to remove light scratches and shallow pits from your windshield. Photo courtesy The Eastwood Company.

REMOVING GLASS

If you haven't already removed your windshield, read on. Because of their size and seeming permanence, windshields and rear windows appear intimidating. Not to worry. You have to exercise a little caution handling them, but no special skills are required to do a good job of replacing them.

Locate a Replacement—If your car has a curved windshield, locate a

THINGS YOU'LL NEED:

- Heavy leather gloves
- Goggles
- Tin snips
- Screwdrivers
- Grease pencil
- Utility knife
- Putty knife (stiff)
- Carpet piece 3 x 5 feet
- 3M Weatherstrip cement
- Automotive silicone sealer (available at glass shops)
- Rubber moldings and seals
- Black filler strip
- Electric drill and fine bits

replacement before removing your old one. Replacement windshields can be hard to come by for some older cars. Old glass shops, or dealerships that have been in business for a long time are a good place to start. Hobby publications such as *Hemmings Motor News* can be helpful too.

Remove Molding—Begin by removing the garnish molding around the windshield on the inside of the car. Be careful not to scratch it with your screwdriver. Put the screws in a Ziploc bag and tape it to the molding, then wrap the molding and store it where it won't get scratched or bent.

Cut Gasket—Next, cover the hood and dashboard of your car with blankets, then put on thick gloves and goggles. The windshields on cars made before the 1960s usually come out from the inside. To remove them you need to cut away the lip of their rubber seals from the inside with a utility knife.

SOURCES FOR RUBBER GASKETS

Metro Molded Parts Inc.
11610 Jay Street, P.O. Box 33130
Dept. 46, Minneapolis, MN 55433
(612) 757-0310

Steele Rubber Products
1601 Hwy. 150 East
Denver, NC 28037
(800) 544-8665

Cutting off the lip releases windshield from its frame. When pressure is applied to push glass out, there is less chance of breaking it. Photo by Michael Lutfy.

Wind wings usually come out as a unit and are held in by small screws. Check gears and replace them if broken, then clean and grease them.

Removal—Get a friend to push gently from the outside while you pry the rubber from the inside with a putty knife. Be prepared to catch the glass when it pops free, and be careful not to allow it to fall down and scratch the dash. Don't be tempted to prove your manhood by working without gloves and goggles. Fifty-year-old glass can shatter unexpectedly and expose sharp edges.

If your car is a later model with a pop-out safety windshield, cut away the gasket around the outside. Carefully pry any decorative metal trim out of the seal and store it out of harm's way, then cover the hood with several thick blankets. Now get a couple of friends to stand outside and catch the windshield while

you push from the inside. Put on your high-top work boots and heavy Levi's before getting into the car. Now slide the seat all the way back and gently push the windshield out with your feet. This is the method I prefer, however, you can push with your hands as shown below.

Rear Windows

The same instructions apply to back glass as for windshields. Once again, if the glass is curved, make sure you can get a replacement before removing your old window.

Roll-Ups

The side windows on most cars are a little more complex than stationary windows, but they yield to a systematic approach of removal.

Remove the Reveals—Carefully unscrew the garnish moldings or reveals around the side windows. Don't lose any of those chrome screws or little eyelets. It's not easy to find correct replacements. Put them in baggies and store them with the moldings in a safe place.

Whisker Moldings—The whisker moldings in which your side windows glide up and down are usually held in by tiny screws or rivets. Begin by unscrewing or drilling out the fasteners holding the top molding in place. Also remove the fasteners holding the upper part of the side whisker moldings in.

Pull the upper whisker moldings out toward the inside of the car. Now roll the window up all the way into the moldings so the sash and regulator lever are above the level of the door. With your grease pencil, note on the inside of the window which way is forward, which way the sash channel faces and its position on the glass.

When removing windshield, push gently and evenly at the top center of the glass.

ORDERING NEW GLASS

T ry to find a source of auto glass that has been in business awhile and has an employee that understands old cars. If there isn't one near you, check hobby publications for sources. If your car has only flat glass, take your windows into a glass shop to be copied.

Tell the glass shop to cut your new windshield and back windows about 1/16" smaller than the originals all the way around, because replacement rubber tends to be thicker than original. Side windows should be cut same size and the edges carefully dressed.

Be sure to tell the glass shop you don't want any "bugs" in your replacement glass. A bug is the glass manufacturer's logo which has been sandblasted into each large piece of new glass. Modern "bugs" don't look like old car originals, and if the glass cutter isn't careful, you could wind up with a modern bug upside down in the middle of your windshield. I've had it happen.

Some glass shops can sandblast original style bugs into your newly cut windows in the right places if you want them. If you're lucky enough to find such a shop, have them do it. It could mean more points at your next show.

Glass in wind wings comes out of its channel easily if you soak assembly in gasoline. Rubber gasket should come out of frame easily. If it doesn't, heat frame with a propane torch.

Detach the button on the regulator arm, then slip the window up and out of the cat whisker moldings. Roll the regulator back down. Be careful while you're working not to get any of the grease that is likely to be on the regulator and sash on your upholstery.

Separate Glass From Sash— Sometimes you can carefully pry sashes away from the glass by slipping a narrow screwdriver in between them and gently prying. But most likely, you'll need to soak the assembly in gasoline to partially dissolve the seal holding them together. Let it soak at least half an hour before trying to pull them loose. But be careful not to wash off your notations as to sash location and direction. Work outside, don't smoke, and keep a fire extinguisher handy.

If you intend to replace your car's whisker moldings, remove the old ones now. Don't forget the ones that fit at the bottom of the window frame on either side of the glass.

VENT & QUARTER WINDOWS

Getting wind wings out takes a little

effort and care, but they aren't as tough as they look.

Remove Panel—You will probably have to remove the inner upholstery panel in order to get to the vent window assembly. Pry the fasteners loose with a special tool for the purpose, available from The Eastwood Company, or use a stiff putty knife and work very carefully.

Unscrew the Assembly—The vent

window and its frame come out as an assembly and are held in by tiny screws. Remove the window, then put the screws back in their holes so you won't misplace them.

Remove Glass—Take out the screws holding the window pivots to the frame. Soak the window assembly in gasoline to separate the glass from its chrome surround.

Door latches and window regulators should be removed, cleaned, repainted and lubricated with a little grease.

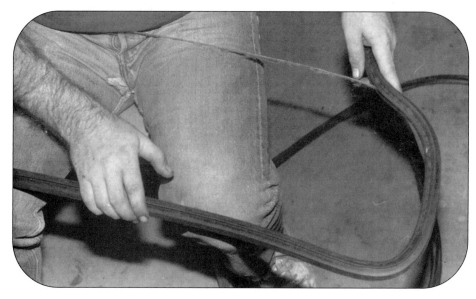

Put a little silicone sealer in the groove, then press the windshield gasket into place. Cut it about 1/8 inch long to allow for shrinkage and to make a tight fit in the car.

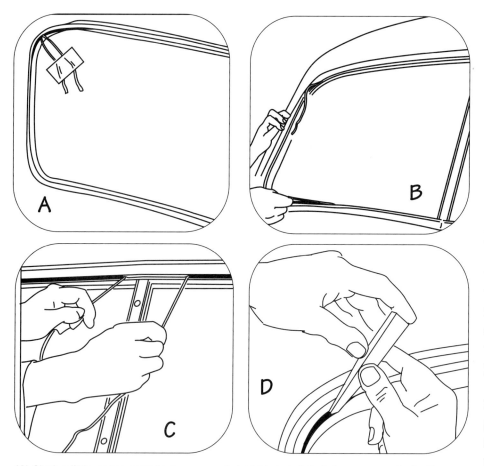

(A) Slosh a little soapy water in groove on windshield gasket that goes over car body, then wrap a strong piece of string in groove and tape ends to glass temporarily. (B) Have a friend press the windshield into the opening from inside the car, then slowly pull string so gasket lip slips out over sheet metal at bottom. (C) As helper presses glass into place, slowly keep pulling the ends of the string until you wind up at the top of the windshield in its center. (D) If there are any places where the lip of the gasket didn't quite pop into place, use a tongue depressor, popsicle stick, or piece of wood to work the gasket out over surrounding sheet metal.

Old rubber that is stuck in the frame that holds the wind wing can be removed by heating the frame with a propane torch to soften the rubber, then pulling it out.

INSTALLATION

This is the fun part. All you need to remember is work slowly and carefully and don't force anything. Use carpet remnants on your work surfaces to prevent your new glass from getting scratched or chipped.

While you have the upholstery panels off, remove the side window regulators, clean them, and put fresh grease on them. If they are rusty, strip them clean of corrosion and give them a coat of rust inhibitor paint before lubricating them. If you're doing a four-door sedan, don't get the regulator mechanisms mixed up. Clean and lube the wind wing gears too. Then reinstall everything. Evenly tighten the screws holding the mechanisms in.

Windshields

Measure carefully, then with a grease pencil, mark the center of the top of your new windshield. Now cut one end square on the rubber seal that is to go around it. Press the rubber seal in place on the glass starting at your center mark. Work your way around the glass until you arrive at the top center again, then cut the excess rubber off squarely, leaving about 1/8" excess so the joint at the top of your windshield will be tight and flush when your windshield is in place.

Next, pull the seal off and squirt a thin bead of 3M Weatherstrip Cement in the groove that the windshield rides in. Then reinstall it on the windshield, pressing it in place firmly as you go.

Installing—Wrap strong twine in the groove of the lip that fits over the body of the car so the ends of the twine cross at the bottom of the windshield with a foot or two of excess. Now mix up a small batch of soapy water and slosh it in the groove with the string.

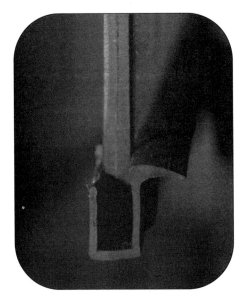

If your side windows use rubber gaskets in their sashes, put a thin bead of silicone sealer in the gasket channel before pressing it onto the glass.

Make sure sashes on side windows are put on new glass in the same position as they were on the old glass and facing the correct direction. Don't mix them up on four-door sedans.

The next step takes two people. Have your friend or spouse get in the car and set the lower lip of the windshield gasket on the frame, then press the windshield gently into place. From the outside, slowly pull the string toward the front of the car so the gasket lip slips out onto the outside of the body of the car. If the gasket doesn't pop into place all around, use a tongue depressor or popsicle stick to coax it into place. Don't use a screwdriver for this task; its sharp edges will scrape the paint.

If your car has a two-piece windshield, put one side in first, then the center rubber, then the other side. Keep your hood and dash covered and protected while you work.

Reinstall Reveal Molding—On most older cars, the *reveals,* or *garnish moldings,* help hold the windshield in. To reinstall them, press them into place, then screw them down loosely. Be careful not to scratch them with your screwdriver. Now tighten them down evenly a turn or two at a time until they're snug—but don't over-tighten them because doing so can cause stress in the windshield. The result of over-tightening will be a crack the first time you hit a good bump with the car.

Rear Windows

Rear windows go in just as windshields. The same instructions apply. Windshields and back windows on later cars are installed from the outside, but the techniques outlined above will work.

Roll-Up Windows

It is important to get the sashes and winding mechanisms installed correctly and aligned properly. A little patience is required, but there is nothing mysterious about installing side windows.

Sashes—Clean, then paint the sashes with rust inhibitor enamel. Carefully note the location of each sash on your new glass. Curl the black filler strip and press it into the sash. Be sure to use the correct thickness for your car. It comes in 1/32" and 1/16" thicknesses.

Some cars use a sweeper-type rubber seal between the metal sash and the glass. If your car is made that way, install the seal on the glass using 3M Weatherstrip cement, then coat the groove in the seal with the same cement and slide the glass in place. Leave the sweeper gasket a

Leave gaskets a little long, then cut them to fit at time of installation. Fit the gaskets carefully, as they will be all that stands between rain and your newly upholstered door panels.

Measure your old whisker channels, then cut new ones to fit using tin snips. File the ends to smooth them.

Grease sashes and window regulators before coupling them together. For easy access, roll regulator up as high as it will go.

Put whisker channels loosely into place in door, then pull them toward inside of door. Now make sure it is facing the right way, then slip side window into place and attach its sash to the regulator. Roll the window all the way down and finish installing upper channels.

little long at each end so when you install the window in the car, you can cut it to run tightly against the cat whisker channels in order to keep water out.

Install Side Whisker Channels— New whisker channels are glued, then screwed, in place. Measure the slot in the door where the two vertical channels go, then cut new whisker channels to fit in place tightly top to bottom. It's a good idea to miter the tops of the side whisker channels as well as the top piece, so the top channel is held in place at the corners.

Put a little 3M Weatherstrip Cement on the lower halves of the side whisker channels, then slip them in place in the door. Drill new holes in the channels and frames, then screw the lower channels in place with small flat-head screws. Make sure they tighten flush with the inner surface of the channel so they won't chip your new windows.

If your car requires whisker moldings on each side of the glass at the bottom of the window, snap and glue them in place in holes provided at this point.

Slide in Windows— Roll the window regulator up all the way until its lever is up past the window frame. Gently pull the whisker moldings out of their slots from the inside. Make sure the sash regulator slot is facing the right direction, then slip your new glass and sash assembly in place and connect it to the regulator button. Roll the window all the way down into the door.

If your car has a rubber gasket on the sashes, cut them to fit tightly against the whisker channels before installing the glass.

Install Upper Whisker Molding— Glue and screw the upper whisker channels in place, then do the same for the top channel. Now roll your window up to see how it glides in its channel. If it binds at any point, loosen the regulator mechanism and reposition it until things work smoothly.

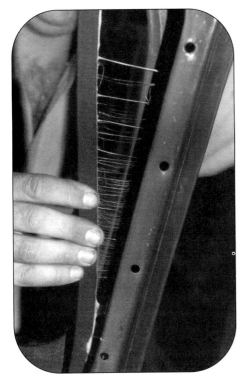

Glue whisker moldings in place using 3M Weatherstrip cement. Do upper part, then roll windows up and do lower part. Follow instructions on cement tube for best results.

Wind Wings & Vent Windows

Coat the inside of the chrome frame of the vent window with a little mineral oil. Now form the black filler strip into a U shape and push it into the frame. Depending on the shape of your window, you may need to cut some V-shaped slots in the sides of the filler strip in order to relieve it around tight inside curves.

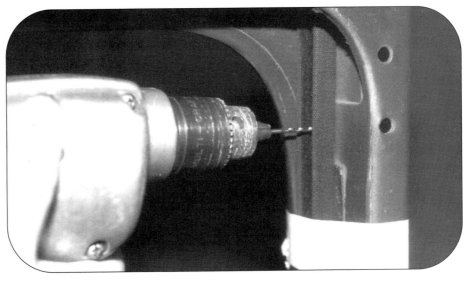

Drill new holes, then install small flat-head screws to help hold moldings in place. Use masking tape to keep molding from creeping while drilling. Make sure screws are tightened down flush so they won't chip glass.

Slip in Glass—Coat the inner surface of the filler strip with more mineral oil, then slide the glass in place. It should go with only a little pressure if you've used the correct thickness of filler strip.

Install Rubber Gasket—Shoot a little silicone sealer on the underside of the rubber gasket that fits in the door and push it into place. Masking tape can be used to hold it in position until the sealer sets up.

Reinstall Vent Windows & Regulators—Slip the window in place in the door frame, then install the winding mechanism, if your car is so equipped. You may have to move the mechanism around on its screws to get the window to work properly, but a little patience will pay off in this area. When you're finished, pop the upholstery panels back in place and reinstall the various handles.

Even though your windshield and rear window are set into a rubber gasket that overlaps the body of the car, they are still not watertight. Shoot a thin bead of automotive silicone sealer under all of the rubber gaskets around your windows to take care of this problem. Be careful not to get any of the sealant on the exposed paintwork of your car, as it may damage it. ■

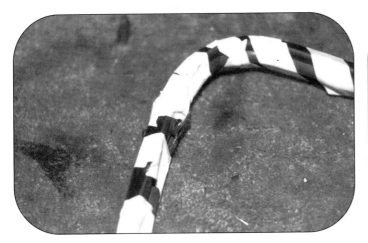

Put a little silicone sealer in quarter-window frames then press rubber gaskets into place. Use masking tape to hold them tightly in place until sealer has cured.

When you install window garnish moldings, use a paper punch to make holes in masking tape, then place tape around holes to prevent screwdriver nicks. Tighten moldings evenly in place, but don't over-tighten them.

CHROME TRIM

14

As I mentioned previously, paint and chrome are the two things that combine to create the first—and most powerful—impression of your show car. Many home restorers have done first-rate paint jobs. Unfortunately, only those who own (or have the use of) a chrome shop are able to do their own plating. But even when you turn your parts over to a professional plater, you can make a big difference in how your job turns out. Here are a few tips from experienced restorers who, for the most part, also send their work out.

DISASSEMBLY & CLEANING

If you removed the brightwork to paint your car, you only need to prepare it for the plater. But if you aren't going to paint your car and just want to do the chrome, soak all of the screws and bolts with penetrating oil before trying to remove them. Tap on stuck bolts with a small ballpeen hammer to loosen them, but don't tap on surfaces that show. Don't force anything. Trim items are often very hard to find.

Disassemble Completely—Any chrome items that are riveted or screwed together, such as 1930s headlight buckets will need to be taken apart. Otherwise a condition called *nickel shadow* will likely appear around joints. Nickel shadow is a yellowish area that does not have any chrome adhering to it. It may not be too evident when first polished, but it will soon tarnish and stand out badly.

Inspect—Try cleaning your trim pieces to see how bad the plating really is. Often, chrome just needs a good polishing. What looks like pitting is really only dirt. Chrome is expensive

Chrome like this is no accident. It takes careful preparation on the part of the restorer and a lot of experience on the part of the plater, but it pays off on the judging field at shows.

Fifties car designers were obsessed with chrome. The more the better, seemed to be the guiding rule of the day. All chrome must be removed before it can be plated, and pieces that are riveted or screwed together must be disassembled. Otherwise, chrome won't adhere to the nooks and crannies, resulting in nickel shadow.

and the buffing that must be done to produce a good job wears items down. Don't replate unless you need to. Are any of the parts from your car made of cast pot metal? If so, you will need to select your plater with care. Are any items badly pitted, rusted, or broken? If

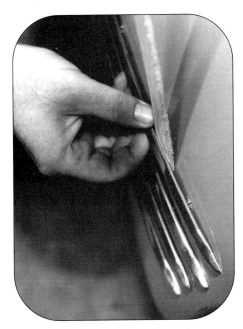

If chrome is held on by clips, it can be carefully popped off using a wedge-shaped piece of wood. Don't use a screwdriver. You'll scratch your paint if you do. If you can get behind the chrome, squeeze ends of clips together with pliers to help the process.

so, replace them if possible. Chrome is very thin. Pits always show when re-plated. And rusted pieces can sometimes get so thin that they disintegrate when the plater tries to work with them.

Wrap & Strap—Wrap screw or bolt threads with masking or electrical tape so the threads won't get plated too. Plated threads will be thicker, so nuts will not go back on. And because chrome is so hard, it is difficult to chase plated threads with a die.

Tape long, thin strips of trim to a 1" x 3" piece of wood in the appropriate length, so they won't get bent in handling, and so the person running the buffing wheel will have something to help brace the part. Overzealous buffing without backing can warp and even crumple fragile items.

CHOOSING A PLATER

Try to find a plater that does old cars as a specialty, or at least has experience with vintage trim. Go to a local car show and ask people whose car's chrome looks good where they got the work done. A production shop will give you a

reasonably good job if your parts are pristine to begin with, but if you need any special work done on them, they will likely be at a loss as to how to do it correctly. Raised lettering and ornamental grooves can be obliterated by careless buffing. And pot metal will be eaten up and virtually dissolved by conventional plating methods. Only an experienced specialist who understands pot metal alloys can be trusted with these precious pieces.

Don't be afraid to send your parts to a good shop in another part of the country, if necessary. Check them out carefully first though. And work out the terms and delivery date for the finished job before you send your parts. Also, take photos and list every item. Send a copy of the list with your order, and keep one for your files.

Don't be tempted to choose a plater solely on price. Good plating is expensive but worth the investment. As of this writing, it can cost in the

When you pick up your chrome work from the plater, look it over for nickel shadow. It will show up as subtle yellowish patches. If you suspect nickel shadow, breathe on the discolored spot. Moisture will condense on nickel and make it more evident. If you don't send such work back to the plater, it will tarnish and look like this. Note dull patches on steering wheel hub.

neighborhood of $1,100 to $2,000 to have the chrome work done on a typical car from the forties or fifties. You might get lucky and find someone who will do the job for less, but make sure you know what quality of work you'll be getting before you trust your irreplaceable items to him.

Check Your Order—Chances are, the chrome shop will return your parts wrapped in plastic or newspaper. Unwrap them and inspect them before taking delivery. Make sure there are no scratches, grooves or buffed-off details. And make sure any repairs were done correctly. Also check for nickel shadow. If you think you see a golden tint on any of your chrome, exhale slowly on the area. The moisture from your breath will make the nickel shadow stand out. If you detect any, have the shop re-plate the part.

Finally, get out your list and make sure you are getting all of your parts back. Also make sure nothing is broken. Reputable platers are usually extremely careful to keep track of your work and to handle it with care, but accidents can happen.

Replacement & Repair

Sometimes, on deeply pitted pot metal parts, you can have the plating shop strip off the old chrome, buff out the small imperfections, then copper plate the part. At that stage you take the part home and fill the pits with silver solder, then file them smooth. If you decide to try this, make sure you use only solder recommended by your plater.

Cast New Pieces—Some trim items are not repairable, but nearly impossible to replace. If yours are like this, don't despair. It is possible to cast new ones using the old part as a mold. Have any new parts cast in brass. It is easy to clean up and it takes chrome well. Call foundries in your area and tell them what you need.

It might pay to have several parts cast

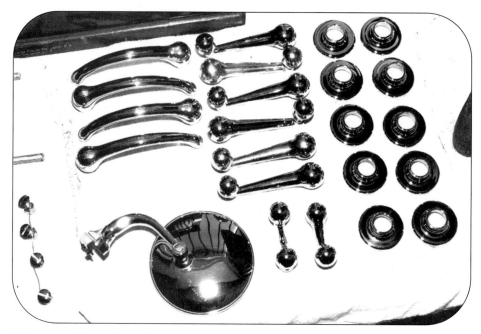

Before accepting work from the plater, take careful inventory to make sure you have gotten back everything you sent.

from the mold the founder will need to make. You might even be able to offset your costs by selling your extras to other hobbyists who own your same make and model of car. Some hobbyists have even made a retirement business of replacement castings.

Installation

Use masking tape to protect painted surfaces that might get chipped or scratched. Wax painted surfaces that will have chrome against them, and paint your chrome pieces in the areas that mate against the car and will not show. Make sure all parts are on straight and level and meet up with each other properly before

tightening fasteners. Don't tighten nuts down so tight that you crack the paint under trim items. Use new lock washers and just snug things up, rather than torquing them down.

Waxing—Chrome deteriorates very quickly if it is not kept protected, especially if you live near the sea or in a damp climate. The best defense against corrosion is a thick coat of wax. Never use bathroom cleanser or abrasives to clean chrome, and don't use wax that has abrasive cleaners in it. Some classic car collectors rub a thick coat of wax on their trim pieces prior to long-term storage and don't wipe it off until they are ready to drive the car again. ■

Be careful when installing chrome as well. You don't want to create any paint chips. Clean and wax the paint underneath before installing the pieces. Make sure all pieces are straight and level, then be careful not to overtighten the fasteners. Doing so could crack the paint around the hole. Photo by Michael Lutfy.

UPHOLSTERY

15

Automobile interiors have changed dramatically over the years. Upholstery has gone from utilitarian leather in the early days when cars were steered with tillers; to mohair, brocades, and broadcloth in the '30s and '40s when cars were dignified; to naugahyde and other synthetics in the '50s and '60s when plastics were in. Leather, which was used originally because of its durability, has now become a luxury item. The ways these materials were installed varied with the era too. But no matter which period your car came from, there is no magic to doing its interior. Here are some tips.

UPHOLSTERY TIPS

Upholstering a car is no more difficult than any other part of a restoration; it's just that most guys are unfamiliar with the process. An upholstery class at the local junior college is the best way to pick up the necessary skills, especially if you are working on a car made during the period from the '20s through the '50s. Seats in such cars had a lot in common with your living room couch. They had tied springs and stuffed cushions, and were sewn together in the same way as furniture. And the fabrics they used back

Your classic's interior must be in top shape if it is to score big in a concours show. All areas, from seat covers, carpets and kick panels, to headliners, chrome bezels and door handles, can be restored to better than new condition with careful planning and basic skills. Some of the work, such as making custom seat covers, may be better left to a professional unless you have an industrial sewing machine and know how to use it. Photo by Michael Lutfy.

Removing your car's door panels can be tricky. There are special tools made for the purpose available from The Eastwood Company catalog and I highly recommend them. If you can't wait, you can sometimes pop panels loose using a curved putty knife, but you must work carefully.

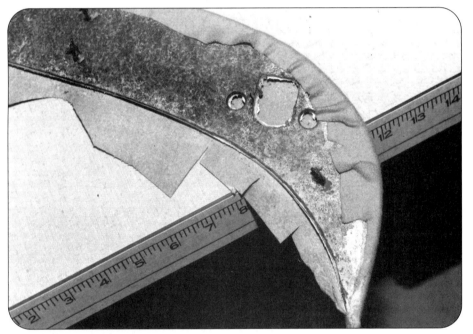

New fiberboard panels should be cut to replace old warped ones. Fastener snaps are put in place next. Fabric is then cut to shape slightly larger than fiberboard panel and glued in place. Holes are cut last.

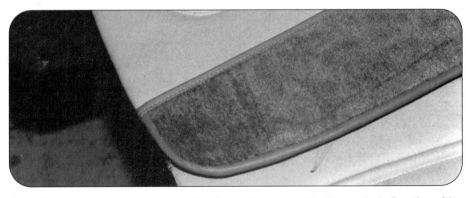

Carpeting covers lower door panel and is edged with matching leather or vinyl. Practice with scraps until you can sew straight seams.

then were not much different than household interior materials today.

Research—How many times at a car show have you been lured over to a beautiful classic car only to discover that it has an interior that looks like it was made from the stage curtains of a condemned adult theater? Unfortunately, it's a common experience. But the saddest part is, the installation is often done very well. It's just that the choices of colors and materials are ghastly. But let's not be too hard on such a car's owner. His is an easy mistake to make.

Automotive manufacturers have entire departments of professional designers trained to do nothing but interiors. That's because, except for the paint scheme, it's the most important part of a car's appearance, and one of the easiest areas in which to blow it. How do you avoid the problem? The obvious answer is to replicate exactly what the car's designers did originally. For each color, or combination of colors of paint, an interior was carefully chosen. Your chances of being able to improve on the designer's choices are slim. Besides, if you show your car, you can bet there will be at least one judge that remembers exactly what its upholstery was supposed to be. And, he'll deduct a lot of points if it isn't correct.

So do your homework. Try to find sales brochures, specification books, or old photographs that show your car's interior. Join a club for your make and attend their meets. Try to find an original example of your car, and take pictures of it. Inquire about sources of correct fabrics, and whether kits are available to do your car. Take special notice of details, such as *windlace* (the rolled piping that goes around the doors to keep drafts out), as well as edging, types of stitching, and grain pattern if your interior is leather or vinyl.

Check Underneath—Often, when a car is reupholstered, they put the new interior right over the old. Pull a door panel out of your car and check to see if

Fabric is folded over and cut out to relieve fasteners. Glue it in place, stretching it evenly as you do.

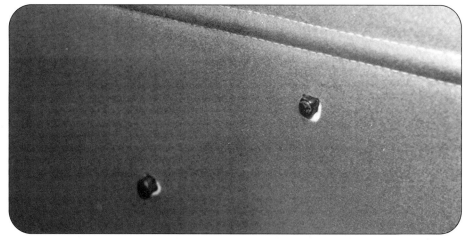

Door handle splines are cut out with a sharp, single-edged razor blade after panel is fitted.

the original material is still under the replacement fabric. If that is the case, you can carefully remove the later, incorrect material, and use the original cloth underneath as a color and pattern

Headliner is made using old one as a pattern if possible. In this mid '30s car, the top bows and sills were made of wood so headliner is merely tacked or stapled in place.

sample. You may also find remnants of your car's first interior stapled to the undersides of seats and kick panels.

Order Swatches—There are a number of suppliers of classic car upholstery materials that advertise in hobby publications. One with a good reputation is: LeBaron Bonney Co., 6 Chestnut St., Amesbury, MA 01913. (508) 388-3811. Other good suppliers are: Bill Hirsch (800/828-2061) and Kantor Auto Products (800/526-1096) both in New Jersey. Any of the these sources will send you swatches of the original types of fabrics they offer for sale. They will also send pieces of windlace and trim as well. Ask them for samples in the colors and patterns available for your car. Be sure to tell them your year, make and model, and whether your car had deluxe or standard trim.

When you receive your swatches, check them carefully against your reference material, then, outdoors on a clear or hazy day around noon, check the colors against the colors on your car to see if they look right together. The reason for doing this check at midday is because sunlight is neutral in color at that time. It is very red early or late in the day, and it will affect how you see colors at those times. Don't compare colors indoors either. Artificial lighting can throw off your perception completely.

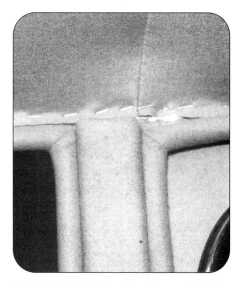

Windlace is carefully mitered to create right angles around doors.

New scuff plates are a perfect final touch to a good interior job. Check hobby and club publications for people who make them. They are available for all but the rarest classics.

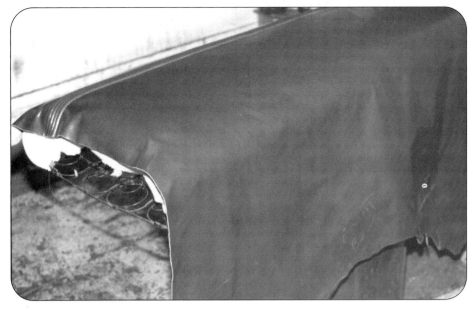

Leather interiors are the most difficult and demanding to do. Here, hide is placed so any scars or blemishes are cut away. Sewing on leather requires great care. If you make a mistake you will ruin the hide. That's because your stitches will leave holes when you try to pull them out.

It takes skill to stretch leather over compound curves without wrinkles and puckers. Make sure surface underneath is smooth and clean.

Order a Kit–If you are restoring a Mustang, a Model A, or an early to mid-sixties Impala, everything you require can be ordered already made up, ready to install. All you need is a utility knife, a heavy-duty staple gun and a good eye. LeBaron Bonney has kits for early Fords. For Mustangs or Chevys, try Texas Mustang Parts (Rte. 6, P.O. Box 966A, Waco, TX 76706. 800/527-1588) or Chevy Interiors (888 Ranchero, Ste. A, San Marcos, CA 92069. 800/451-1955).

Start From Scratch—If you don't want to purchase a kit (or if one is unavailable) you can do an interior from scratch; however, doing so requires a lot of skill, knowledge and an investment in some special tools and equipment. If you really want to attempt it, take a course in upholstery at your local trade school before trying. If there are no such classes in your area, you can work from a book, such as the *Automotive Upholstery Handbook* (available from FisherBooks, 4239 W. Ina Rd. #101, Tucson, AZ. 602/744-6110), but you will need to practice with scraps before you start cutting up expensive fabric.

Tools — Your wife's Singer sewing machine won't work. If you're doing car interiors from scratch, you need a heavy-duty industrial sewing machine with a running foot. They are expensive, but sometimes you can pick one up used. You will also need a large cutting table, a long steel straight-edge, some heavy-duty scissors, and a tack hammer.

Practice — Before you attempt anything with your expensive, original material, practice with cheap fabric of about the same weight until you can sew straight seams without any puckering. Also practice making piping and other trim. Because cars have had so many types of interiors installed in so many different ways over the years, it is impossible in one chapter to cover all you need to know for any particular car, so look for a book that explains how interiors were installed on cars like yours. Sometimes extended shop manuals will tell you quite a bit. Often you can find books in the public library that cover the subject. Don't forget to check used book stores too.

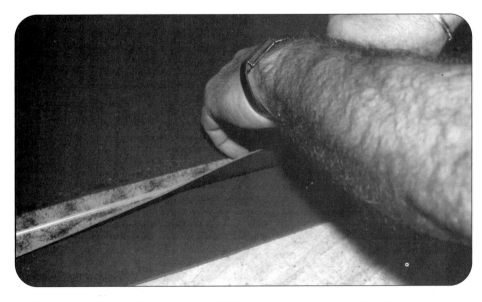

Leather is skived (scraped) down to make it thin enough to go around nylon piping.

On back side of rounded panels leather must be relieved with small triangular cut to prevent wrinkles.

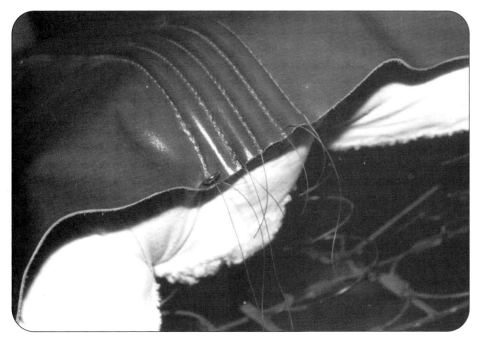

Thread used on leather must be dyed to match hides. Frequent test fitting is the key to preventing mistakes.

Selecting a Shop—If you decide you don't want to try doing your car's interior yourself, there are some things you can do to help make the job turn out right. First, check around with fellow classic car owners to see who does good work in your area. If you don't turn up any leads that way, at least try to determine whether a prospective upholsterer has experience working on old cars. Also, browse around his shop and see what kind of work he does. Finally, order the fabric yourself, or make sure that what the upholsterer orders is correct for your car. You are the one who loses if he gets it wrong. Don't forget to give the upholsterer your reference material so he can see how the car is supposed to be. The difference between first and second place is often in details such as this. ■

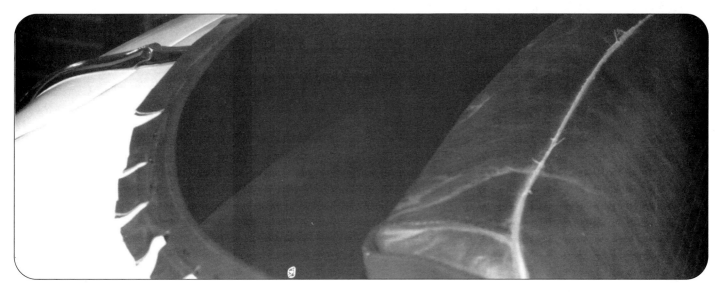

Careful sanding of ash backing was necessary before gluing rubber to it in top boot of author's '38 Packard.

The plastic used to make the steering wheels on many classic cars didn't stand the test of time. Sunlight and summer heat caused it to shrink, crack and fade. While there are services that can recast vintage wheels with excellent results, the process is expensive and the colors seldom match your original. However, you can restore your wheel to its original color and luster inexpensively and easily at home.

Remove the Wheel—Start by disconnecting the horn wire down at the base of the steering column in the engine compartment. Next, depress and turn the horn button so it pops out of the wheel. Put the horn button, spring and any washers or other parts into a baggie for safekeeping.

You will need a steering wheel puller to get the wheel off. They can be rented or purchased at tool stores. Find which bolts in the puller kit thread into your wheel, slip the yoke onto them, and locate the center bolt in the steering shaft hole. Now tighten the center bolt slowly until the wheel comes loose. But be careful. Steering wheels can pop off suddenly with a lot of force.

If your steering wheel has a horn ring, tape it to a piece of plywood to keep it from being bent or damaged until it is time to reinstall it.

Re-Chrome & Polish—If there is any re-chroming or stainless steel polishing to be done on your wheel, now is the time to do it. Some wheels have chrome hubs. They can be re-chromed without removing the outer grip plastic if the plastic is properly taped to protect it. Wrap your wheel tightly with masking

This steering wheel was done six years ago using the method outlined in this chapter and still looks new. Anyone can restore a steering wheel using this technique.

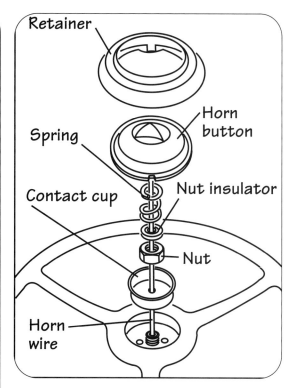

Disconnect horn wire at base of steering box under the hood. Attach a string to it so you can pull the wire and button out of the car, then pull it back down through the tube when you are finished. Horn button usually comes off by depressing it, then turning it 1/4 turn. Tape parts together and store them so they won't get lost.

tape, then have the chrome shop wrap it again with the yellow plastic tape they use to protect threaded surfaces. Buff any stainless trim with jeweler's rouge and a buffing wheel, or have it buffed at the chrome shop.

Open the Cracks—When you get your wheel back from the chrome shop, unwrap the plastic, then tightly wrap the chrome and stainless parts with a couple of layers of masking tape to protect them. Wash the wheel with dish detergent and water, then wipe it down with Dupont's Prepsol (available at automotive paint stores) or any other professional quality degreasing product. Next, file or grind open the cracks in the plastic to a wide bevel so the filler will have a good base. A Dremel motor tool is ideal for this purpose, or you can use small hand files.

Fill 'Em Up—Some guys use two-stage epoxy for this job, but good old Bondo is all you need to fill the cracks in your wheel. The wheels you see in the accompanying photos were done five to seven years ago and have held up beautifully.

Begin by mixing only enough filler to fix a couple of cracks. That's all you'll have time to deal with before the stuff starts to set up. Follow the manufacturer's instructions carefully. Overfill the cracks so you'll have enough to sand down to the shape of the wheel. Use lacquer thinner to clean your tools.

When the Bondo sets to the consistency

of cheese, sand it roughly to shape with #60-grit paper. But don't wait too long; the filler will set harder than the surrounding plastic and make shaping it difficult. Next, sand with #360-grit paper to do the final shaping. Keep working until you've filled all the cracks. Finally, look your wheel over carefully for bumps or imperfections and fix any you find.

Color Matching—Take a knob, or other dash part that is the correct color for your car, to an automotive paint store and have them mix paint to match it. I prefer acrylic lacquer because it is easy to use, but enamel works just as well. If you'd like to try lacquer, put a drop of lacquer thinner on the plastic part of your steering wheel to see if it affects it. If the plastic doesn't soften or craze, lacquer will work fine. Otherwise, buy enamel paint.

While you're at the paint store, pick up some primer, a little clear lacquer or enamel, some anti-fisheye solution and some flexing agent. Make sure all of these items are from the same paint system and are compatible with each other.

Prime It—Wipe your wheel down with Prepsol again, then shoot it with a couple of coats of primer. Let the primer dry thoroughly, then sand it carefully with

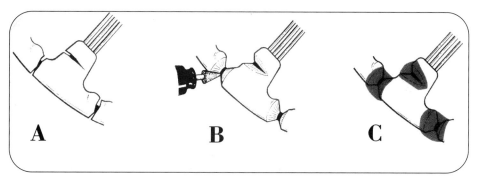

(A) Cracks like these are common in early plastic steering wheels. The sun and heat caused shrinking and cracking. Most such wheels can be restored inexpensively without recasting them. (B) A Dremel tool or small files can be used to hog out cracks to accept plastic filler. (C) Mix up only enough filler to fill a couple of cracks at a time. Overfill cracks, then sand them to shape using #60-grit coarse sandpaper when they harden to the consistency of hard cheese. Finish with #360-grit sandpaper. Use lacquer thinner to clean tools.

A steering wheel puller is necessary to detach the wheel from the column. Tighten bolts into holes in wheel, then slowly tighten center bolt. But be prepared. Steering wheels can come off with a lot of force.

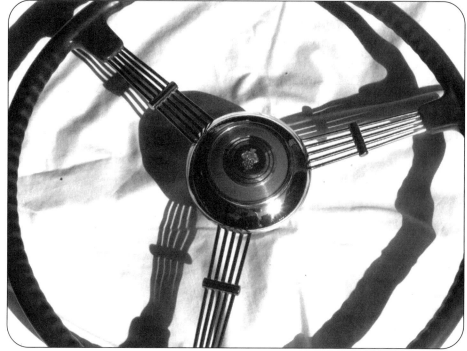

If there is any chrome work or stainless steel polishing to be done, do it first. Wrap plastic areas with masking tape, then plastic electrical tape to prevent damage during plating process.

#360-grit dry paper. Don't use any water; body filler is not waterproof. If you break through the primer while sanding, shoot on a couple more coats and sand lightly again.

Paint It—When your wheel is just the way you want it, and the primer has dried for a couple of days, you're ready to paint. Mix the paint by the manufacturer's directions, add a little flexing agent and a drop of anti-fisheye solution, then shoot on three good coats if you're using lacquer. Allow 20 minutes between coats so your sanding scratches won't swell and show. Let it dry at least overnight, then sand lightly with #400-grit sandpaper and water to remove any orange peel or runs.

Next, if you're going with lacquer, mix a final batch of paint using about 25% clear and spray on three more coats. Now sand your wheel lightly with the #1000-grit paper and water.

If you're shooting enamel, mist on a tack coat, give it a couple of minutes to get sticky, then shoot on a good wet finishing coat. Don't try to sand it afterwards the way you would with lacquer.

Finally, let your wheel cure for a few days, then reinstall it. If you painted it with enamel, let it cure for six weeks, then color-sand it with #1000-grit paper and water. Whether you used lacquer or enamel, don't wax your newly restored wheel for a few weeks until the paint has had a chance to cure. Then, apply a good-quality wax and buff to a high gloss.■

This restored dash needed a restored steering wheel to complement it. Wheel was filled, then painted with acrylic lacquer. A little clear lacquer was added to final coat to get the correct translucent look.

RESTORING RADIOS

17

Radios have been available for cars since the early 1930s. And chances are, unless your car is a real antique, a radio was made to fit it. Some of the early radios were add-ons, with a tuning head attached to the steering column, a box mounted on the firewall, and a speaker mounted separately—sometimes in the roof above the windshield. Runningboards were insulated and used as antennas as was the chicken wire in the top insert on some cars. When manufacturers went to all steel bodies in the late '30s, cowl-mounted whip antennas were developed. In the '60s, FM and stereo became available, and radios went solid state. So for the last 60 years, drivers have not had to suffer in silence.

Neither should you. The old-style, tube-type radios that most collector cars came with are fairly easy to repair and restore, and the sound quality of many of them is surprisingly good. So if your old car's radio hums, but doesn't sing, why not fix it and amplify your touring pleasure?

RECONDITIONING

Clean It—Find a small, soft paint brush and hook up the slot-shaped crevice attachment to your vacuum cleaner. Next, remove the covers on your receiver, then use the brush to dislodge any dust or dirt that has accumulated on the radio's chassis and components. Vacuum up the loosened dust. Be careful not to bump and break fragile components. Pull each tube out, one at a time, and clean under it. Spray their prongs with contact cleaner (available from electronics stores such as Radio Shack), then slip them in and out of their socket several times to help clean the contacts inside.

Clean exposed points on switches with contact cleaner. Spray some in the tuning mechanism (called a variable condenser) and turn it back and forth to loosen corrosion. If your radio has a separate control head with flexible cables going to the receiver, clean the head, then shoot a little WD-40 down the cables to free them up.

Antique, tube-type radios are easier than you think to restore. You don't need to be an electronics expert to do it. Everything you need to fix one is still available.

THINGS YOU'LL NEED:

- Small, soft paint brush
- Vacuum cleaner with crevice attachment
- Contact cleaner
- Small soldering iron
- Solder (60% tin, 40% lead, rosin core)
- Desoldering braid
- Needle-nose pliers
- Pocket knife
- Wrinkle-finish paint

135

Power supply is in walled off section of chassis. It consists of buffer condenser on left, vibrator (metal canister) and rectifier tube on right. Modern, solid-state vibrators last much longer than originals. Make sure you order positive or negative ground to match your car's system.

Test the Tubes—Mark your tubes as to where they go with bits of tape or a china marker. Don't use a graphite pencil, because graphite conducts electricity. Call around to local TV repair and electronics stores to find one that has a tube tester. Take your tubes in and have them checked out. If any are bad, and if the TV repair shop can't furnish replacements, contact: Antique Electronic Supply, 688 W. First St., Tempe, AZ 85281. (602) 894-9503. They have everything you will need to restore your radio, and their prices are reasonable. Not only can they supply all the parts you might require, but they sell books, speakers, speaker cloth, tools and cleaners too. Send for their free catalog.

Wiring

The insulation on old wiring is often stiff and brittle, especially wiring made 40 or 50 years ago. Back then, wiring was insulated with rubber, wrapped with silk, then lacquered. Because these materials were so biodegradable, they didn't often hold up. Look your set over carefully for wires that are burned or scorched, or have crumbling insulation. Check for loose or corroded solder joints too.

Replacement—To replace a bad wire, heat the old solder in the joints with your soldering iron, then when it becomes molten, suck it up with desoldering braid. Be careful not to bump other components with your hot iron. Cut a new wire to the length of the old one. Use the same gauge (or slightly thicker) wire as the one you are replacing. Don't use wire that is finer than your old one because it will increase resistance and cause problems. Strip the ends of the wire with your pocket knife, then gently scrape the corrosion from the terminals that the wire attaches to until they are bright and clean.

To solder in the new wire, heat the metal contacts only enough to get the solder to flow, and use a pair of needle-nose pliers as a heat sink to prevent burning the insulation.

Upgrading Parts

Turn your receiver chassis over. You will see a number of small cylinders with

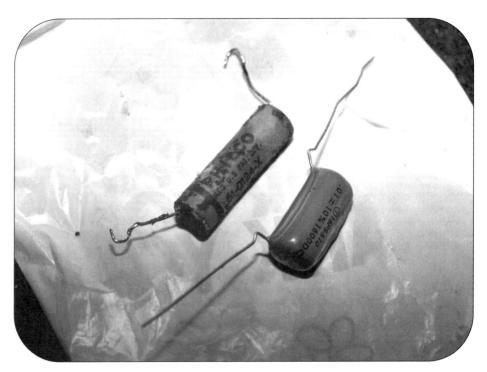

Condensers look like paper tubes with wax in them. Note specifications, then replace them with modern capacitors.

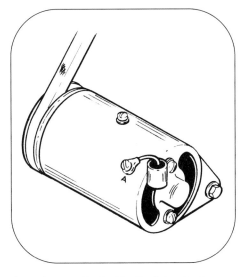

A condenser attached to the A terminal on your generator will help prevent static too, but make sure you don't put it on the wrong terminal. You could ruin the generator if you do.

writing on them and wires sticking out of each end. These are *condensers,* and they don't look like much more than paper tubes filled with wax. If you want dependable service out of your old set, you will need to replace them with the modern equivalent, called a *capacitor.* Capacitors are a major improvement on old-style condensers. Note the capacity and voltage of each condenser, then replace it with a capacitor of plus or minus 25% of the same capacity, and the same, or greater voltage. Capacitors can be purchased at most electronic supply stores.

Vibrator—The most common power-supply arrangement in tube-type radios is a vibrator used in conjunction with a rectifier tube and a buffer condenser. Old-style radio vibrators fail with regularity, as do the rectifier tubes, often marked OZ4G. Replace your radio's vibrator with a new, solid-state, equivalent. It will last many times longer than the original. Modern vibrators are polarity conscious, so make sure you order one that is correct for your car.

The vibrator, buffer condenser, and rectifier tube are often found in a walled-off section on your chassis. The vibrator is usually in a round metal canister, and most often has 4 prongs, but may have as many as 6. If you are uncertain as to which it is, look for a circuit diagram in the access pans of your radio. Also replace the buffer condenser and rectifier tube when you replace the vibrator.

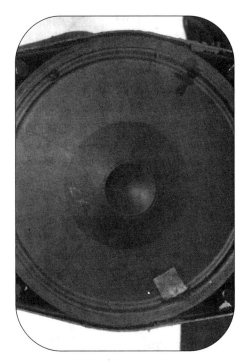

Speakers can be reconed if they are really deteriorated, but if they are only slightly torn, you can patch them with a little Duco cement and vellum paper.

Speakers—If your speaker's paper cone has deteriorated or is badly torn, you will need to get it reconed. Check hobby publications such as *Hemmings Motor News* for people who perform this service. If your speaker only has a couple of small tears, you can easily repair them with small pieces of vellum paper and Duco cement. Just put a drop of cement on a bit of vellum and gently press it into place over the tear.

If your speaker cloth is torn or missing, it's not a big problem; new speaker cloth is available from Antique Electronic Supply in the correct-looking brocades. But if your grille cloth is just a little faded, you can probably save it. Here's how. Remove it carefully from the speaker grille. Place it outside, face down on a piece of Stitch Witchery (a very thin adhesive patch available from sewing shops and dime stores), then on top of that, place a piece of fine, neutral-colored silk. Carefully iron this assemblage. You now have a strong piece of original fabric that you can put in your speaker grille, new side out.

The condensers are located underneath the chassis. Solder them in place carefully so you don't damage neighboring components.

137

Many antique radios are attached inside the car with special bolts. If you are installing a radio in a car that didn't have one originally, you can make attaching bolts by cutting down carriage bolts, then filing them smooth.

Painting

Many collector car radios were painted with wrinkle-finish enamel. Xenolite and Krylon both offer it, and you can order it from The Eastwood Company too. Before you can repaint your radio you will need to strip all of the old paint off. Use heavy-duty paint stripper such as described in Chapter 12, available at automotive paint stores. Don't get any stripper on plastic or rubber parts, as it will ruin them. Wipe the parts down with a rag, dampened with water and dish detergent, to neutralize the stripper and get any oil or grease off of them.

No primer is used with wrinkle-finish enamel. Shoot on the paint in even strokes from left to right, then from top to bottom, then diagonally, letting the paint get tacky between coats. Now place your parts near a heat lamp to accelerate the wrinkling of the paint.

Knobs

If you are unable to find replacement originals, you can make new knobs using a poured latex mold made from a good

knob. When you have a mold made, use casting resin (available from craft stores) to make new ones. Another way to make knobs is to turn new ones on a lathe using plastic stock. Of course, if your knobs are salvageable, it is much easier to fill any cracks with epoxy, then sand and paint them to match the rest of the dash plastic.

TESTING

You can bench-test your radio using a car battery. Make sure you have the polarity right when you hook up the wires. Many cars made from the early '50s on back were positive ground, unlike modern ones. Attach a multi-tester or ammeter in the hot wire from the battery to the radio. When you turn on the radio, it should draw between 6 and 8 amps if your car has a 6-volt system, and between 3 and 4 amps if it has a 12-volt system. If the meter goes up past 9 amps (5 amps on a 12-volt system) turn it off immediately. If you do not have an ammeter, you can hook an in-line fuse holder in the power line with a 9 amp fuse, in the case of a 6-volt system, or a 5- amp fuse in the case of a 12-volt system. If your radio blows the fuse,

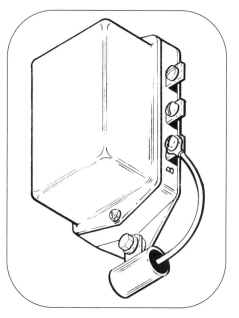

If your radio picks up a lot of motor static, try attaching an ordinary ignition condenser to the B terminal on the voltage regulator. Make sure your connections are clean and tight.

check the vibrator, buffer condenser and rectifier tube. Also check the condensers underneath if you decided not to replace them.

Troubleshooting

If the tuning dial doesn't light up, listen for the hum of the vibrator. If you installed a new solid-state type, its hum will be very faint. If the vibrator doesn't

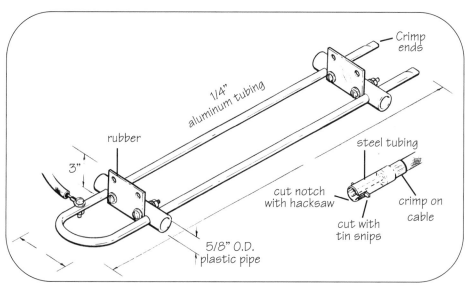

Many cars of the '30s used antennas that were suspended under the running boards. If your car needs one of these, or if you'd rather not spoil the lines of a later car by installing a whip antenna, you can make a hidden one yourself as shown here. The adaptor at the lower right of the drawing can be made to use a modern antenna with an old radio.

hum, the problem could be a blown fuse. Check for a poor connection from the radio to the ignition switch or ammeter too. And make sure the radio is grounded from the box to the firewall or dashboard metal. If none of the above are the problem, try replacing the vibrator.

Lights On/Sound Off—If the dial lights up and the vibrator hums, take the access pan off of the back of the radio and check the tubes. Grip each tube and move it around in its socket so it will make better contact. With the radio on, check each tube by tapping on it with a pencil eraser. If one howls, chatters or makes odd sounds, replace it. Also clean and check the clip-on connections that attach to some tubes.

If the tubes are all good, make sure your antenna is properly insulated where it attaches to the car, and check its connection at the receiver. Also check for a bad connection or a bad ground at the speaker.

Weak Reception—If you have poor overall reception, your antenna may need trimming (adjusting). On the side of most early receivers is an antenna adjustment screw. If you are near power lines, take your car away from them to make the adjustment. Tune your radio to a weak station around the 1400 mark on the dial. Now slowly turn the adjustment screw back and forth until the reception is optimal.

Interference—If there is static when the engine is running, install carbon-core ignition wires if your car has the copper-core types. If that doesn't help, try installing condensers on the voltage regulator, distributor, and generator. Use ordinary distributor condensers and attach one to the B terminal on the voltage regulator and one to the A terminal on the generator. You can also attach one to the hot lead on the coil. Screw them down with structural bolts or screws nearby. If none of the above works, try a ground strap from the muffler to the frame. ∎

Tap tubes with a pencil eraser. If you hear chattering, howling or other odd sounds, the tube is bad. Order new ones from Antique Electronic Supply in Tempe, Arizona.

Hole on left is antenna trimmer adjustment. Hole on right is where antenna attaches.

LICENSE PLATES

18

A clean, restored original license plate adds a final touch of authenticity to your classic. Photo by Michael Lutfy.

You can make your antique license plates look as good as if they were done by the pros at the state penitentiary. And, you won't have to deal with the boys in cell block number 9. Many states allow owners of antique and classic cars to register them with year of manufacture (Y.O.M.) plates. Period plates can add that final touch of authenticity to a restoration, and restoring them isn't difficult. A little paint and some sandpaper are all it takes.

RESTORING PLATES

Take your plates to an automotive paint store and match the colors using their paint chip books. The California plates shown in the following photographs have black letters and numbers on a taxicab yellow background (the photo at left is yellow letters on a black background). Both colors were easy to find. Your plate colors probably will be too. Buy lacquer paint for the numbers and enamel for the background. Also buy a little lacquer primer, lacquer thinner, enamel reducer and some sandpaper. You will need a sheet of #360-grit dry and a sheet of #600-grit wet-and-dry sandpaper.

Strip the Plates—Pick up a can of Drano. Fill a metal bucket with hot water, then pour in the Drano. Suspend your plates with coat-hanger wire, then lower them into the bucket. The Drano will remove the paint and any grease or oil as well. Wear neoprene gloves and eye protection while working, and don't let kids or pets near your project.

Even badly weathered plates such as these can be saved with a little work. The first thing to do is to strip off all of the old paint. Drano and hot water will do the job in a jiffy, but be careful. Drano is dangerous. Wear neoprene gloves and goggles. Keep children and pets away.

It will take only a few minutes to strip your plates. Rinse them thoroughly in clean water. Dispose of the Drano stripper down a household drain.

Rust—A little Naval Jelly, available in hardware stores, and some #360-grit sandpaper is all you need to remove most rust. When you have all of it off, mix up a solution of two parts Naval Jelly to one part water and brush it on your plates to prepare them for painting. Leave it on for a few minutes, then rinse it off with water.

Painting

Priming—Dry your plates thoroughly, then shoot them with a coat of primer. A touch-up spray gun is best for this task, but your trusty regular gun will do fine too.

Numbers—Mix up a little of the color for the numbers in lacquer and shoot them. You must use only lacquer, not enamel, for this job, because cured lacquer will not be disturbed by the enamel we will be shooting over it for the background. But lacquer, when shot onto enamel, will cause it to craze and lift, and lacquer shot over lacquer, or enamel shot on enamel, will melt into the paint underneath and it will not be possible to wipe it off the numbers. Let the numbers

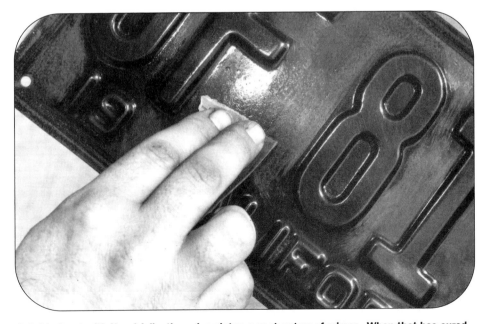

Get rid of rust with Naval Jelly, then give plates a coat or two of primer. When that has cured, spray on the lacquer for the numbers. Let it dry thoroughly, then rough up areas to be painted with background color.

dry for a few days before going on to the next step.

Background—Lightly scuff the areas between the numbers on your plates with #600-grit sandpaper. Be careful not to touch the numbers or letters. Mix the enamel for the background according to the directions on the can, then shoot only the fronts of your plates, one at a time.

Wipe It Off—Wrap a lint-free rag around your finger, dip it in enamel reducer, then wipe the still-wet enamel off of the numbers. Rub gently and change your rag frequently. Don't be too fussy about the edges, you can come back in a couple of minutes with Q-tips dipped in thinner and clean them up.

Rear of the Plate—After the fronts of your plates have been allowed to cure overnight, shoot the backs, then hang them up to dry for a week before installing them on your classic. ■

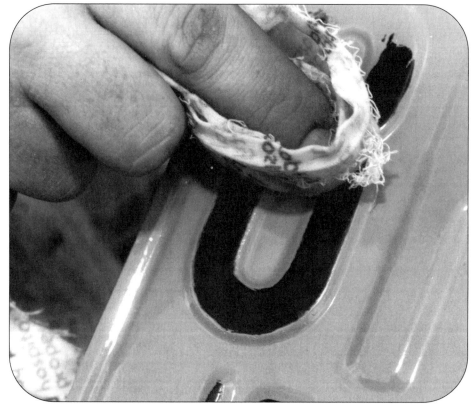

Spray on background color in enamel, then wipe off numbers with a rag soaked in thinner while paint is still wet. Clean up edges with Q-tips.

Finished plates look as good as new. Many states will allow you to register your classic with Y.O.M. (year of manufacture) plates. They are a great final touch to a correct restoration.

19

DETAILING

A great architect once said "Beauty is in the details." Concours car show winners know what he meant. The quality and depth of detailing is often the difference between winning and losing. Detailing means more than waxing and buffing. When it comes to show quality, detailing includes trim, undercarriages, tires and wheels, upholstery and interior trim, emblems, glass and paint chips.

UNDERCARRIAGES

Detailing is done from the bottom up. You begin with the chassis and finish with the paintwork and upholstery. The idea is to do the dirtiest work first. Cleaning a chassis that has been on the road for years is a filthy, time-consuming job, but competition at shows is keen. You can bet the other guy's running gear will be sanitary.

Many people take their car to a steam cleaner, or blast their chassis with a pressure gun at a do-it-yourself car wash. Such devices will remove a lot of muck quickly, but will also blow dirty water into places it shouldn't be, such as into the ignition system, or crevices in the bodywork, or even onto upholstery panels and paint. It's safer to clean your classic by hand. It's hard work, but the results are better, and you don't run the risk of damaging irreplaceable parts.

Cleaning

Grab your scrapers, wire brush and

A good detailing job can easily be done with preparations available from most auto supply stores and a couple of brushes and rags. Wear goggles and gloves when working with caustic solutions, and wear a good mask when painting.

THINGS YOU'LL NEED:

- Liquid dishwasher detergent or trisodium phosphate (T.S.P.)
- Bucket
- Sharp scraper or putty knife
- Assorted wire and bristle scrub brushes
- Squirt can and cleaning solvent
- Electric drill, wire brush wheels, sanding pads
- Course steel wool
- Rust remover
- Paint
- Goggles and rubberized work gloves

solvent and roll under the car. Caked-on grime can be removed with the sharpened scraper. Soften stubborn, hard-to-get, greasy dirt with the squirt can and solvent, let it soak in for a few minutes, then scrub it with a wire brush.

Next, mix a strong solution of dishwasher detergent and water in the bucket (T.S.P. works well too), then scrub as much of the chassis as you can with a stiff bristle brush. Especially filthy areas can benefit by slopping on plenty of solution, then for added punch, shaking some powdered laundry detergent into it. Let the stuff set for a few minutes so the chemicals in the soap will have time to do their job, then scrub the area again. Rinse thoroughly afterwards, and don't get any of the wash solution on your skin. It's surprisingly caustic.

Prep It—Brush off any loose rust with a wire brush, then get things as clean as possible with your electric drill with a wire brush chucked into it. Use a sanding pad on broad, flat areas. On many cars it

will not be possible to get at a few areas up in the suspension, but make every effort to get everything as clean, and as grease- and rust-free as possible.

Paint It

Those of us ambitious enough to do frame-off restorations on cars that will be trailered to and from shows, can bead-blast chassis components to perfect cleanliness, then paint them with Dupont IMRON. But most home restorers who like to use their cars don't want to go to that extreme. Rustoleum is the best alternative. It has the correct semi-gloss appearance like the paint most manufacturers used originally, and it does not require a completely rust-free surface to adhere properly. You can also use The Eastwood Company's *Chassis Black* for the perfect match.

Begin the task by covering tires and other items that could be affected by overspray with plastic tarps or newspaper. Spray your undercarriage using aerosol cans or a compressor and touch-up gun. Use pieces of cardboard as shields where necessary. Shoot on a couple of coats of rusty metal primer first, let it dry for a day or two, then shoot on the top coats.

Some parts of the running gear and suspension will have to be painted colors other than black. Shock absorbers came in a lot of different colors at different times in automotive history. Try to match the original color for yours. Talk to members of the club for your marque to determine original accessory colors, or write to manufacturers like Monroe or Delco for information they might have. Transmissions were usually painted the same color as the engine. Use the correct color of engine enamel to give yours that factory fresh look.

ENGINE COMPARTMENT

To compete at shows, your engine compartment must be more than clean; it must look showroom new. Not only must

Parts removed from your car's engine can be stripped of paint and grease with a solution of Drano and hot water. We put 3 cans of Drano in about 6 inches of water in this small galvanized wash tub and it did the job nicely for all of our engine accessories. Wear neoprene gloves and goggles while working, and dispose of the stuff down your laundry tub drain, not on your lawn. The stuff is dangerously corrosive and caustic.

Use Naval Jelly or other rust remover to get rid of corrosion and etch metal for painting. Wear gloves for this operation too.

manifolds and pull them away from the engine.

Cleaning

Duct tape over any holes in the block to seal them from moisture, and then scrub the engine clean of all dirt and grease. Use the detergent solution and a scrub brush, as well as the solvent can if necessary. Finally, wash the engine down with a good degreaser such as Prepsol or Pre-Kleeno (both are available at automotive paint stores).

Painting

Scuff any painted areas with #400-grit sandpaper, and use a metal-prep etching solution or Naval Jelly to etch any bare metal areas. Now mist on a very light tack coat of engine enamel, let it get sticky, then shoot on two or three finish coats. Let each coat dry before applying the next.

By the way, primer is not used with most engine paint. Engine enamels, high temperature coatings for manifolds, and specialty paints are available from your local auto supply, or you can order them from The Eastwood Company catalog.

If you're unsure as to color, do some

things be painted the correct colors, but ignition wires, hoses, hose clamps and fan belts must all be correct and looking better than new. Engine accessories must be clean and freshly painted. These are things you would do as a matter of course if you were doing a complete restoration, but they can also be done with the engine in the car if you're just detailing for competition.

Cleaning an engine is much like doing the undercarriage except you get to stand up. Use the same tools and techniques as you did with the chassis. But before you get started, there is some disassembly work to be done.

Remove Accessories—Remove all of the engine accessories so you can clean and paint them, and so you can detail the block. Attach clothespins to the ignition wires, numbered according to the cylinders they go to, then remove the distributor. Disconnect the battery at its terminals, then use clothespins, or tape, to tag wires that go to the starter and generator. Now remove these items,

along with any pumps, carburetors, air filters, fans and pulleys or other items that will get in the way of painting the block. Wrap the wire harness with plastic trash bags and masking tape to keep it dry and free of paint overspray. Loosen exhaust

These engine accessories were primed and painted using underhood aerosol spray enamel from The Eastwood Company catalog.

Eastwood also offers these authentic-looking paints for engine accessories.

This air filter was stripped, then small dents were taken out. A piece of sheet metal was wrapped around its cylindrical portion to hide larger dents that were inaccessible.

Sheet metal seam was soldered, then filed with fine files and sanded with #400-grit sandpaper.

research among fellow owners of your type of car to make sure you know how your engine was painted when it came from the factory. Old advertising and sales literature can also be a good source of information.

Coat Manifolds—Use only high temperature coatings that will take 1000 degrees Fahrenheit without burning off. Before painting the manifolds, clean them to bright metal with a hand drill and wire wheel or sand blast them. Use new gaskets when you re-attach your manifolds to the block.

Clean & Paint Accessories—Scour the fan, pulleys, radiator tanks, generator or alternator, starter, distributor and pumps of dirt and rust, then wipe them down with Prepsol and scuff them with sandpaper. Shoot them with Eastwood's Under Hood Black or Rustoleum. Many restoration shops use Rustoleum for the chassis, as well as engine accessories, because it holds up well, is easy to apply, and it has the correct semi-gloss sheen.

Air Filter

For some reason, classic car air filters take a beating. They are usually dented and rusty if they are still on the car at all. Finding factory correct ones can be difficult, and when you do, they usually show their age. But luckily, they aren't as hard to restore as you might think.

Reconditioning—First, empty any oil out of your filter, then wash any copper or steel filtering medium with gasoline. Finish cleaning it with lacquer thinner. Next, strip the parts of your filter to bare metal using automotive paint stripper. Now, with sandpaper and a hand drill with a wire wheel attachment, remove all vestiges of rust.

Fix any minor dents in the top or sides of your filter with plastic body filler. Cover major dents in the sides of a cylindrical filter with a new piece of metal. Measure the height and circumference of your filter's side, then have a tin shop cut a new piece of thin sheet steel to cover it with. Carefully wrap the new piece of metal around the canister, then clean, tin and solder the seam. File it smooth with hand files.

Prime and paint your filter with the proper color of enamel. When the paint has had a few days to cure, add the correct decal; they are available through hobby publications or possibly from a club for your marque.

Before you install your new air filter, clean the exterior of the carburetor with lacquer thinner and a stiff toothbrush to remove any varnish deposits.

Reassemble—Clean and paint, as necessary, all visible nuts and bolts on your engine, then reinstall all of the accessories. Replace any incorrect or worn hoses, hose clamps, belts or ignition wires with new ones. Use new gaskets where required. Finally, apply new decals where they're supposed to go. Now stand back and allow at least half an hour to admire your work. Your new engine compartment should look great!

PAINT DETAILING

If your car's paintwork is not too thin to be polished, it can be restored to its original shine and depth with a bit of work and care. The maze of high-tech sounding

Next, air filter was primed, sanded, then painted. Even if you use aerosol cans, you should wear a good paint mask (available from automotive paint stores) while painting, because the paint is no less harmful to your body than it is when shot from a spray gun.

A proper decal is the finishing touch to our restored air cleaner. Decals were ordered from classified ads in hobby publications such as *Hemmings Motor News* and *Classic Auto Restorer*.

but if you wish to know more, an excellent source is HPBooks' *Automotive Paint Handbook*. I learned auto detailing basics from a pro named Percy who plied his trade behind a local car wash back in the '50s. Used car dealers in our area relied on Percy's expertise to make their inventory irresistible to buyers.

Rubbing Compound

Paint that is oxidized and flat can be restored to its original luster using ordinary rubbing compound. The pros use power buffers and special concoctions that can get the job done quickly but, unless you're already proficient with them, do your show car by hand. A buffer in inexperienced hands can burn right through paint and ruin a finish that could otherwise be saved.

Other things to remember, even when polishing by hand are: Go lightly on lids, roofs, hoods and tops of fenders. Chances are the paint will be most worn in these spots, so such areas will require a light touch to avoid cutting through to primer. Never rub the sharp edges of hoods, doors or other panels. The paint in these areas is thin—even when new—and it buffs off to bare metal in a hurry. Before you begin, remove any brightwork or chrome items that can be taken off easily.

Buy professional quality rubbing compound and polish from an automotive paint store if possible. Otherwise, the products available at your local auto supply will do. Follow directions on the container. Most rubbing compound manufacturers recommend that you work a small area (2 feet by 2 feet) at a time. Use a soft cloth that is folded into a pad and slightly dampened. Work with your hand flat, and do a circular or cross-hatch pattern so your fingers won't make grooves in the finish. Take only enough paint off with the rubbing compound to restore a shine. Rubbing compound is very abrasive and will cut paint quickly, so be careful.

and glitzy products available is truly confusing. Sealers, compounds, glazes, finish-restorers, swirl removers, etc. are common names applied to what used to be just plain ol' wax. But paint care

technology has progressed in recent years, and the types of finishes possible with some products is truly amazing. It would be beyond the scope of this book to get into the finer points of product selection,

After rubbing out and polishing your car, give it a coat of glazing compound, or, if you drive it frequently, a coat of non-abrasive wax such as Harlys.

Clean excess wax from around decorative items and grooves with a toothbrush or other soft brush.

Paint Chips

Touch up any nicks or small scratches with touch-up paint mixed to match your car's finish. If you don't have any touch-up paint and don't know the paint code, remove a small part and take it to an automotive paint store. They should be able to match it. Build up such areas by daubing paint into them with a fine brush until the spot is above the surrounding paint. An excellent kit, called the Action ChipKit®, is available from Pro Motorcar Products, 22025 U.S. 19 N., Clearwater, FL 34625. 800/323-1090. It includes everything you'll need, except for the touch-up paint, to fix paint chips.

On cars finished with lacquer, give touch-ups a week or so to dry, then lightly sand them with #1000-grit wet-and-dry paper and a rubber sanding block so they blend with the rest of the finish. But don't try sanding on a car painted with enamel, because if it doesn't have special hardeners in it, you will ruin it.

Polishing

Next, go over the car again with a fine polishing compound to remove scratches, then wax it with a non-abrasive wax. Alternatively, if you keep your car indoors

and covered most of the time, just give it a coat of glazing compound, available at automotive paint stores.

Stainless Steel—Stainless steel items, if they can be removed from the car, can be polished with a buffing wheel and jeweler's rouge, or you can use stainless steel polish. Chrome should also be polished and given a coat of wax. Use a toothbrush to remove any excess wax from grooves between ornamental items and the body.

REVITALIZING RUBBER & VINYL

Percy, my old mentor, used to go over all of the rubber and vinyl items on a car with saddle soap. It helped protect them from the elements, and it cleaned them up and gave them a new-car sheen. Just rub it on, then buff it with a soft rag. I still use this trick. If you want a more contemporary answer to the problem, Armor All, STP Son Of a Gun and Meguiar's Intensive Protectant work well.

Black silicone sealer is good for filling small cracks. Just squirt it on, let it set up, then trim it with a sharp single-edge razor blade. Before silicone sealer, the common cure for cracks in rubber seals was Henry's Roofing Cement (another of Percy's techniques). The stuff stinks and stays sticky for several days, but it molds into cracks easily and sets up to look remarkably like rubber.

There are a number of preparations made for cleaning and protecting rubber, but saddle soap is a good, inexpensive alternative that has been in use for years by professional detailers. Black silicone cement is good for fixing cracks.

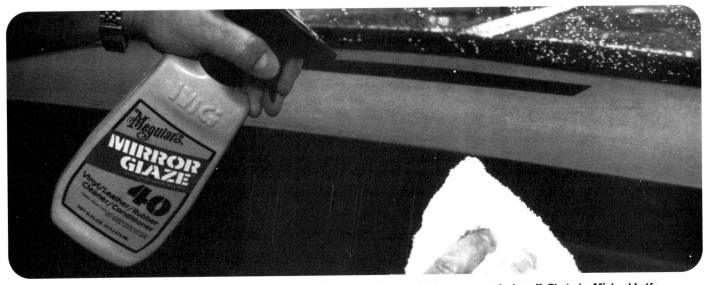

Meguiar's makes a superb interior vinyl, leather and rubber conditioner and cleaner. Just spray on and wipe off. Photo by Michael Lutfy.

Here is a typical judging sheet from a car show. Notice that points are divided about evenly between interior, exterior and engine and chassis. If any one of these areas is less than pristine, you will lose points. 197 out of a possible 200 is what it took to win a first-place trophy.

White sidewall tires are best cleaned with detergent and water, unless they are old and stained. If detergent and water don't do the trick, try Westley's Bleche Wite.

UPHOLSTERY

Next to paint and chrome, your car's upholstery will do more to help (or prevent) taking home a trophy than just about anything else. Factory correct materials, straight stitching, and the right color scheme are absolute musts. Beyond that, it must be clean and in good repair. Here are some winning techniques.

Vacuum It—Use a small, hand-held vacuum cleaner to gently remove dust from your car's upholstery. Dust is your interior's worst enemy. If your interior is made of leather, hold the vacuum slightly away from the surface to avoid scratching.

Wash It—Wool fabrics can be cleaned with a little Woolite and lukewarm water, but don't get the upholstery soaking wet. If you do, stains, caused by dirt in the padding, will develop. Leather can be cleaned with Lexol pH, which is what the professional detailers use, or you can use a mild solution of non-detergent castile soap and water. Dry the surface quickly with soft towels. If you clean with Lexol, follow up with their leather dressing and protectant

Small tears in seats or dashboards can be fused together with Vinyl Fusion, available from The Eastwood Company.

to restore your interior's original luster and suppleness.

Clean vinyl interiors with a vinyl cleaner such as Armor All, or use any of the many other, similar products. Saddle soap will work on vinyl too. Just wipe it on, then polish it with a soft cloth.

Stains & Tears—Grease or food stains can be removed from wool fabrics with *Energine*, which is a solvent used by dry cleaners. (Sometimes, patches can be made by using surplus fabric that is tucked up under the seats and stapled. Re-stitch leather or vinyl in the original holes.) If your vinyl interior has small tears, they can usually be fixed with a vinyl repair kit. Most kits use a plastic cement to weld the material back together. They are available from auto stores or The Eastwood Company. Just follow the instructions with the kit. ■

MAKING GASKETS

20

Gaskets for old cars can be hard to find or may be obtainable only in expensive sets, but you can make your own, inexpensively and quickly. All you'll need are the items listed in the sidebar on the next page. Sheet cork can be purchased at your nearest auto supply store and comes in various thicknesses. Get the rubber-impregnated kind; it holds up better and is easier to cut. Fiber gasket paper is also available at auto parts and hardware stores. Rubber is used for some applications. Neoprene is the best replacement for it.

Don't be tempted to use cardboard or manila envelope paper for gasket material, as it is not strong enough, nor is it impregnated with the necessary oil resistant resins that keep gasket paper from disintegrating.

Order hole punches from the Eastwood catalog or, in a pinch, make your own out of pieces of metal tubing. Just cut off about a 4-inch length of the tubing with a hacksaw, then sharpen one end with a file.

Always buy the correct type and thickness of paper or cork for the application. If you choose a material that is too thin a seal will leak, and gaskets that are too thick will allow parts to deform when they are tightened into place. Use a remnant of your old gasket as a gauge when picking out your material.

Almost any gasket or seal can be made easily and quickly with a few hand tools. Be sure to buy the correct material and in the right thickness for your particular application. Take your old gasket with you when you go to the auto supply store.

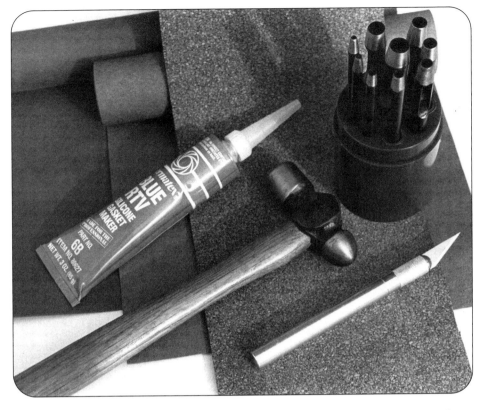

Hole punches, a small hammer, a straight-edge and an X-Acto knife are all you need to make most gaskets. Hole punches can be made from thin-wall tubing if necessary.

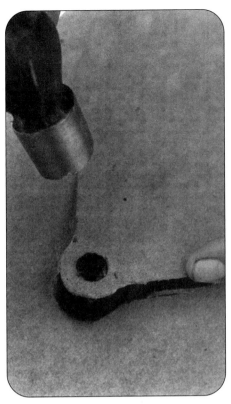

In a pinch, a gasket can be made by placing fiber material on a part and tapping with a ballpeen hammer to cut the material. Clean up the edges of your new gasket with fine sandpaper.

THINGS YOU'LL NEED:
- **Fiber, cork or rubber gasket material**
- **X-Acto knife or razor blade**
- **Hole punches**
- **Sealant**
- **Ballpeen hammer**
- **Metal straight-edge**

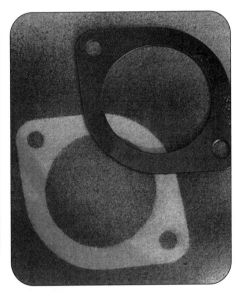

The simplest way to make a pattern for a new seal is to place the old one on gasket material, then shoot it lightly with cheap aerosol spray paint. Lift off the old gasket and you have your pattern.

MAKING THE PATTERN

The easiest way to make a pattern for the gasket is to lay your old seal on the new material and mist it with quick-drying aerosol spray paint. Shoot straight down with the paint so the holes won't be misaligned.

If there isn't enough of your old gasket to do the spray paint trick, or the casting you are working with is quite large (such as the banjo housing on a differential) hold a piece of gasket paper in place on the opening of the part for which you need a seal, and lightly tap around it with a ballpeen hammer to create an outline. Tap a couple of bolt holes clear through

with the round end of the hammer, then install a couple of bolts loosely in the holes to hold your paper in place while you continue tapping. When you remove the paper, you will have an embossed outline to cut along.

Many mechanics cut out gaskets for large, heavy castings merely by tapping until the gasket paper is cut through. Doing it this way leaves ragged edges that need to be cleaned up with fine sandpaper, but the gasket produced by this method will work fine.

Don't tap on delicate castings such as those used on carburetors; instead, trace carefully around the outsides of the parts with a sharp pencil, then measure the thicknesses of the mating surfaces of each part and draw them onto your gasket paper.

Cut It Out

Work on a flat, soft, wood or plastic

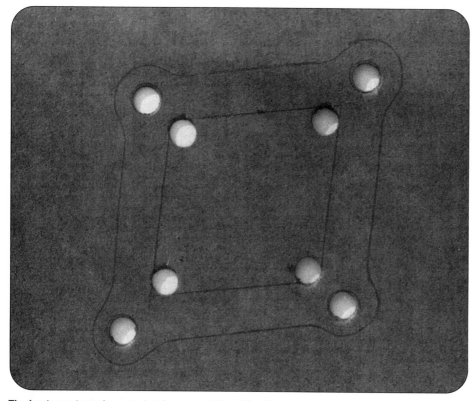

The best way to make a gasket is to carefully outline the old one on new material. Punch holes first, then cut it out with your X-Acto knife.

several light passes rather than trying to cut clear through on the first try. If you apply too much pressure while trying to cut cork, you will distort the material. The unfortunate result will be a gasket that won't quite fit.

Installation

Use Gaskacinch or Permatex Blue silicone sealer to attach your new gasket to a mating surface. Silicone sealer should be used sparingly, and should be allowed to skin over for a few minutes before parts are bolted together. Only use sealer on one side of a motor pan or valve covers. That way you can remove these parts later if need be, and you won't have to make a new seal.

Tighten all attaching bolts or screws evenly and don't over-tighten. Doing so will deform pans and castings and cause serious leaks. Cork seals should only be snugged into place. If you keep tightening, they will squeeze out from between the mating surfaces. Rubber seals usually only need a thin coating of grease to seal. ∎

cutting board. Punch your holes first, then cut any radiused corners by tipping your hole punch so you only cut with part of it, or use your X-Acto knife or a razor blade

and a round object of the correct diameter to trace along.

Cut the straight lines next. On thick material, such as cork or rubber, make

Here is the finished gasket ready to install. If you are cutting through thick cork or other material, make several light passes with your knife, rather than one heavy one. You'll have better control that way.

If your car is equipped with mechanical lifters, sooner or later it will need a valve adjustment. Telltale signs are tappet "clattering" under the hood, or a rhythmic "chuffing" emanating from the exhaust. Also, the valves will need adjusting after the initial break-in period (500 miles) of a new or rebuilt, mechanical lifter-equipped engine. Some engines need a valve adjustment every 6000 miles. The procedure is relatively simple and performed with a few hand tools.

Periodic valve adjustments are necessary to keep most older engines running right. If their tappet tolerances are too loose, valves will stay closed too long, causing the engine to lose power dramatically. Or worse, if tolerances are too tight the valves won't close completely, denying adequate cooling contact with valve seats. The result will be burned valves. Either way, you lose.

An old Nash six, Buick straight-eight or Chevy six is easy. The adjusters for these vintage overhead valve engines are under a cover on top of the engine. However, because the mechanism that drives overhead valves is more complex,

Valves on most old flathead engines are adjusted with the engine fully warmed up and running. Slip a flat feeler gauge of the correct thickness according to the specs in your shop manual into each gap to check for clearance. Exhaust valves often get tighter as time goes on, and intake valves sometimes get looser.

THINGS YOU'LL NEED:

- New valve cover gaskets
- Permatex or silicone sealer
- Feeler gauges
- Tappet wrenches (L-head engines only)
- 100% cotton work gloves with fingertips cut off
- Timing light (for engines that require valves be set cold)

it goes out of tolerance quicker. As a result, these engines need more frequent adjustment.

Flathead engines, like Dodge or Plymouth sixes, Pontiac straight-eights and inline Packards, have their valve adjusters down on the side of the engine,

so they're difficult to get at. But once these engines' valves are set, they stay that way for a long time.

Many old car powerplants, such as later overhead valve V8s, are equipped with hydraulic lifters that never need adjusting. And flathead Ford V8s aren't provided with any means for adjustment other than grinding valve stems to the correct length while the engine is apart. But these are the exceptions. Most classic era cars need periodic valve adjustments to stay healthy.

OVERHEAD VALVE ENGINES

Most old American cars must be thoroughly warmed to operating temperature before their valves can be adjusted, and they must be adjusted with the engine running. Work outdoors to avoid carbon-monoxide poisoning. Run your engine at fast idle (about 800 rpm) for at least 20 minutes before beginning work. Don't rely on your temperature gauge to tell you when your engine is warm enough. It only shows you cylinder head temperature. An engine isn't thoroughly warmed until all of its metal parts have expanded to their maximum. If you adjust the valves before everything reaches full operating temperature, you'll get the tolerances too tight and you'll soon have burned exhaust valves.

Exhaust manifolds get skin-searing hot when an engine is operating normally. Therefore, I recommend you wear protective work gloves to keep from getting burned. Make sure they're 100% cotton, because synthetic materials will melt and cause painful burns. Cut the fingertips off so you can feel what you're doing.

Remove Valve Covers—Set the engine back to a slow idle speed but with no bucking or rolling. (Don't idle it back too far because the cylinder walls won't get enough oil if you do.) Next, evenly loosen any screws or nuts holding the valve cover on, then grasp it and gently

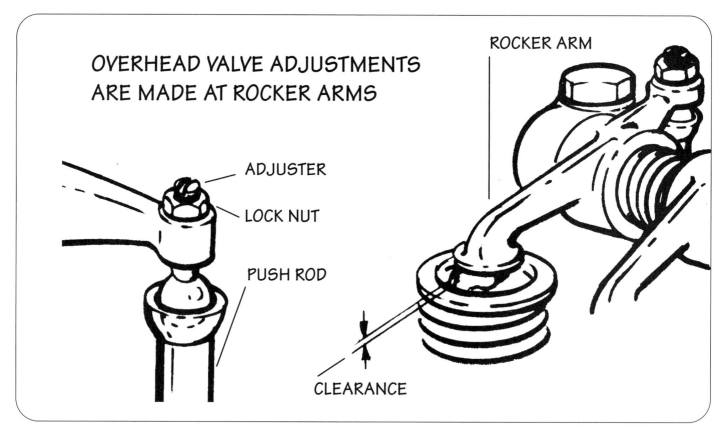

OVERHEAD VALVE ADJUSTMENTS ARE MADE AT ROCKER ARMS

ROCKER ARM

ADJUSTER

LOCK NUT

PUSH ROD

CLEARANCE

Overhead valves are easier to adjust than those on old flathead engines, but they need attention more often. All you need to adjust overhead valves are feeler gauges, a wrench and a screwdriver. Most old car engines require that their valves be set while the engine is warm and running.

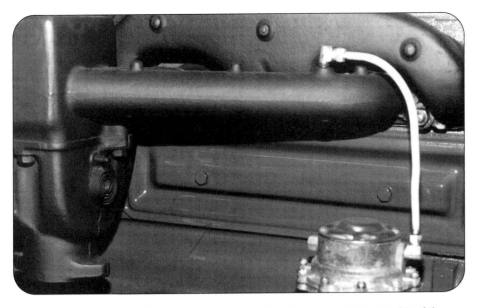

Valve adjusters on inline flathead engines are under these tappet covers on the side of the engine. You may have to take the wheel off and the inner fender pan out on some cars in order to get at them. Pop them loose carefully so as not to damage their cork gaskets.

Don't use any sealer on the mating surfaces between the valve cover gasket and the block. The oil pressure isn't high in this area of your engine, so there is no need to seal both sides of the gasket. And you will be able to easily remove the cover without ruining the seal when it's time to do another adjustment. Don't over-tighten the fasteners. Valve covers only need to be snugged into place. If you over-tighten them, they will warp and overly compress the gasket, and leak as a result.

Check for Leaks—Top off your engine's oil supply, then start it up and check for drips. Let it run for at least five minutes. If you don't see any telltale trickles, the job is done.

rock it from side-to-side to pop it free. If necessary, slip a sharp putty knife under the cover and gently pry it loose. Try not to damage the gasket. Valve cover gaskets, if they're not damaged or overly compressed, can be re-used two or three times before they need replacing.

Adjusting—Shoot a little oil on the valve stems to make sure they're not sticking in the guides, then adjust the clearances with the adjusters at the ends of the rocker arms. Usually, all you need is a box wrench, screwdriver and feeler gauges. Set the clearances to the correct dimensions for your car. A tune-up guide or shop manual will give you the correct specifications.

Adjust all of the exhaust valves first. Valves are set correctly when you can just slip a feeler gauge of the correct thickness between the tip of the rocker arm adjuster and the valve stem, but the next thicker gauge won't fit. If you do a lot of high-speed driving, it's a good idea to set the valves on classics from the thirties and forties about two thousandths looser than called for in the specs. They'll be a little noisy, but they will be less likely to burn when you cruise at speeds near the limit of your old car's design envelope. Double-check your work before

proceeding.

Reinstall Valve Cover—If your old gasket came off in one piece, and isn't nicked, torn, or compressed and brittle, you can re-use it. Otherwise, install a new one. Coat the valve cover sparingly with silicone sealer or Permatex, then press the gasket into place. Clean any excess sealer off of edges, because globs of silicone sealer can break loose and clog tiny oil galleries in your engine.

FLATHEAD ENGINES

The same warm-up time is required for flatheads as overhead valve engines. The 100% cotton work gloves are critical when doing side-valve engines because of heat and the proximity of the exhaust system. Wear a long-sleeved cotton shirt to protect your arms too.

Access—To get at the valves on many flathead inline engines, you must remove

Flat feeler gauges and tappet wrenches are needed to adjust valves on a flathead engine. Tappet wrenches are identical to standard, open-end wrenches except they are thinner.

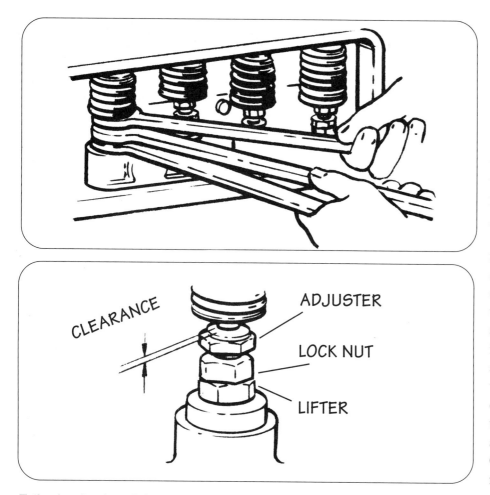

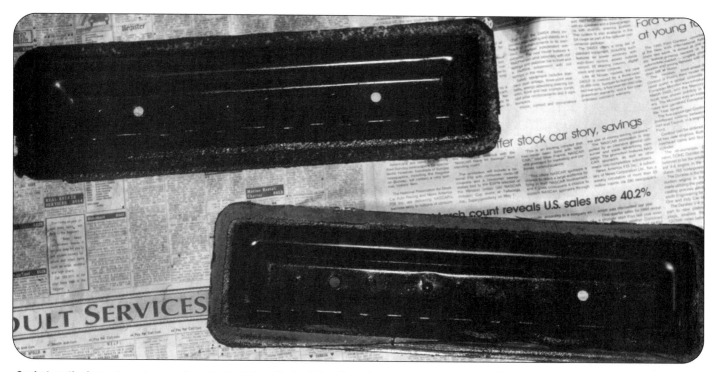

Flathead engines have their valves in the side of the block instead of on top of the engine. You will probably have to remove the front wheel and inner fender apron to get at them. Earlier flathead engines, made in the '30s, require three wrenches in order to make the adjustment. After about 1940, only two wrenches were needed because tappets were self-locking. Valves are usually set warm with engine running.

the front wheel and inner fender panel, then climb in under the fender to reach them, because the tappet covers are on the side of the engine, under the exhaust manifold.

Pop Tappet Covers Loose— Sometimes you can pry them off with your fingers, but often as not, you'll need to slip a sharp putty knife under them to free them. Try to avoid tearing the gaskets.

Adjustment—Flathead engines require tappet wrenches for valve adjustments. Tappet wrenches look like ordinary open-end wrenches except they're thinner so they can fit on the adjusters. If your car was built after 1940, it is probably equipped with self-locking adjusters so you'll only need two wrenches. But if it was made in the '30s or earlier, you'll need three wrenches: one to hold the tappet still, one to unlock the adjuster, and one to make the adjustment. Check a shop or owner's manual for your make to determine which kind of lifters you have, and what the valve settings should be.

To adjust the later, self-locking tappets, you only need to loosen the lock-nut with

Gasket on the lower tappet cover slipped out of place the last time the valves were adjusted, causing a major oil leak. Place covers face up on clean newspaper while working so dirt and grit won't get into them.

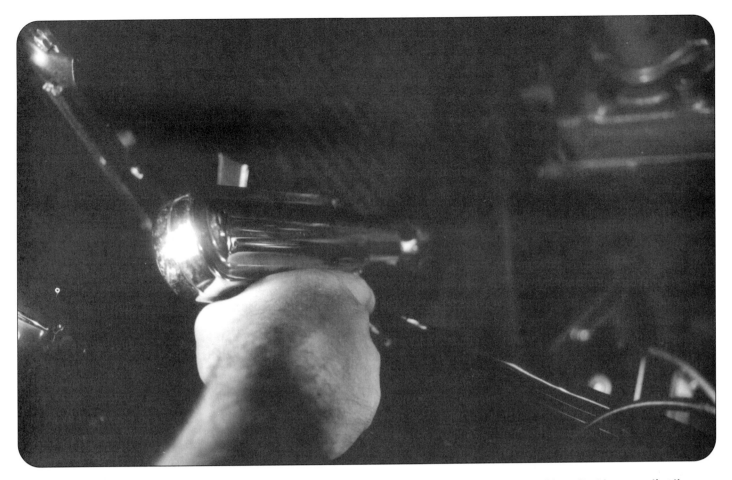

If your car's engine requires the valves to be adjusted cold, use a timing light to get each set of valves in position. Start by connecting the light to the number one spark plug wire, then slowly turn the engine over until the light flashes. Valves are now in the closed position and can be adjusted. Do each cylinder in turn.

one wrench, then make the adjustment with the other. Again, do all of the exhaust valves first, then adjust the intake valves.

To set the old-style tappets, hold the bottom wrench that keeps the lifter from moving in the same hand as the wrench that unlocks the adjuster. Loosen the lock-nut just enough to make the adjustment using the third wrench in your other hand, then squeeze together the two wrenches holding the lifter and lock-nut so as to secure the tappet at its correct tolerance. Check your work carefully. Readjust any tappets that aren't precisely correct, then reinstall the valve covers as outlined above.

Check for Leaks—Run the engine at least five minutes at fast idle and watch for oil streaks, especially at the corners of the covers. Fix any you see before returning the car to service.

SETTING VALVES COLD

Many old cars, including Volkswagen Beetles, MGs, flathead Studebakers and Model A Fords, require their valves to be set cold, with the engine shut off. The task is not difficult, but it usually requires a timing light to do it properly.

Make Sure Engine Is Cold—Engines that require their valves to be adjusted cold must be allowed to sit for several hours before attempting the job if they have been in use. Classic car engines, especially those made of cast iron, hold heat for a long time. For valve adjustment purposes, cold means room temperature, or about 70 degrees F. A summer day in Tucson or winter day in Green Bay is not suitable for valve adjusting.

Find Top Dead Center—Carefully remove the valve covers and place them on

old newspaper to keep them from getting dirty. Now connect your timing light to the number one spark plug. Slowly crank the engine until the light just comes on.

When the timing light flashes, the number one piston is at the top of the cylinder on its compression stroke. Both the intake and exhaust valves will be closed, so their springs will be fully compressed and their adjuster gaps open. Set the tappets as described above. Now attach the timing light to the number two cylinder and keep working along until you have adjusted each set of valves. Recheck your work, then reinstall the valve covers and top up your engine's oil. Start it up and check for leaks.

With the valves in proper adjustment, you'll be able to drive in serene silence, knowing that your classic's engine is performing at its peak. ■

STORAGE

After going to all the work of restoring a car, few of us want to risk undoing even part of our efforts by driving them in inclement weather. For those who live in snowy climates, it is essential that you store your collector for at least 4-6 months. Also, collectors who own more than one car often must let certain ones sit idle for long periods of time. Wealthy collectors and museums sometimes go so far as to store their cars in special sealed rooms containing only dust-free, dehumidified air. Most of us can't afford such extreme measures, but want to prevent the deterioration of our cars nevertheless.

LONG TERM STORAGE

As a general rule, any car stored more than six months is considered to be long-term storage. It is always best to run a car occasionally rather than let it sit idle for long periods of time. But, circumstances sometimes prevent this.

The ideal place to store a vehicle is in a well-lit, heated garage that has a wooden floor. A wooden floor absorbs moisture—thereby reducing the possibility of rust formation. Heat does the same thing but its benefits are more readily apparent in the colder, damp

Long or short term, storing your collector car properly requires that you follow some basic procedures. Of great importance is the garage. It should be heated and preferably have a wooden floor, which absorbs moisture better than cement. Make sure the garage is leakproof as well. Photo by Michael Lutfy.

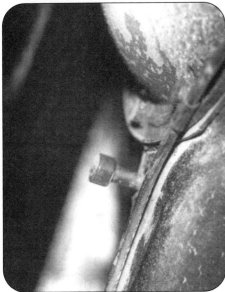

Differentials and transmissions have small vents to relieve pressure and heat buildup. When a car cools after having been driven, moisture condenses in your transmission and rear end and causes corrosion and pitting of bearings. To avoid damage, change these oils before storing your car.

months. Heat dissipates moisture and dries the air out. However, most garages have cement floors which absorb moisture but also release it rather quickly. To combat this, plastic sheathing can be placed on the floor and then covered with plywood. The plastic acts as a moisture barrier and the wood absorbs any moisture that gets past the plastic. Bags of silica gel placed in the garage also absorb moisture.

Change or Drain Fluids

Take your car out for a drive and warm the engine up thoroughly, then change the oil and filter. When oil is heated and circulating, it picks up and emulsifies or suspends harmful chemical contaminants and particulate matter. Drain it while it's hot. Just be careful and wear gloves, because hot engine oil can cause painful burns. Refill the engine with new oil. Don't forget the extra quart for the filter.

It is also a good idea to drain and refill your transmission and differential with fresh gear lube. Both of these mechanisms have small vents on them to relieve heat and pressure during operation. Unfortunately, after using the car, these devices cool, so moisture condenses in them and rusts gears and pits bearings.

If the universal joints on your car have lube fittings, carefully fill them with fresh grease. But don't apply too much pressure, because you can easily ruin the seal on them if you do. Next comes the chassis.

With a garden hose, wash all of the dirt and road salt from the wheelwells and suspension. Pack the front wheel bearings. (You might as well, since you're doing all the other servicing anyway.) Then apply clean grease on all of the steering and suspension fittings. Get a service chart for your car and do all of the other little chores it outlines, such as lubing the generator, distributor and starter, if required. Also top off refillable shock absorbers and the steering box.

Bleed Brake Fluid—The best insurance against brake deterioration is to purge the system of the conventional polyglycol fluid, then clean the system and fill it with DOT 5 silicone brake fluid. If you don't want to go to that trouble, at least drain your system of old fluid and refill it with fresh. For more details on silicone fluid, see Chapter 9.

Drain Fuel Tank—If you are only going to be storing your car for a few months, add a can of gasoline stabilizer to delay fuel deterioration. It's available through hobby publications and it really works. If you are going to store your car for more than six months, drain the tank completely, then start the engine and run the rest of the gas out of the lines. Old gasoline will clog carburetors and cause valves to hang up in their guides to the point where they sometimes have to be driven out with a hammer and drift. Clean or replace fuel filters.

Drain Cooling System—If you are going to be storing your car over the winter, drain the cooling system completely. Old-style cooling systems that were designed to have only water in them required antifreeze in the winter to prevent the water from freezing, but why go to the trouble of putting in antifreeze if you are not going to drive the car? Just drain the system and leave the petcocks open and the radiator cap off so air can circulate. Disconnect the heater hose and drain the heater too.

If you don't drain the system, don't count on "freeze plugs" to save your block from freezing and fracturing. They are usually down too low on the block to be effective. And they are not put in the engine to relieve pressure, as many people believe. They are actually there to fill holes that the foundry needed in order to let the casting sand out of the waterjacket after the block was poured.

Battery

The battery must be stored carefully if it is to survive, but first, take out the spark plugs, put a tablespoon of oil in each hole, then crank the engine over a few times to coat the cylinder walls. Put the plugs back in. Now disconnect the battery cables and remove the battery from the car. Wash it down with a solution of water and baking soda, then top it up with distilled water. Store it on a shelf in a dry place. Don't store your battery on concrete, because concrete holds moisture which causes the battery to discharge. Instead store it on a wooden or rubber

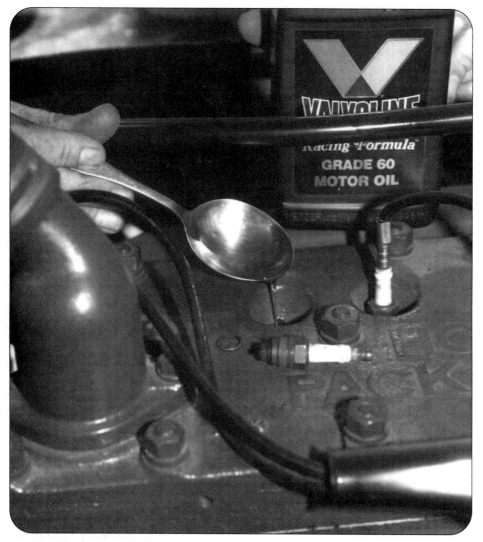

Remove each spark plug and put a tablespoon of oil in the combustion chambers. It will help keep rings free and protect metal surfaces from corrosion.

surface to minimize discharge. Clean up the battery cables, then coat the ends with white dielectric grease. Tighten, then coat any other exposed connections, such as those on your voltage regulator, starter and generator.

Other Details

Carburetor—If you live in a moist climate, put a plastic bag over the carburetor to keep condensation out. You can also bag the exhaust pipe tip too, or stuff it with rags to keep out rodents and debris.

Clean Upholstery—Vacuum your car's interior, then coat it with silicone dressing if it is synthetic, or use Lexol Leather Conditioner or Meguiar's if it is

leather. If your car has a wool interior, put some mothballs in strategic places, then put a couple of opened boxes of baking soda on dishes on the floor to absorb moisture and odors. Leave the windows down a crack to let air circulate.

Wax It—Give your entire car a good waxing before storing it. Coat chrome surfaces but do not buff them off until you are ready to remove it from storage. It will protect better that way. Use Armor All, saddle soap or a similar rubber protectant on the rubber items and tires.

Raise Car—There is often debate on where to place jackstands or block—under the frame or suspension. Basically, it is best to put the stands under the suspension points. Then, remove the tires

and stack them in a corner, placing cardboard between each tire and covering them to prevent fading. Finally, depress the clutch, then block it in that position with a length of 2" x 4" and a flat piece of plywood against the front of the seat cushion. Clutch plates often stick together in storage, sometimes to the point that they have to be removed from the car to separate them.

Car Covers

Even though the car is inside, you will want to cover it to keep dirt off of it, and to protect the finish. There are many types of covers available to choose from. Even though collector cars aren't driven much, they still need protection from dust and other outside debris, especially when they are in storage.

Car covers are available specifically made for your car or you can save a few dollars by getting a "one size fits many" that accommodates cars approximately the same size as yours. The most important consideration when purchasing a cover is selecting the right kind of fabric for your specific storage application.

Types of Fabrics—Cotton flannel fabrics breathe, allowing air to circulate through them. They are soft and easy on the car's paint and wax. They have no fluid resistance so they should only be used in the dry environment of a garage.

Cotton/polyester fabrics have poor fluid resistance and they trap heat and moisture. Their stiffness can harm your paint and remove wax and they can also fade. When they are treated with a chemical repellent, they lose their ability to breathe. Nylon fabrics have the same deficiencies as cotton/polyester.

Plastic films should be avoided because they don't breathe, they trap heat and moisture, their stiffness can damage your paint, they shrink in the cold and stretch in the heat, and they provide only minimal hail and nick protection. Vinyl films should also be avoided for the same reasons.

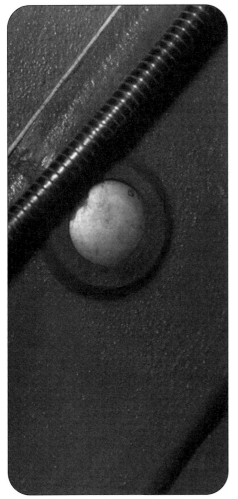

Drain and replace your car's coolant. Check the block for weeping soft plugs in the casting. Replace any that are leaking before refilling your car's cooling system. Use antifreeze if you live in a cold climate. Freeze plugs won't protect your block.

Composite covers made from several layers of material combine the best of each type. For example, a cover made from Kimberly/Clark's Evolution 3 fabric is made in four layers which allow the cover to breathe, repel fluids and provide protection against hail and nicks. Another benefit is that an Evolution 3 cover will not rot or mildew if folded and stored while it is wet.

If you only plan to use a cover in the garage, then a simple cotton cover is sufficient. If the car is kept outside or if it will be trailered, then the Evolution 3 fabric will provide the best of all worlds to keep the car's finish clean, dry and scratch-free. ■

Store your classic in a watertight garage. Never place it in a barn with a dirt floor. Moisture will attack it from underneath if you do. Cover your car, even in the garage, to keep dust from settling on it.

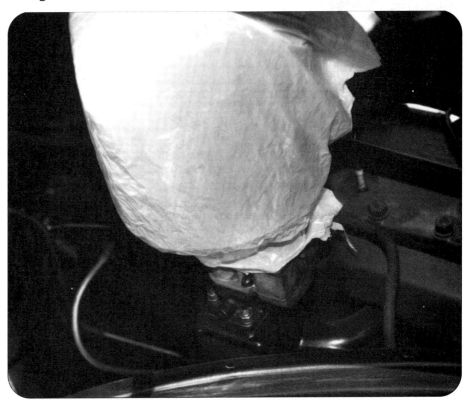

A plastic bag pulled over the carburetor and tied at the bottom will keep moisture from entering. Another bag over the tailpipe will protect the exhaust system.

INDEX

ABOUT THE AUTHOR

Jim Richardson purchased and restored his first vintage car, a 1939 Oldsmobile, in 1960. He has been an avid collector and restorer ever since. Over the years, he has personally restored to show condition a number of cars, including several classic-era Packards. Many of his restorations have taken first-place honors at prestigious concours shows. For the last five years, he has been a contributing editor to *Classic Auto Restorer* magazine, writing how-to feature articles on automotive restoration. He lives in Long Beach, California.